FOSTER CARE OF CHILDREN

CWLA STUDIES OF THE CHILD WELFARE
LEAGUE OF AMERICA

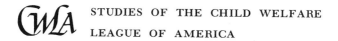

Foster Care of Children

NURTURE
AND TREATMENT

DRAZA KLINE

HELEN-MARY FORBUSH OVERSTREET

1972

COLUMBIA UNIVERSITY PRESS
NEW YORK AND LONDON

TO THE MEMORY OF

Margaret Wilson Gerard and Charlotte Towle

FOREWORD

When a child has to be uprooted from his family and placed in a foster home or in group care with substitute parents, the feelings, thoughts, and behavior of all concerned have certain universal characteristics. Powerful psychological forces are aroused that affect the lives of all, for good or bad. The child welfare agency and its social workers, although aware of the objective conditions that created the problem, must, like a hospital and its doctors, act as a positive instrument to salvage the human personalities caught up in the problem.

The authors of this book are among the most experienced leaders in the field of foster care. Over many years they have distilled a practice wisdom and crystallized it into a placement casework skill of the highest order. Using theoretical discussion and many case examples, this book presents that wisdom and skill in their most up-to-date form. The authors are aware of the importance of ethnic and cultural considerations, of newly emerging treatment methods, and of environmental change in preventing placement; but they have confined themselves to using the medium of the caseworker-to-child/parents/caretakers interchange as the most direct and comprehensible way to convey the essential concepts of nurture and treatment when placement is in the child's best interests.

Generally speaking, child welfare and the foster care system hold a low priority in American politics. The Child Welfare League of America exerts continuous efforts to raise the status of children in our culture and to advance our child welfare system to the highest priority, an achievement that would make a quality service available to those children who really do have to live apart from their families. For the teachers and practitioners who help those who must survive in separation, the League considers this book indispensable. It is also a necessary foundation for all practitioners concerned with temporary and partial forms of physical separation of children and parents—day care, day treatment, homemaker service, hospitalization.

This book is the product of collaboration between the Child Welfare League and the U.S. Children's Bureau. Its writing was financed through the Children's Bureau (and subsequently the Community Services Administration) as part of the League's Coordinated Program of Research in Foster Care. Subsequent publications reporting research conducted under this grant will deal with the related issues of decisions to place children in foster care and strategies for maximizing children's return to their natural families. The League wishes to express its appreciation to the authors for their contribution to improvement of practice in foster care and to the Children's Bureau for making this contribution possible.

Joseph H. Reid
Executive Director
Child Welfare League of America, Inc.

PREFACE

This book represents an expansion and reformulation of concepts and practice principles familiar to foster care casework and elaborated and tested clinically in our work at the Illinois Children's Home and Aid Society. Under the creative and far-sighted leadership of Lois Wildy, then executive director, major changes in the programs were introduced more than fifteen years ago. At that time the present collaborative team was formed not only to make needed changes in the existing foster home program but also, in association with other colleagues, to develop small residential treatment facilities for young children and adolescents and clinical programs for placed children of all ages, their parents, and their siblings. The objectives of this closely interrelated constellation of services were, primarily, to provide the treatment of choice for the agency's clientele, and, secondarily, to try to learn more about how to increase the effectiveness of foster care services. As expected, it was found that the knowledge gained from each of the services helped to illuminate the others.

Over the years a pattern of collaboration was established which has been carried into the authorship of this book. One of the authors (Overstreet) continuously carried experimental practice in connection with each of the programs. The other (Kline) took responsibility for the writing that emerged from joint formulations of practice principles in connection with this experimentation and that of other members of the staff.

It was in response to the request of colleagues in the agency and across the country and at the invitation of the Director of Research of the United States Children's Bureau that this volume was undertaken. Its content is addressed to practitioners, students, and teachers.

The limitations of space imposed by a single volume confronted us with the issues of what to include and what to omit, what to emphasize in detail and what to condense or telescope. We were guided in our decisions, first, by the explicit needs brought to our attention repeatedly by a diversity of practitioners with varying educational backgrounds and functioning in various types of agencies, and, second, by our own convictions regarding basic aspects of practice that appear to us to be indispensable to the welfare of placed children and their families. Consequently we have focused on only those basic concepts that apply to children in placement regardless of social, ethnic, and economic differences, and for whom foster care is the treatment of choice. We have provided detailed examples of systematic decision-making processes and of illustrative technical procedures within the framework of theoretical concepts that can be directly connected with practice.

We are aware that foster care is still used in many places, not as the treatment of choice, but as a substitute for other suitable services which have not been made available. However, we have not addressed ourselves to this problem nor to this clientele, as the problem embraces the need for broad social and economic reforms leading to prevention and to the provision of appropriate services, subjects which far exceed the purpose of this book. Our purpose, here, is to focus on the identification of family conditions that require placement as the treatment of choice and on treatment measures appropriate to this clientele.

We have, reluctantly, omitted discussion of current experimental developments in the use of group methods, manpower development, and delivery systems. They are large and complex subjects in themselves, well beyond the scope of what could be effectively encompassed in this volume. These important trends hold promise of modifying and improving service, but only to the extent that they are closely related to individualization of the clientele and to the underlying dynamics of foster care as a unique system of nurture and treatment. It is our hope that our efforts will contribute, indirectly, to the efforts of others in these important developments.

ACKNOWLEDGMENTS

The many persons to whom we are indebted include, foremost, our colleagues at the Illinois Children's Home and Aid Society—social workers and special consultants—with whom we worked and from whom we learned for nearly two decades. Among them, special thanks are due to the many staff members who undertook to record their work in sufficient detail to provide case materials for what was then current study and teaching, and for its potential illustrative use in this book. Their names do not appear here because of the large number of persons involved. All case material is anonymous.

We are especially indebted and deeply grateful to the friends and colleagues who gave us their encouragement and generous help with the manuscript in various stages of its preparation. Rachel Marks and Lois Wildy read the entire first draft. Rita Dukette and Ner Littner read parts of the second draft. Each made invaluable suggestions about organization and content. Charles Gershenson's encouragement and confidence contributed immeasurably to our proceeding with the project.

We wish to thank Carl Schoenberg, who reviewed the final manuscript for the Child Welfare League of America and who made valuable editorial suggestions. Thanks are due to Doris Stude for her excellent work in typing the final draft of the manuscript.

Finally, we are grateful to our respective families who gave us their warm support throughout and provided comfortable quarters in which to work while we were in the process of changing our home base.

The writing of this book was supported through the Child Welfare League of America by a grant from the United States Children's Bureau of the Department of Health, Education, and Welfare, which we greatly appreciate.

Draza Kline

Helen-Mary Forbush Overstreet

Blue Ridge Summit, Pennsylvania
May, 1971

CONTENTS

FOSTER CARE OF CHILDREN

CHAPTER I

AN OVERVIEW

The task of conceptualizing foster care services for children has challenged practitioners and teachers ever since the recognition that the needs of placed children were not met simply by transferring children from a disorganized environment to an organized one. Some of the difficulty in conceptualization arises from the fact that foster care as a social service is markedly different from other relatively well conceptualized social services in that it combines both care and treatment of the child and thus is unique in its functions, structure, and procedures. The care and treatment components are inseparable in practice and influence the content and process of the total service beginning with the intake study and terminating with the child's discharge from service. The combination of care and treatment represents a dynamic system of services, within which the participants interact with and influence each other. In order to understand the dynamic interaction and transactions that take place within the total service, it is necessary to understand each participant (person and institution) individually and the ways in which each influences and is influenced by the others.

The major participants in the foster care service system [1] are the

[1] Human systems theory offers a promising framework for a more useful conceptualization of foster care services than has been available in the past. Within this frame of reference all of the individuals and social institutions that participate in each placement situation can be viewed in their interactions and transactions, their reciprocal influence on each other, and the fluid states of equilibrium and disequilibrium within the service system.

In this book the use of the term "system" is based on this description: "Every system is composed of parts which in relationship to one another com-

child and his parents, the surrogate parents [2] and their family or
other social institution, and the caseworker and the agency. A brief
discussion of these participants and their situations will be presented as a prelude to the succeeding chapters.

The Child and His Family

The foster care agency typically sees families at the point when
placement of a child (or children) is under consideration or has already taken place, privately or by the order of a court. While there
are individual differences in the causative factors (economic and
social conditions, individual psychodynamics of the parents and
children, and family dynamics), some conditions of families and of
individual family members in this situation are common to most of
them.

Few parents who need more than temporary care [3] for their children reach this point of crisis without having passed through painful struggles within themselves and within the family. In most instances, when the problem extends beyond a temporary situational
crisis, the causes can be seen in both severe internal (personality)

---

prise the whole not simply in summation, and each part or subsystem has its
own components. In and of itself, a system is a patterned process of action
which has adaptive purposes in the living economy. Each system maintains its
organization or wholeness by regulatory devices which are homeostatic or
equilibratory by goal-seeking, for example, drive reducing activity. In addition
goal-changing activities such as exploratory behavior are actualizations in response to external conditions impinging on the system's potentialities and
which result in novel reactions as in evolution and creativity. Every system
resists disintegration by realignments of gradients, partial sacrifice of structure
or function, or by hardening its boundaries to decrease permeability and open-
ness. Finally, every system is in patterned transactional processes with all others which constitute its environment, to a degree dependent on intersystemic
closeness, significance for viability and external stress." (Roy R. Grinker, Sr.,
M.D., "Conceptual Progress in Psychoanalysis," in *Modern Psychoanalysis*,
Judd Marmor (ed.) Basic Books, 1968. p. 33.)

[2] The term "surrogate parents" is used to cover foster parents and those
child care staff who may be in a parenting role in group facilities.

[3] Temporary care represents a special and limited set of conditions, needs,
and consequences which will not be dealt with comprehensively in this volume.

problems of the parents and external (environmental) problems, interacting with each other. Superimposed on these stresses, the parents and other members of the nuclear family are confronted by a solution to the crisis which, in its very nature, introduces further anxiety and conflict. Contemplated or actual dissolution or partial dissolution of the family as an organic entity typically sets up three interacting responses: (a) the parents feel a sense of failure and loss and they fear the changes that may be engendered by this loss; (b) the children experience dread of impending catastrophic change, fear of loss of their home and family, and fear of the unknown future; (c) the reactions of persons outside the nuclear family—relatives, friends, members of the community—are usually negative in at least some aspects. These three sets of responses have such a major impact on the total family equilibrium that they alter it radically, beyond the limits of the fluctuating equilibrium characteristic of the family's life when it is not threatened by dissolution.

In their internal reactions to the stressful solution, parents almost universally experience a profound sense of failure and fear of loss. In regard to the sense of failure, Whitehorn described the causes of anxiety in a way that is especially pertinent. He emphasized that one of the sources of great apprehension is connected with failing in one's duty, and that this apprehension arises "in large part because one dreads the reactions of other persons" (1). In our culture and in our subcultures, the failure to provide for the care of children within the family represents a supreme failure in one's duty and usually is a devastating blow to parental self-esteem. In addition, placement of the children makes this parental failure highly visible to the other members of the nuclear family and to the extended family and community. All family members then become acutely vulnerable to the external pressures, which derive from cultural and social expectations in addition to heightened internal and intrafamilial pressures.

For the parent the fear of loss has diverse components, based on the dynamics of personality development (2). It includes:

1) Fear of losing the child's love. This fear is not totally unrealistic since the parent has failed the child in the parental role, and

ordinarily has experienced more than the usual negative feelings between himself and the child. He usually is not aware of the complex, insistent, and ambivalent nature of the child's attachment to him or of the fact that the child's individual identity is closely bound up with the parents and the family identity.

2) The parent's wish and need to be rid of the stress of the child's care, which he has been unable to manage successfully. In most cases the guilt that is engendered by both his failure and his wish operates as a heavy psychic burden.

3) Reactivation of painful separation anxiety (3). This type of anxiety is normally associated with early childhood development and tends to be reactivated in adulthood in the face of separation from important persons. There is considerable evidence that many of the parents of placed children have experienced traumatic separations and losses which were not resolved in their own childhood. Consequently in the placement situation the parent suffers from reactivation of his early trauma and the contagion of the separation anxiety felt by his children.

4) Anxiety about the unknown future equilibrium of his life without the child and his potential for re-establishing the family. The relinquishment of full responsibility for the child's direct care opens a door to an unknown outcome in the parent's psychic equilibrium. It provides an opportunity for potential regression or recovery; for further deterioration or a new equilibrium within which he can manage his life more effectively. While these potentials usually are not fully perceived, the expectation of undefined change in his own adjustment frequently is felt and feared by the parent.

The child's anxiety about the expected separation may include fear of annihilation, feelings of helplessness, rage, distrust, and worthlessness. The breakdown in the family and the communicated anxiety of the parents, sensed and observed, create a dread of impending catastrophe. The environmental disintegration brings some degree of personality disintegration in the child. His initial reactions and his subsequent adaptation, after placement, depend in part on his age, ego development, and the effects of his previous separation experiences. A special aspect of his reactions grows out of normal developmental ambivalence. Because every child consciously or unconsciously feels some ambivalence toward his parents, wanting and needing them but at times wishing to be rid of them, the actual separation may seem to him to be a consummation of his hostile wishes and confirmation of his dangerous, omnipotent ability to bring about such a consummation. He almost invariably sees this action as a punishment for something about him that is bad, something that makes him unacceptable to his parents. He feels strong hostility to his parents for doing this to him, hostility that may be conscious or may be repressed or denied. The degree to which he consciously experiences his anxiety, fear, and anger, and his defensive ways of handling them, depend upon his age, maturational level, and individual personality structure. Because, in varying degrees throughout his childhood, he is realistically dependent on adults for care and lacks familiarity with the outside world, he responds with profound fear of the unknown, strange world that lies ahead of him. His present situation, regardless of how bad it may be, at least is known. In the interim between leaving it and becoming familiar with and safe in the new situation, he is a badly frightened child, regardless of what superficial impression he may give. The effects of the separation and early experiences with his parents influence his future adaptation and he is especially vulnerable to crises, loss, or disruptive change.

The reactions and attitudes of relatives, friends, and members of the community show themselves in various ways. Usually these reactions are not experienced as supportive by family members, but rather they add to the environmental stress. Grandparents, especially, are important. They react in terms of their own parental patterns as seen in the familial relationships of their children, and with the particular child who is now an adult and a parent, unable to care for his own child. Sometimes the intimacy of the relationship between the grandparents and the nuclear family group is such that they form an integral part of the family's psychological system (4).

Attitudes of relatives and friends, further removed from the family, may be observed either in direct contact or through the eyes of parent-clients. Those who are members of religious groups, informal social groups, or organized community groups reflect considerable anxiety about the disapproval they expect. Even the parent who has no roots and seems to be identified with no social group suffers from the attitudes of co-workers and employers and in relationships with landlords and neighbors. School personnel, in their roles as educators, react in the context of their particular role expectations. As would be expected, the problems in the family become manifest to the teacher because they interfere, in some way, with the child's school attendance, social behavior, or learning. Reactions and interventions of teachers are managed in various ways, but to the child and the family they are experienced as external pressures, since even the most constructive approach is implicitly a criticism.[4]

In cases other than clear-cut temporary situational crises, exploration of the family situation, when placement is under consideration, usually reveals that the family situation before the application was fraught with problems of social and personality breakdown, usually in one or both parents, and exacerbated problems with the children. The crisis that precipitates the move toward placement of the children as a solution to the problems is triggered by either some added external, environmental pressure or some internal, intrapsychic stress in a member of the family, either a parent or a child. The triggering stress introduces a change in the family equilibrium. If, for example, one parent experiences some added environmental or internal stress which is expressed in some kind of symptomatic behavior, there follow reactive feelings and behavior in some other family member (spouse or child) that alter the family equilibrium, which is already out of balance. Individual tension and anxiety are heightened and the remnants of family equilibrium may disintegrate. In many instances, some thought of separation and placement of the children has been present in the past, introduced either by a parent or by an outside agent.

After placement of the child, the family members no longer constitute an organic entity; nevertheless, the psychological ties of the individuals to each other persist and are influenced by the effects

---

[4] This reaction should not be viewed as an environmental pressure that, per se, should be modified. The role of the school personnel in identifying children's problems and family situations that represent potential hazards to children and families is of the utmost importance in regard to both preventive and therapeutic measures.

of the family separation. Each member is confronted with the psychological task of adapting to the changes in the family relationships and making new relationships.

The Surrogate Parents

The surrogate parents (in a foster family or an institutional setting) are responsible for the direct care and nurture of the child and have the most intimate interpersonal involvement with him. The natural parent's involvement, once the child is placed, is primarily on an internal feeling and thinking level; he no longer has direct responsibility for the child's care and is removed from the daily interaction that takes place in child-rearing and family or group living. Likewise, the caseworker, although responsible and accountable for the child, must be a step removed from the direct interaction involved in living with the child, in order to discharge the vital functions of maintaining a balance in the relationships and providing, securing, and unifying the various actions needed on the child's behalf.

The role of the surrogate parents, then, is more heavily weighted with emotional and practical demands and investments, different from and more intimately associated with the child, than those of other persons in the foster care system. The surrogate parents must respond to four distinct aspects of change that accompany the placement of a child: (a) the needs and demands of the foster child; (b) the reactions of their own family or group members and the change in the group dynamics that occur in reaction to the presence of an added child; (c) the participating role of the natural parents; (d) the agency's role and expectations and the adaptation to and use of the supervisory-helping functions of the caseworker in respect to the new child and his family.[5]

---

[5] The subject of the child care worker's role and functioning in group care facilities is not included in this volume. It is thoroughly covered in various publications on the subject of group care. (See especially Morris Mayer's bibliography, reference no. 16, p. 131 in *Foster Care in Question*, Child Welfare League of America, N.Y., 1970.) It should be noted, however, that despite the similarities discussed here, child care workers' roles and tasks differ in important ways from those of foster parents. The group care facility is not intended

These changes alter the equilibrium within the facility and necessitate a reintegration to include the foster child, his parents, and
the agency. Once established, the equilibrium in the relationships
may remain relatively in balance for long periods of time. However, such changes as illness of the surrogate parents or their group
members, changes in the composition of the group, and emotional
problems in the new child or other members of the group, may introduce a disequilibrium ranging from minor to crisis proportions.
Likewise, disequilibrium may be introduced from outside, by one
of the other participants in the service. For example, a mentally ill
parent or relative may unexpectedly announce a wholly unrealistic
and undesirable plan to seek the return of the child; the caseworker on whom the surrogate parents have come to rely may
leave the agency; a change in agency policies may directly affect
the foster child and the surrogate parents. Re-establishment of a
stable equilibrium may be partly within the problem-solving skills
of the surrogate parents, but, at the very least, to the extent that
the disequilibrium is caused by changes in other participants, the
problem-solving role is shared with the caseworker.

The Caseworker and the Agency

The caseworker, representing the agency, is the central person in
the dynamic system of the service. He maintains an overview of

---

to and cannot provide a facsimile of family life. The staff member does not
utilize his family life on behalf of the children; on the contrary, it is usually
desirable to separate his personal life from his job. His role is defined in accordance with the purposes and structure of the setting in which he is employed. He is expected to learn to modify lay attitudes, learn certain professional skills, adapt his functioning on the job to the needs of the individual
children and the group, and learn to work as a member of an interdisciplinary
professional team.

The caseworker's role with child care workers differs greatly from his role
in working with foster parents. The role may differ from one group facility to
another, depending on the total role network as conceived and defined by
each group care facility. It is essential that the caseworker learn from each ad-
ministrator about the role expectations in order to function appropriately in a
variety of group care settings.

the individuals and groups, their situations, needs, and actions, and the ways in which they relate to and interact with each other. He observes the changes, and he plans and carries out case strategies to meet emerging needs, to prevent crises when possible, and to aid in the restoration of stability to the interpersonal and intergroup equilibrium. He initiates actions that are intended to bring about an environment that benefits the child sufficiently to assure his progression along lines of healthy maturation.

The caseworker's identifications with child, parents, and surrogate parents, determine largely the emphasis and direction in the ongoing plans. The caseworker's professional aims are to find and maintain a reasonable balance in these identifications and to see, from his position, the needs of each and their influence on each other. The caseworker carries a professional and ethical obligation for objectivity and self-awareness, but it is rare for a practitioner in any of the disciplines operating in a complex set of interpersonal relationships, roles, and situations to maintain a self-regulated, even balance in identifications. In this connection, the agency supervisor or consultant, or both, can have an important function in the foster care system. Because they are a step removed from the operational level of interpersonal relationships, they can bring to the practitioner the opportunity to ventilate and assess his feelings and regain needed objectivity.

The place of the agency in the life of the placed child is a peculiarly important one. What the agency does for the child will heavily influence his future destiny. In the agency lies the responsibility for the realization of the promise inherent in the assumption of parental authority. The image of the good parent holds promise that each child's welfare will be the prime consideration that governs the agency's actions, within the limits of its means. In its role as the ultimate parental authority, the agency's philosophy and value system are reflected in the services it provides and the ways in which it provides them. These actions influence the child's environment and the interaction that takes place between and among the participants in the foster care system of services. One of the major examples of this is seen in the agency's philosophy and practice in relation to the parents and family members of the placed child. If the agency views the child and his family as its client-group, and in this context gives a priority to the services extended to parents and siblings, each individual in the service system experiences a set of psychological and practical conditions distinctly different from those in which the agency assumes no major service commitment to the parents or siblings of the placed child. The caseworker is directly affected. Work with severely disturbed clients in any setting is difficult. Work with the disturbed parents of placed children inevitably arouses some ambivalence in the practitioner. Many of the parents do not initiate or maintain active involvement with the agency; thus, the caseworker must take the initiative in developing a working alliance with the parents. This initiative is possible when service to the parents is a defined and expected function, built into the agency's practical arrangements and working conditions, and strongly backed by supervisory leadership and support. The agency, in providing for a total, integrated service to the family, supports the positive side of the ambivalent feelings of the staff member toward the parents, and his professional maturational pattern is implicitly supported and encouraged.

When the agency is unable to provide these conditions, the caseworker may be in conflict and the child and surrogate parents are adversely affected by the resulting attitudes.

The various enabling services of the agency—financial procedures, public information practices, and the like—form an additional part of the total image of the agency's value system, as seen by the individuals within the service system and by the community in which it operates. To make this principle more concrete, on the financial level foster parents tend to feel more valued if their checks arrive promptly or within a day of the expected dates than they do if the agency's procedures are inconsistent. In the realm of public information (alternatively called public relations) some agencies who do not identify the children emphasize that the privacy of the placed child should be comparable to that of a child living in his natural family. Thus, the agency enacts its own value system in overt and subtle ways that influence the environment of both the child and the surrogate parents.

The agency's professional commitment to the use of available knowledge about child development and family relationships is reflected in the services it provides to facilitate the physical, psychological, and social development of the child and his family members. The surrogate parents, in receiving supervision and help from the agency, identify with its value system or reject it, as does the caseworker, in varying degrees. The ramifications of these identifications spread into the family relationships, the casework relationship, and the wider community.

Conclusion

Three features of the foster care service, which have far-reaching influence on its structure, content, and process, can be extrapolated from this overview. First, is the inseparable union of care and treatment. Care of the child in any placement facility requires an environment that is therapeutically oriented at least to the degree that the meeting of normal needs in daily life is augmented by understanding of the child's reactions to the separation experience and by modifications in his care [6] which are adapted to this understanding.

Second, the psychological effects of separation and loss occupy a central position in the reactions of placed children (and their parents), not only at the time of placement but also at subsequent periods of stress. This high degree of vulnerability to loss, change, and disrupting experiences requires, as a corrective living experience, the stabilization, reliability, and continuity of key relationships.

Third, the foster care agency, through the caseworker, is the central unifying agent in the foster care system to insure stability and continuity to the greatest extent possible. The distribution of child-rearing responsibilities and authority among various individuals and institutions (parents, agency, surrogate parents, court) not only segments the functions but also makes the structure inherently

[6] Hereafter the term "care" will be used to denote both the care and treatment components of the service.

susceptible to fragmentation and discontinuity. The foster care agency has the central task of coordinating and unifying the services, defining roles, and facilitating communication among the participants in the service system. The degree to which an adequate maturative environment is provided for each child is largely determined by the coherence and integration of the agency's philosophy, policies, and practices.

REFERENCES

1. John C. Whitehorn, M.D., "Guide to Interviewing and Clinical Personality Study," *Archives of Neurology and Psychiatry,* Vol. 52, No. 3.
2. Irene M. Josslyn, M.D., *Psychosocial Development of Children,* Family Service Association of America, New York, 1948. D. W. Winnicott, M.D., *The Maturational Processes and the Facilitating Environment,* International Universities Press, Inc., New York, 1965, pp. 15–93.
3. For a summarized review of the main theories of separation anxiety and a comprehensive bibliography, see: John Bowlby, M.D., *Separation Anxiety: A Critical Review of the Literature,* Child Welfare League of America, Inc., New York, 1962.
4. James Anthony, M.D., and Therese Benedek, M.D., *Parenthood,* Little, Brown and Company, Inc., Boston, 1970, pp. 185–206. Benedek's presentation of grandparenthood is pertinent to the understanding of grandparents' reactions to a placement experience in their family.

CHAPTER II

THE DIAGNOSTIC INTAKE STUDY
AND ITS USES

Introduction

The diagnostic study and evaluation of the child and his parents form the cornerstone for planning of care and treatment. One of the chief sources of difficulty in the use of foster care as a treatment method is the failure to utilize the diagnostic study as an instrument for determining whether placement is needed; for evaluating the prognosis for parental rehabilitation; and for determining the type of care and treatment needed by the child. The systematic use of a psychosocial diagnosis as the basis for planning does not rule out errors, eliminate failures, or guarantee success. As in the treatment of any pathological condition, the severity and complexity of some conditions inevitably exceed the technical skills and resources available at any given time. However, a treatment plan based on a diagnosis of individual and family dynamics eliminates the much higher rate of risk resulting from action unrelated to a systematic diagnosis and planning and facilitates the growth of a body of tested knowledge within each agency and within the field.

The foster care caseworker, in the intake process, should learn in a direct relationship with the parents, if they are available, how they see their situation, its causes, and its solutions. Although a referring source may have concluded a study, or the child may already have been removed from his home, the foster care agency brings to its study specialized knowledge about placement which other types of agencies do not possess. The estimate of the prognosis for rehabilitation of the family, and the probable duration of care, can be obtained best from direct experience with the clients. In some instances, when referral to the foster care agency takes place after the child's removal from his home by the action of a court, the agency, on the basis of its study, may recommend the immediate restoration of the child to his family.

An equally important purpose of the agency caseworker is to utilize the intake study process to develop a working alliance [1] with the parents. Thus, the interview with the parents is viewed as the central procedural approach to the intake study, regardless of the age, whereabouts, or legal status of the child—unless the parents' legal rights have been permanently terminated. There are, of course, exceptional cases in which the parents have abandoned or become separated from the child, have left the community, and have demonstrated beyond doubt that, for the child's welfare, the abandonment should be left undisturbed. The parent who is chronically mentally ill, hospitalized, and unable to participate may also be an exception, but in many such cases a visit to the hospitalized parent may be indicated when approved by the hospital medical staff. Some parents in this situation are able to take reassurance and comfort from the firsthand contact with the agency representative responsible for the care of the children, and the children are reassured by the knowledge that the caseworker has seen the parent and can bring together for them some of the fragmented parts of their lives. The same holds true for the parent who is confined to jail or prison. If the relationship with the child has been important, some direct contact initiated by visit or by mail during this period serves both the parent and the child and contributes to the beginning of the future working alliance.

The interview with the available parent, as the initial and central procedure in the study, provides information regarding the child and the family. Hearing directly from the parent his story of the problem and the situation, how he thinks it came about, how it has affected his life, and what he sees as the solution is of chief im-

[1] See pp. 167–73 for detailed discussion of "the working alliance" with parents.

portance in telling the caseworker about him as a person and a parent and in revealing the emotional climate in which the child has lived.

The establishment of a working alliance with the parent, which begins at this point, may become one of the ultimate determining factors in the outcome of the service. If for any reason an alliance is not initiated at this point, it becomes increasingly difficult to establish one subsequently because the agency's action in moving ahead with a plan for the child without the prior participation of the parent can in many instances become an obstacle to the establishment of such a relationship. The parent experiences or interprets the agency action either as affirmation that his isolation from the child is desirable or as evidence of depreciation, neglect, or some other harmful attitude toward him on the part of the agency.

Much has been said in the past decade in the professions of both social work and psychiatry about the relevance and lack of relevance, uses and misuses of personal history as a part of the diagnostic intake study. Much has been discarded in those settings in which the personal life history has no specific relevance to the aims of the service and the treatment approaches needed to achieve those aims.

In the foster care agency the scope and content of the intake study and the relevance and use of the personal life history of the child and the parents are of particular significance because of the special uses of the study and its far-reaching influence on decision-making and planning. In general, when placement of a child is not involved individual or family treatment plans that are derived from the initial diagnostic assessment are fluid and modifiable. Re-evaluation and modifications of the treatment approach are intrinsic to the treatment process. By way of contrast, in the foster care agency the decision to place a child and the selection of the placement facility are not fluid and modifiable aspects of the treatment process. Should it be necessary to change a child's placement as a result of insufficient information or incorrect diagnostic assessment of the information, there are grave disadvantages to the child, lesser but serious disadvantages to the parents, and concomitant erosion of the agency's resources (foster parents or child care staff, and professional staff invested in the service to the child and family).

The necessity for such decisions gives the diagnostic study a prominent position as one of the most critical aspects of the foster care service. A full understanding of the purposes and uses of the intake study serves as the guide to the timing and selective gathering of information, the use of various diagnostic procedures, and the relevance or lack of relevance of individual and family history.

Evaluating the Need for Placement

There are two major stages in the intake study process: the exploratory stage and the full study for placement. The central purpose of the exploratory stage is to determine whether placement is one of the needed services. If it is not and other service is needed, this stage may be completed by offer of the appropriate service or by referral elsewhere. If it is determined that placement is one of the needed services, the intake process proceeds to the stage of the full study for placement. Two contrasting case examples will illustrate the content and process in the exploratory stage. The first case (Abbott) shows the focus and scope of a study that does not lead to placement. The second case (Bryant) shows the differences in content when the exploratory process moves in the direction of placement. The diagnostic judgments for decision-making center around these areas:

1) The nature of the crisis and the presenting problems.
2) The ego functioning of the parents in their major life roles and their capacity to cope with the current family crisis.
3) The family's situation, organizational level, and resources.
4) The developmental status and condition of the children.

THE ABBOTT CASE

Mr. Abbott, the father of two children, Jack, aged four, and Bonnie, aged two, applied for foster home placement for both children. He gave the following information spontaneously: The mother had deserted the family a year earlier and had disappeared. The children were living with the paternal grandparents, but the father thought they were not receiving adequate care, as their diet was inadequate, their daily routine was not sufficiently stable, and because of their Puerto Rican background the grandparents spoke Spanish, which he thought might confuse the children. He worried about his son's development because he seemed afraid of his grandmother when she scolded him. Mr. Abbott explained that he visited the children after work every day, had dinner, and spent the evening with them. On weekends he took them to his apartment to get them away from one of his sisters, who was mentally "not right" and sometimes went into unpredictable rages. He wanted the two children placed together; he planned to continue to see them each evening and to take them home for weekends.

The interviewer did not enter into a discussion of visiting arrangements, as this was not central to the purpose of the interview at this point, and would have diverted the focus from information needed for determining the nature of the problem or the crisis that motivated the father to request placement of the children at this specific time. Instead, the interviewer picked up and explored the father's comment about his sister's rages. The father thought this sister, aged thirty, was mentally defective in some way. She had always been retarded. Her rages, which were directed toward her parents, had been an increasing problem, and the family had considered the possibility of her needing hospitalization. When asked, the father said she had never attacked the children, but he worried about this possibility.

The other family members in the home were a teen-age sister attending high school, a sister, aged twenty, employed as a nurse's aide in a community hospital, and a brother, aged twenty-two, who had just returned from military service. Inquiry revealed that there were no economic problems. All the male members of the family had stable jobs in various aspects of mechanical repairs and maintenance. The father paid a reasonable monthly rate to his parents to cover the cost of the children's care.

The interviewer asked if Mr. Abbott could tell her a little more about his wife. He recounted the highlights of his marriage. His wife had been only sixteen when they married. The first child was born five months later. They had been "going steady" since she was fourteen years old. He knows now that they were both too young for marriage. His wife was "sloppy" in caring for the home, didn't wash the dishes or keep the children clean. Meals were never served on time. She let the children play until they fussed, then fed them and put them to bed. There was much marital conflict centering around her inadequacies as housekeeper and mother.

Several times after he criticized her, she took the children and went to her mother's home. There were two long separations, the last one final; the mother deserted and left the children with the father. She has not returned or asked to see the children. He was, presently, in the process of obtaining a divorce.

The interviewer then turned to a detailed exploration of his concerns about the children. In relation to his concern about diet, she asked about their general health and nutrition. The father described both children as "very healthy." They had recent medical examinations, and he took them to the doctor for their regular medical care, immunizations, and the like. There had been no diagnosis of nutritional deficiency. In his parents' home the daily routine was "casual"; his two sisters shared in the care of the children and his older brother "gave advice" to everyone about their care. The father's tone as he gave this last piece of information revealed antagonism and distaste, but exploration of his concerns about the children's care produced little evidence of inadequate care.

When asked how the grandparents felt about the children, the father said, "Oh, they are crazy about them. They want them." He went on to explain his own point of view. His mother treated Bonnie "like a queen," but when she got mad at Jack she was so harsh with him that he shivered. He spontaneously recalled that his mother had sometimes talked to him that way when he was growing up. His affect suggested that his mother's favoring Bonnie was painful to him.

When the father's initial anxiety had subsided and he seemed to be feeling comfortable, the interviewer said she would like to ask some specific questions in order to get a more complete picture of what the children might need and in what ways the agency could help him. The father was open in his responses. The questions, which were focused on critical areas of child development, indicated that both children seemed to be developing healthily in habit training, age-appropriate independence, play, sleeping and eating patterns, and initiative. They accepted and used care from the family members and went to adults for help or comfort when they were upset. They were always glad to see their father when he arrived after work. The interviewer commented that on the surface it sounded as though they were doing reasonably well; was there anything more that the father could add that might help us understand the problem? The father observed that it seemed as though he might have no reason to be so worried about their development, but the family situation seemed unstable to him. He was asked when he first began to feel concerned about this. He explained that everything had been all right until recently. He thought things got worse when his brother came home from military service. He then expressed intense feeling about his brother's taking over and telling everyone what to do, including the father.

In further discussion the father moved from requesting placement to expressing a need for help. He and the interviewer identified his need for help in evaluating Jack's development, the suitability of the family for continued care of the children, and his own anxieties in relation to his children and parents. The interviewer explained that there were alternative ways to proceed. One would be for her to visit the family and talk with the family members. This would provide an opportunity to see the children with the family and talk with them enough to get some impressions of what the next steps might be. Mr. Abbott favored this procedure without waiting to hear the alternative. There followed some discussion of how his family would view such a visit, as well as his interpretation of the service and its purposes as he might want to present it to them. He said he had already told them about his intention to look into the possibility of a foster home for the children. He now could see that placement might not be the answer. He decided he would tell them this but that he wanted the case-worker's help with other problems.

The home visit took place as planned and confirmed the tentative diagnostic impressions reached in the first interview. Subsequent service focused on helping the grandparents with commitment procedures for the daughter, who needed hospitalization for what was diagnosed as an organic psychosis. Intermittent interviews were planned with the father to deal with his overdetermined reactions to stresses in the family and to keep in touch with the family situation. The goal was seen as a preventive one: to provide the services needed to maintain the grandparent's home as an adequate one for the children and to help the father adapt to the psychologically complex demands of the family interaction and his parental role.

Analysis of the Interviews

The nature of the crisis did not appear to be environmental or external. The extended family had successfully used its own problem-solving techniques to weather the crisis of the mother's desertion. The home of the grandparents in which the children lived seemed to be intact and free from critical problems. There was little indication of any major change in the current family situation to trigger the request for placement. These observations led to the inference that the crisis or precipitating stress was internal, and further led the interviewer to think along the lines of possible environmental occurrences that might have had special psychological meaning to the father.

There was no major disruption of the new family unit. Neither the grandmother's seeming favoritism of Bonnie nor the sister's disturbed behavior was new. According to the information offered, only one change had occurred in the family which altered the family equilibrium: the return of the brother and his role in the dynamic system of the family. This change did not seem to create an external crisis, but Mr. Abbott's strong affect suggested that it may have caused an emotional crisis within him, in the context of a family situation which was already stressful to him for other reasons, and that this crisis precipitated his request for placement of the children. In many instances when the crisis requires placement of the children, there is an actual or threatened breakdown in the continuity of care in the home.

The father's *ego-functioning* in his roles as wage earner and parent, and by inference, as a member of his nuclear family, seems to be adequate. He had a stable employment history, paid for the children's care, took responsibility for securing their medical care regularly, and spent each evening with the family group. The children's ability to relate to him positively and to the family members suggests that there was a degree of family unity and cohesiveness that made this possible.

Further evidence of the father's adequate ego-functioning and capacity for constructive handling of family relationships was seen in his independent action in seeking help and in his preparation of the family for the caseworker's home visit. These observations yield useful evidence of ego-functioning and the dynamic pattern of interpersonal relationships within the family. How does the father interpret to the family members his application for service? Does he need help, and is he able to use it, to consider constructive approaches to the necessary family involvement in the service? Subsequently, how does he carry out the plans in the direct interpersonal relationships?

The level of family organization and its resources are often reflected in the nature of the crisis. In this case, the grandparents, their children, and grandchildren appeared to comprise a basically stable family unit. The children were loved, valued, and seemed well integrated into the total family system. The major sources of stress were the extremely disrupting effect of having the mentally ill daughter in the home and the return of the brother. The grandparents, although unable to resolve this problem independently, used the agency's help to secure needed hospitalization for their daughter.

The condition and development of the children, evaluated on the basis of the observations of both the father and the caseworker, showed no major problems but rather confirmed the assessment of adequate parenting and of a relatively stable environment in which their needs were being met sufficiently to promote their growth.

The direction of movement in the exploratory interviews provides further diagnostic clues which can be assessed in conjunction with other observations in the diagnostic process. As the father and the interviewer examined the reality of the family situation the movement was away from the initial request. It became apparent to the father, as well as the caseworker, that the situation did not appear to require so drastic a remedy at this time. The father asked few questions about foster care. When the parent wants placement and sees this as the only solution, he usually pursues questions about the service. His strong motivation goes hand-in-hand with serious impairment in some interrelated areas of functioning in major life roles.

LIMITED FOCUS OF
EXPLORATORY INTERVIEWS

It has been implicit in the analysis of the information sought in the initial interview that focus on longitudinal life-history information should be avoided in this stage in the study process. Such information usually is not needed to make a gross diagnostic assessment of the central problem and to formulate the tentative outlines of service needs. To the contrary, obtaining longitudinal history at this point has several disadvantages. It tends to distort the focus on the conditions surrounding the problem, to obscure the purposes of the exploratory stage of the intake process, and to confuse both the client and the interviewer, since neither one knows its relevance. Since it has no mutually understood purpose, it not only causes confusion, but for some clients it may interfere in their use of service. Premature exploration of life history is experienced by some applicants as an invasion of privacy. Hence, it interferes with the development of confidence in the interviewer. For some, excessive anxiety is mobilized beyond the limits of what the ego can sustain, and the applicant may be driven away despite his need for service.

The importance of the caseworker's orientation to well-formulated diagnostic focal points cannot be over-emphasized. The movement toward or away from placement takes its direction from examination of the critical elements in the client's situation. When the movement is toward placement, there must be discussion about the agency's services and policies and how they operate, the agency's expectations in regard to shared responsibility for the care of the child in placement, the impending changes in the parental role, and the parent's hopes and expectations. The reciprocal responses of applicant and caseworker to the shared information about the actual operations of the foster care service become a major dynamic in the decision-making process. The parent's ambivalence about the separation and its various secondary implications, often manifest in resistance to agency policies or procedures, may require some preliminary working through to enable the parent to move ahead into the stage of the full study. In many situations the movement toward placement heightens the family crisis. If critical problems arise, it may be necessary to initiate temporary treatment intervention to protect the family from secondary damage which results from extreme family disintegration.

THE BRYANT CASE

The Bryant case shows the operation of these added factors when the applicant and the caseworker move toward placement in the exploratory interviews. Mrs. Bryant, the mother of two boys, Dick, aged seven, and Ted, aged five, was a client in a family agency for several months before she was referred to a foster care agency. The family agency caseworker reported that Mrs. Bryant and the two boys had always lived with the maternal grandmother, who recently became an invalid following a stroke. Mrs. Bryant had been brought to the family agency by a member of a community church group who said that the family, then living in a cluttered, filthy, cold apartment, was without food.

Mrs. Bryant, who is in her early thirties, had been employed intermittently as a waitress, "bounced from one job to another," and received public assistance when unemployed. The referring caseworker believed that the children should be placed because the mother was unable to use help to improve her situation or to give the children adequate care. They were not overtly mistreated, but they were seriously neglected. They were often hungry, dirty, and unsupervised. Dick had not been started in school, and neither child had been given inoculations for communicable diseases.

There was no father in the home. Mrs. Bryant had been divorced from her husband before the birth of the older boy. She claimed that Mr. Bryant was the father of both boys, but he denied it. Appeal to the court for support for Dick and Ted had been denied.

Mrs. Bryant could not mobilize herself to look after the children, although she was not currently employed. She wanted placement, but could not follow through on a referral on her own initiative. The family service agency caseworker accompanied Mrs. Bryant to the foster care agency for her initial interview. The interviewer observed that the mother seemed shy and ill at ease. Mrs. Bryant said she wanted the boys placed, but she "couldn't say exactly why very easily." She said she wasn't able to give them the proper supervision, especially when she was working. The maternal grandmother couldn't get around any more to look after them. The mother shrugged her shoulders and looked helpless. She gave no reason why Dick wasn't in school; she just hadn't sent him. The grandmother had always taken care of the boys until she became ill.

She described the boys vaguely, saying that "they are pretty good." Ted stays in better than Dick and amuses himself. Both make friends readily and like children of their own age. They sleep well and eat well, have no illnesses, and have had no need for medical care for several years. Last year for about three weeks they stayed with a family that knew them from the neighborhood settlement house, and were not homesick. They like toys and animals, are energetic and lively, but need direction.

In talking about foster care, Mrs. Bryant said she would not want the boys separated, but again she could give no reason. She frequently turned to the family agency caseworker to help her in the interview. This caseworker raised questions about the foster care agency's service and procedures, reflecting some of the questions she and Mrs. Bryant had discussed previously. The interviewer explained briefly the steps taken by the agency to get acquainted with parents, to understand the situation thoroughly, and to work together toward a decision about what plan would be best for the family. Mrs. Bryant said she thought that if she could place the boys for a few months she could find a job and then take them home. The interviewer explained that the decision about the length of time was an important one. Usually the agency found that if only temporary relief was needed it might be provided in other ways. If Mrs. Bryant would like, they could talk together about her whole situation and consider carefully what would be best for her and the boys. Mrs. Bryant wanted to proceed in this way, and was given an appointment for another interview.

The second interview was held in the home after the mother had canceled several office appointments. The caseworker proposed the home visit because she was concerned about the reported neglect of the children and the mother's passive, depressive affect in the first interview. The mother gladly accepted the proposal. There was minimal discussion about the family's preparation for the visit. Mrs. Bryant confirmed that her mother and the boys knew that she had asked the agency for foster care and agreed to tell them about the caseworker's expected visit.

Interviewer's Notes

Mrs. Bryant and her mother were at home in the small, crowded, three-room apartment in a run-down neighborhood. Clothing and boxes littered the rooms. Mrs. Bryant looked clean, but her hair was uncombed. She appeared blank and dull, but became more alive and better able to express herself as the interview progressed. Her mother was poorly dressed and talked in a monotonous tone with little inflection, saying over and over again that her son wanted to put her in a nursing home. She complained that the land- lord threatened to smash Dick's nose all over his face if he played in the hallway or on the stairs. She said she would do the same to him if he touched the boy. Mrs. Bryant said that she didn't like to hear about that anymore. The interviewer tried to focus the begin- ning of the interview on the mother's problem of needing care for the children, what she had thought about it since the previous in- terview, and how she felt the agency could help her. Mrs. Bryant responded that it was impossible to find reliable sitters for the children. She and her mother rambled over various complaints about sitters, their high cost, and their neglect of the children. The interviewer inquired about relatives and other family members as possible resources. Mrs. Bryant said she had two brothers but each had his own troubles taking care of his own kids. She dismissed this discussion and talked about her trouble with her public welfare income. She prefers to work; she planned to look for another factory job "after the boys are settled."

The interviewer referred back to the first interview regarding the mother's understanding of the agency's services, how it worked, and what further questions she might have. Mrs. Bryant recalled what she had been told, that the caseworker would want to talk with her several times to see what would be best for her and the two boys. She recalled also that the agency questioned the desirability of temporary care. The interviewer asked whether she had thought further about this. She said that at first she thought about placing the boys for a short time until she could get a steady job, but now she could see that they would be better off if placed for a longer time, if she could see them. She seemed dubious as to whether this would be allowed. The interviewer said this would be important for her and for the boys, explaining that the frequency of visiting was arranged on an individual basis for each family. It is important to arrange regular visits so that all know what to count on. Mrs. Bryant was relieved to know that visits were held at the agency and that the caseworker would be present to help her and the children get accustomed to the changes. She then asked about medical care. The caseworker explained that the agency maintains a medical service with a nurse and a pediatrician. The details of medical procedure and the rationale for this as a part of the agency's responsibility when it undertakes the full-time care of a child were discussed.

Mrs. Bryant inquired about financing. She was told that parents are expected to pay in accordance with their income, and that the caseworker and the parent review income and expenses together as a basis for the agency to set the fee. The plan is reviewed periodically or if circumstances change.

After a lull, the caseworker asked whether Mrs. Bryant had thought any more about how she would feel about having the boys live away from her. The grandmother interrupted, saying, "Oh, she'll be happy to have them gone." Mrs. Bryant, in a child-like, pouting way, said, "I will not, mama." She continued, in a more mature tone, to explain that she had to make better plans for them, that she had to work, and that her mother could not take care of them any longer.

After another lull, the interviewer returned to ask whether there were other things the mother was wondering about. Mrs. Bryant asked how the agency got foster homes and how she could be sure they were good ones. She was told about the study, selection, and supervision of foster homes. She asked if the agency placed many children in the same home; she wanted the boys to be together. The interviewer explained that the agency usually tried to get to know the children, what they are like, and what they need and then tried to select the place that seemed best for each of them. This would be talked over with her, but she could be assured that if the children were not placed together they would at least have regular visits with each other and with her. Ordinarily there are family visits with all of the family members at the same time, unless there is some reason for a different plan.

Mrs. Bryant then began to talk about the boys, seemingly wanting to give a positive picture of them, but her mother interrupted to say that they were learning foul language from the boys in the neighborhood. Dick has been asking for a bicycle lately, and can't understand that the family can't afford it. When the grandmother talks to them about living in a foster home, she says they will have more room to play. The interviewer asked the grandmother how the boys react to her talk about moving. She said Dick told her he doesn't want to move, but when the boys don't obey her she tells them they will have to go to a children's home, where there is a big fence so they can't get out. Mrs. Bryant interrupted. She did not like her mother saying that to the boys; she must have them placed because she could not take care of them. The interviewer supported the mother's nonpunitive explanation.

Mrs. Bryant then asked if the children would stay in one home

or would have to move from home to home. She was given an ex-
planation of the agency's efforts to place children, and of the coop-
erative relationship between caseworker and parents to work out
the ways for parents to participate which contribute to stabilizing
the placement. She was also told about the caseworker's work with
the children and foster parents or child care staff to help them in
the necessary ways.

At this point Dick and Ted came in. They sat on the couch
between their mother and grandmother. They patted and caressed
grandmother, who responded warmly. There was little interaction
with the mother. The boys were both dirty and poorly dressed.
They acknowledged their mother's introduction, saying "Hello."
The interviewer asked them about their play. They talked about
their baseball games, which they enjoyed. Dick printed his name,
and Ted's, and said he was going to school in the fall. They began
to fight over some marbles, and the grandmother yelled at them,
saying "the lady" was going to take them to a children's home be-
cause they were so bad. The mother yelled at the grandmother not
to say that. Dick, the elder of the two, cried and crawled behind
the couch. He seemed to be much younger than his age and gave
the impression of possible mental retardation. Ted did not cry. He
delighted in "needling" Dick, but there were indications that when
he was angry or frightened he teased or laughed inappropriately.

Before leaving, the caseworker talked with the boys in the pres-
ence of the mother and grandmother. The caseworker explained
the agency's work and why she was there, emphasizing that she
and the family would try to become well acquainted before decid-
ing where it would be best for the boys to live.

Analysis of the Interviews

The content and process of these two initial interviews took an
entirely different direction from that of the Abbott interviews, even
though the areas of information sought by the interviewers were
comparable. The differences in direction stemmed from the differences in the problems and motivations of the applicants and the
diagnostic inferences reached by the interviewers.

The crisis in the Bryant family was precipitated by the major en-

vironmental change of the physical incapacitation of the grandmother, who was the main child-caring adult. The crisis was preceded by serious economic and psychological problems.

The ego functioning of the mother, as parent and as wage
earner, was inadequate to achieve minimal success, currently and
in the past. Her inability to solve the current environmental problem was a continuation of a long-standing pattern of helplessness
and dependency. She had never taken direct responsibility for the
care of her children and had not been able to provide the supplemental parenting required to secure health care, education, or a
minimally adequate income. She developed no job skills, although
she preferred working to caring for the children, and had a history
of moving from job to job. Further evidence of severe ego disfunction was seen in her inability to seek help. When the family was
without food, a neighbor took Mrs. Bryant to the family service
agency. When she applied to the foster care agency for service, she
was accompanied by the caseworker.

In the course of the interviews, Mrs. Bryant's interest in foster
care did not waver. She did not move away from the request; instead, she consistently focused her questions on the specifics of the
agency's service. Mrs. Bryant's helplessness and entrenched pattern
of dependency on others, her chronic failures in work, parenting,
and home-making, and her marked depressive affect revealed pervasive maladaptive ego functioning.

The children showed overt disturbance in their social behavior
in the community, possible retarded intellectual development, and
potentially severe emotional disturbance evidenced by inappropriate affect and infantile behavior. The observable problems suggested serious environmental deficits and warranted thorough diagnostic exploration.

The mother's inability to use help from the family service agency
in any area other than the referral for foster care was consistent
with the total diagnostic picture and served as confirmation of the
potential need for placement. This combination of problems is typical of those of many families in which placement of the children is
needed and cannot be averted by less drastic treatment measures.

The intensification of family tensions and the increased *family disorganization* observed in the home visit to the Bryants are typical reactions to the beginning of placement planning. The observations in the home visit provide clues to the treatment measures that might be needed as a part of the study process. In this case, the grandmother's threats to the children (which probably reflected her guilt over the necessity to place them), the tension between mother and grandmother, the intense anxiety revealed in the children's behavior, and the landlord's recent threats regarding Dick's behavior suggest potential sources of future crises and the need for specific preventive intervention.

The first step in the treatment intervention was taken by the caseworker when she talked with the children, in the presence of the mother and grandmother, to clarify her role, and to define the future relationship. The direct discussion tends to reduce anxiety about the unknown and to communicate the caseworker's nonpunitive supportive attitude.

The communication of the caseworker's attitude is of considerable therapeutic importance, since each of the family members is dealing with a great deal of shame, guilt, or fear of punishment, and all are fearful of what appears to them as a catastrophic impending change. The caseworker's relative freedom from anxiety and her objective responses help to alleviate the intense anxiety of the family. In a sense, the caseworker lends an auxiliary ego to the family from which to draw support during the most acute period of disintegration.

The Full Study for Placement

The full study should expand in comprehensiveness and depth to confirm the need for placement and to yield adequate information for the following purposes:

1) Prediction of the probable duration of placement and of the potential for family rehabilitation.

2) Determination of the other services needed by the child and other family members.

3) Selection of the appropriate placement facility (type of foster home or type of group care).

4) Preparation of surrogate parents for the child-caring tasks through the caseworker's selective sharing of information about the child and his family and interpretation of anticipated needs.

5) Planning and structuring the contacts between the placed child and his nuclear family members in the initial period after the placement. (Later observation may indicate the need for modifications in the visiting plan.)

Ordinarily it cannot be concluded, on the basis of exploratory interviews, that foster care will be needed. The parents' responses or the caseworker's subsequent findings in the course of the study process may alter the diagnostic assessment of the need for foster care as a treatment measure. However, when the initial interviews move in this direction they are likely to prove consistent with the future findings.

It should be noted that the purposes extend beyond those of a clinical study for treatment because of the necessity to select the child's new environment, provide for his education and health care, orient the prospective surrogate parents to his needs, and plan his future contacts with the important persons from his past life.

If the parent is available to participate in the study, and as work proceeds, there must be continuing explanation to him and other family members about the nature of the steps to be taken and the reasons for these steps. Obviously, the caseworker can clarify the purposes of the various steps in the study only if he is entirely clear about them himself. Clarification of the relevance of information sought by the interviewer holds a particularly important therapeutic potential when placement is under consideration. The relinquishment of responsibility in one of the parent's vital life roles opens the door to potential regression. Some degree of regression may take place, inevitably, but offering service can be designed to strengthen the client, as much as possible. When the client knows the purposes of the proposed steps, if he is able to perceive their meaning, he has an opportunity to relate to these purposes, and to be an active rather than a passive, compliant participant. If the parent appears to be too disturbed or too disorganized to integrate the information, a simple explanation of the steps in the study is indicated.

Discussion of content which is usually relevant to a comprehensive study for placement follows.

LIFE HISTORY OF PARENTS

It is implicit in the foregoing discussion that learning about the current situation and problems, the conditions that led to the problems, and the family's problem-solving efforts has involved the exploration of the current functioning of family members in their important life roles. These include marital, parent-child, and work relationships, and the health, education, economic, and social conditions of the family.

Beyond this, how much and what aspects of the longitudinal life history of the parents are relevant to fulfilling the purposes of the full intake study? What lines of exploration yield information that contributes to essential understanding? There is considerable latitude for adapting this aspect of the history-taking process to the parents' wishes and needs. Given the far-reaching uses of the study, a fairly full longitudinal life history is potentially useful. But understanding the childhood genesis of the parents' problems is not essential to help the children in placement. It may become so at some point in helping the parent with a specific problem, at which time the needed information can be secured. For purposes of a tentative prediction of duration and outcome of foster care, it is important to understand the patterns of adaptation and the chronicity, duration, severity, and repetitious patterns of severe maladaptive behavior in the parental and other life roles.

Parents ordinarily tell a good deal about themselves spontaneously. Some offer a great deal of information, not only about their current situation, but also what brought them to it. In so doing they may recall their experiences in growing up and recount their marital difficulties, their economic pressures, and the like, as a part of the total context in which they see their present situation.

The necessity to place a child often stimulates the parents to recount some of their own childhood experiences and to relate them in some way to the present situation with their children. It is important to listen, to take note, and to be aware that any information the parent offers spontaneously is of immediate diagnostic usefulness in understanding his feelings about placement, as well as of potential future usefulness. Such spontaneous recounting of life history opens the door for purposeful direction by the caseworker, through expressing interest or well-directed, responsive questions or comments about areas that are pertinent. With such clients, a longitudinal history of significant childhood experiences usually can be obtained.

For others, who are guarded and defended about the years before marriage and the establishment of a family, the exploration of childhood history on the initiative of the caseworker may not seem relevant, and the guarded attitude may serve an important defensive purpose.

LIFE HISTORY OF CHILD

A full and detailed picture of the child's current functioning and of his life history is the ideal goal of the study of the child (3). It can seldom be fully achieved, but in many cases a reasonably well-documented history can be obtained. The detailed longitudinal history of the child, from birth to the time of placement, has considerable value in three important areas: (a) it helps the caseworker understand the child's current developmental status and provides the basis for a diagnosis of problems that are manifest or are latent and may emerge later, during placement; (b) it contributes to the caseworker's knowledge of the child's specific strengths and vulnerabilities and enables the caseworker to anticipate his needs in the placement experience; (c) it is the source for providing the child with information about himself at times in the course of his placement when such information adds to his self-understanding or meets his need to establish continuity between past and present.

A convenient and useful framework for the study of the child can be based on five major areas of information: (a) interpersonal relationships; (b) health; (c) habit-training and performance; (d) intellectual and educational status; and (e) sublimations (other than education) and socialization.

The sources of vital information are the parents, substitute parents or child-caring adults if they have been substantively engaged in the child's care, school personnel who know the child, social and medical agencies that have served the child and/or family, court records or reports, others who know the child in group activities or other important functions, the caseworker's observations, and, in selected instances, diagnostic psychological tests. The child himself, when he is sufficiently mature, may give significant history.

Exploration of current functioning as the first step in the study has two advantages: the parents usually are able to relate to it and see its rationale; and the diagnostic assessment helps identify the areas of major emphasis in seeking etiological factors and identifying points of regression or trauma.

INTERPERSONAL RELATIONSHIPS

Often the inexperienced caseworker is at a loss to find productive lines of exploration to obtain a picture of the child's relationships with parents or parent surrogates. Inquiry into the major areas of parental care is illuminating.

Exploration can center around the major parental functions (physical care, affection, training, supervision, protection). These areas open the door to viewing the interaction between child and parent. The focus of exploration is determined in part by the child's age. For example, in a study of a preschool child, the caseworker might explore the child's reactions to being washed or bathed; how he responds to limits or discipline; how he reacts to the parents coming and going; what eating and sleeping and elimination habits are; what is the family's customary way of showing affection; how the child takes help, asks for what he wants, and so on. In this context of specific parenting functions the quality of the relationship with the child emerges. A similar approach may apply to the school-age child, with increasing emphasis on observing the degree of age-appropriate initiative, freedom, and increasing independence in his various activities.

The child's longitudinal life history may be given spontaneously by the informant as he picks up on earlier stages to explain the present behavior, or, as often happens, to alleviate his feelings of frustration, bewilderment, or guilt over some episode for which he feels responsible. This discussion opens the way for the interviewer to pursue pertinent earlier history with appropriate, responsive questions and avoids the relatively sterile question-and-answer approach that caseworkers are sometimes compelled to resort to. Often the history of interpersonal relationships is revealed most meaningfully when the caseworker explores the child's early feeding, weaning, toilet training, walking, and talking history. The mothering relationship, the parental roles, and parents' feelings about the child as they functioned in these roles emerge as we learn how the child responded and behaved. In short, any focus in the history involves both discrete facts and interpersonal interactions.

The child's relationships with siblings usually focus on what they do together, how they do it, how they behave toward each other, and what they do independently of each other.

Relationships with individuals outside the nuclear family have special value in revealing the appropriateness of role relationships and the child's capacity to differentiate his responses to adults whose attitudes and roles differ.

Relationships with peers during the school years become increasingly important in assessing the child's emotional health, anticipating and understanding the loss of peer relationships that he will experience with a change of environment, and evaluating his future movement along developmental lines in this area.

Throughout the assessment of patterns of interpersonal relationship, the caseworker should be especially sensitive to information that will help him to anticipate the child's reactions to loss, the patterns of relating that are pertinent to the selection of his new environment, and to the specific kinds of help that he may need.

At times caseworkers are troubled by the fact that information about the child is colored and unconsciously distorted by the parents. Recognition of this psychological phenomenon actually adds a dimension to the understanding of the child's environment. The way in which the parent perceives the child has been a part of the child's environment and psychic equilibrium. Information about it is most important in helping the caseworker understand the child, the parents, and the family dynamics. Such information, as perceived by the parent, can be checked against other observations of the child, and manifest discrepancies can be evaluated as a part of the total diagnostic assessment of the family members and their inter-relationships. What the parents tell, in their account of the child, is a reflection of what actually happens among the family members. For example, the following is a mother's account of her problems with her twelve-year-old daughter, Cathy, for whom she was requesting an emergency placement:

The mother feared that while she was away at work Cathy would "get in trouble with boys." She had warned Cathy repeatedly, but it was useless. Cathy reacted with anger and denial. The mother, asked when she first began to worry about Cathy's relationships with boys, replied that it was when Cathy entered puberty: "After all, she's just a kid. She doesn't understand these things." The mother recounted how she sat her daughter down and tried to tell her about boys. She has frequently warned her since then. The interviewer asked if anything had occurred to make the mother feel that Cathy had a problem of this kind. She responded, "No, but I thought she should be warned." The caseworker commented, "But you are especially worried now?" The mother responded that recently, while she was at work, Cathy stayed home from school and had a boy in the house. Upon questioning, Cathy admitted that he had "rubbed against her." In this brief recital, the mother revealed that one aspect of her relationship to her daughter was her expectation of sexual acting out, and that this had been unconsciously communicated through repetitious, spontaneous warnings and through her high level of anxiety. For reasons directly involving Cathy's relationship with her mother, Cathy had moved toward the expected behavior.

The mother reported what she perceived: the child seemed obstinate, willful, and disobedient in response to her efforts at guidance and training. The caseworker, however, perceived that the child was responding to the mother's unconscious expectations expressed through her irrelevant warnings. These expectations aroused curiosity and fear. Thus the parent's subjective account of the child's history, development, and behavior may reveal otherwise hidden aspects of the child's environment.

HEALTH HISTORY

Discussion of health status and history, an important subject in itself, may be a suitable place to begin if the parent does not seem able to start with current family relationships. This information, ordinarily nonthreatening to the parent, provides an opportunity for him to reveal his attitudes and reactions to the child's physical development and childhood illnesses. Often parents spontaneously recall a great deal about the family situation at the times when illnesses occurred and about the family interaction in response to the stress. This spontaneous recall is of value in understanding not only the child's physical health history but also his psychological development. A long and early history of successive minor illnesses, upper respiratory infections, and accidents is a clue to possible early, serious affectional deprivation and resultant somatization. However, it is only a clue, not evidence, and the value of the clue is to suggest further areas of exploration to confirm or rule out the possibility of serious and persistent deprivation. If such extreme deprivation has been experienced by the child it is likely to be reflected in his capacity for relationships, his status at various maturational stages, and his current functioning in the crucial areas of living.

The child's current health status also has immediate implications for service. A physical examination secured through the family physician or through the agency's medical facilities sometimes uncovers an acute need for immediate medical care.

The history of illnesses, inoculations, and immunizations is part of the working material of the agency's medical service, which assumes responsibility for the child's care. The entire discussion of this factual information is, in addition, an integral part of the preparation of the parent to transfer this aspect of parental responsibility to the agency. Parents' anxieties about medical care are likely to reflect either their sense of responsibility or their fears that "something will happen" to the child. Such fears may have their genesis in conscious experiences or unconscious conflicts but, regardless of the etiology, direct and clear information about the agency's medical services, practices, and policies is the first level of approach to modifying this anxiety. Usually the caseworker includes information about the standards of medical care, the policies pertaining to keeping parents informed of children's health, authorizations needed for major surgical procedures, and any other major policies.

EDUCATIONAL STATUS—THE SCHOOL AS RESOURCE FOR STUDY INFORMATION

One of the most important and productive sources of information for assessing the child's current developmental status and for planning for his future is the school. Teachers and other school personnel have at their command observations of the child that contribute to an understanding of all aspects of development. Intellectual functioning and learning level and behavior in the classroom are, of course, the teacher's main focus of attention. But the child's behavior in the school yard, his relationships with the teacher and with peers, his attendance and health, his general physical appearance and condition, his affect—all come under the over-all observation of the teacher. The school's contacts with the parents are another important source of information. Some teachers are not aware of the relevance of these observations to the caseworker engaged in a diagnostic study, but teachers often are responsive to explanation and interpretation.

The use of a written school report or a telephone call to a teacher is not an adequate means of using this resource. Exchange of information in a face-to-face, well-directed interview is a different order of communication. It is responsive communication, governed by principles of interviewing, and it creates optimal opportunity for involvement and for moving both participants to a level of observation and understanding that neither can achieve alone. Occasionally, school personnel are uncooperative or appear to be unsuited to their jobs. This fact cannot be evaluated from a printed form or a telephone call, but it is an important piece of information against which to evaluate the child's school performance and attitudes toward school attendance.

At times the current teacher does not know a child because he has only recently been admitted to the current class or the present school. In such instances, it is well worth the time to seek out the previous teacher. Not only is the child's current functioning of importance; one often picks up information here about deterioration in learning, attention, appearance, relationships, and the like. Or, at the other extreme, one sometimes learns that a child who is doing poorly at home is doing well in all or most areas of functioning at school. This fact may have bearing on the ultimate decision regarding the necessity for placement.

An educational diagnosis of a child who is having learning difficulties may be as important to his future development as a medical diagnosis for a child with health problems. Undiagnosed and untreated, poor school work, like other symptoms, for many children becomes a source of continuous erosion of self-esteem, concrete confirmation of personal deficiency, and disapproval from adults. The condition or symptom becomes a potent secondary source of damage to, and interference with, healthy development. Learning problems stem from varied causes. Some children who have been moved from school to school and lack any continuity in their educational experiences have gaps in learning which can be corrected by augmentation of the school program with tutoring. Some are in that large group of children who have had insufficient opportunity for learning during the pre-school years at home. Others are innately retarded intellectually. Others are going through phases of internal turmoil or external environmental stress that interfere with their attention span and ability to concentrate. Others have distinct learning disabilities that result from organic damage. Still others have learning disabilities that are associated with internalized conflicts.

Some public school systems have facilities for making an educational diagnosis which can be shared with the foster care agency; others do not. The aid of specialists, such as a psychologist experienced in diagnosing educational problems, may be needed for an accurate assessment of the problem and for specific treatment recommendations.

THE SELECTIVE USE OF DIAGNOSTIC PSYCHOLOGICAL TESTING

In many residential treatment centers, the diagnostic study routinely includes a battery of intelligence tests and projective techniques administered and interpreted by a psychologist who is a member of the clinical team. In the multifunction foster care agency such routine testing for personality diagnosis is ordinarily not available and, fortunately, it is not necessary in all instances. Selective use of diagnostic testing as an adjunct to the psychosocial history is needed when the data obtainable are insufficient to provide an adequate diagnostic assessment of the child, or when the problems of the child are complex and obscure and require illumination through tapping unconscious processes. In either event, however, a battery of diagnostic psychological tests cannot substitute for a psychosocial diagnosis based on even the most limited information. Observation of current functioning and the quality and use the child makes of relationships with adults who are in helping roles are the essential determinants in selecting a facility for the child. Psychological testing is an adjunctive tool only. In relation to diagnosis for placement, projective techniques may help to clarify such factors as internal reactions to stress and what constitutes stress for the individual child, or to identify crumbling defenses not yet apparent in behavior, and to evaluate underlying capacity for close relationships. These factors have particular value when the child's disturbance raises borderline questions about the kind of environment he needs and can use.

In school-age children intelligence levels often can be assessed adequately through school performance and results of tests administered by the schools. If so, the use of intelligence testing can be reserved for preschool children and school-age children who present problems of educational diagnosis. In the Bryant case, for example, neither child was in school; both gave the impression of limited intellectual functioning; and the mother and grandmother had no discriminating perceptions of intellectual functioning. In such circumstances, establishing the level of intellectual functioning through the use of tests is a desirable diagnostic step as a basis for selecting an appropriate facility.

DIRECT DIAGNOSTIC OBSERVATIONS OF THE CHILD

The caseworker's direct observation of the child is one of the key procedures in the diagnostic process (4). This appraisal utilizes both the intuitive feeling responses of the caseworker and specific observations in defined areas. The caseworker's intuitive responses to the child add to the diagnostic information derived from other sources and substantiate or differentiate the kinds of subliminal responses he elicits in people by subtle or overt behavior. Regardless of the setting or the structure in which the contact takes place, useful observation includes these areas:

1) The child's appearance: physical characteristics and demeanor.

2) The interaction between the child and adults and peers who are present.

3) The use of toys and play and reactions to participation of others.

4) Motor coordination and skill-motor activity.

5) Speech and communication (verbal and nonverbal).

6) Attention span.

7) Initiative.

8) Reactions to brief separations, as observed in leaving and rejoining the parents or parent surrogates.

9) General affect, behavior, and observable symptoms.

Each of these areas of observation is useful only in relation to age-appropriateness and affect-appropriateness. For example, a description of a child's physical appearance and body build has significance only when related broadly to age expectations. This applies similarly to verbalization, play, and all other of the designated areas.

The timing, structure, and focus of early contact may vary widely, depending on the child's age and situation and any particularized aims. The judgment exercised by the caseworker is influenced as much by what the caseworker is trying to avoid as by what he is trying to accomplish. He is trying to avoid introducing unnecessary stress and confusion into the child's situation at this critical point in his life. For this reason, in some cases, informal contacts can be utilized for the purpose of direct observation, as contrasted to a structured interview session. Such informal opportunities for observation may take place in the agency waiting room before or after the parent's interview, in the home during a visit, or in shared contacts with the psychologist, pediatrician, or others who may be involved directly in the study process. In some instances, with the young child, observations obtained in this way are sufficient to amplify the study without the added stress of a one-to-one interview.

Observations of the Bryant children in the home visit illustrate this point. Questions regarding intellectual and emotional development of the two boys emerged. Plans for a complete intellectual and personality evaluation by a clinical psychologist followed. The degree to which the mother's plans had been communicated to the boys prematurely was revealed, and the caseworker included in her contact the specific clarifications that seemed indicated. The emotional stress of premature knowledge of potential placement plans and the children's reactions to the stress were observed. This episode suggests some of the diverse, particularized approaches that can be adapted to the child's situation. When a one-to-one, structured session with the child is needed, the caseworker should be in a position to give the child a brief, simple, specific explanation of the reason for it.

Consideration of the limits of the development of a casework relationship with a child in the course of the study process may seem elementary, but such a relationship is so often a source of confusion that it merits special attention. In any special, short-term relationship with a child it is important for him to know its time limits as well as its purpose. This knowledge tends to protect him from making an unrealistic investment in the relationship and from subsequent disappointment. If the agency's structure of services is such that a transfer of caseworkers is anticipated following the full study, the one-to-one contacts with the child should be limited to the minimum necessary for achieving the study purposes.

The factors that determine, in part, the depth of the relationship are: 1) the length of time spent in each contact; 2) the frequency of contact; 3) the span of time over which the contacts continue; 4) the degree to which the relationship becomes a confidential one.

Technical handling which helps limit the unrealistic development of the relationship includes:

1) Realistic explanation of the purpose of the contacts.

2) Limiting the time with the child in each session to what is essential. Usually this varies roughly from 30 to 60 minutes.

3) Limiting the frequency of contacts to intervals of a few days or a week.

4) Limiting the number of sessions and telling the child what to expect.

5) Avoiding the exploration of unconscious or preconscious feelings and handling feelings on a reality level.

These technical aspects of management tend to protect both the child and the caseworker from an investment in the relationship which is unrealistic for its purpose. The structure of the temporary situation usually can be utilized most productively to achieve the purposes of the contacts when the safeguards and limits are observed.

Prediction of Duration and Outcome of Foster Care

A tentative assessment of the probable duration and outcome of placement and of the prognosis for rehabilitation of the family is drawn from the diagnostic study. Such an assessment is essential to a planned program of care and treatment for the child and as the basis for determining the services needed by the family.

Outcome of placement may fall into one of four major categories: 1) temporary care in which the arrangements for termination can be planned in advance; 2) permanent care through legal adoption; 3) indeterminate long-term foster care; 4) permanent foster care.

Prediction of the probable duration and outcome of placement is essentially a diagnostic problem for the agency rather than one in which the parents' verbalized goals can be accepted at face value. The decision-making process is a mutual one to the fullest extent allowed by the parents' capacities, but the agency alone is responsible for determining what service it should offer. The diagnostic process on which this determination is based includes a careful assessment of the immediate and contributory causes of placement, both social and psychological. The assessment of goals, which is directly related to causes, begins with the agency's first contact with the case.

TEMPORARY CARE

Conditions characterizing the need for temporary care were identified by Sauber and Jenkins in a study of the reasons for placement of children (5). They found that physical illness of the mother as the immediate cause of placement was significantly associated with brief duration of placement. In many such cases, despite the pressures of economic deprivation, dependency on welfare, and single-parent families, there was a core concept of a protective nuclear family. The frequent expressions of enjoyment of family life conveyed a picture of fairly close-knit families and strength in family relationships (6).

The presence of contributory causes introduces complications which tend to interfere with the successful outcome of advance planning and prolong the duration of foster care. Identification of the contributory problems at the outset may lead to recognition of the need for a different service plan.

FOSTER CARE VERSUS LEGAL ADOPTION

In some situations it is clear early in the study that a permanent plan is needed, although the parent may request foster care or may be in conflict about consummating a plan for permanent care. Some unwed mothers, for example, may request foster care in some instances because they are in conflict about relinquishing the child for adoptive placement but have little potential capacity for mothering the child and no foreseeable plan for providing for the child's care. In contrast, some unwed mothers have the potential capacity to care for their children and are able to use a limited period of foster care as a constructive interim plan. Married couples sometimes present a similar problem. Such cases highlight the necessity for the interviewer to move, not only beyond the request into an exploration of the real need, but also to provide the immediate casework help which may enable the parent to make a plan that will meet the need and protect the child. In some cases, the parents and the caseworker may be unable to arrive at a mutually satisfactory goal in the course of the intake process. In these situations the agency, for the child's protection, may be confronted with the necessity to offer a service which is not the best solution to the problem but is the better of the immediately available alternatives. The treatment strategy may require planning for immediate goals or a step toward the realization of long-range goals.

THE ANDERSON CASE

Anita Anderson, a seventeen-year-old black unmarried high-school girl, requested foster care for her baby. She wanted to complete high school and get a job. She felt confident that she would be able to find a way to make a home for the baby after she became self-supporting. At the outset her plan was vague and unformulated. However, she was able to consider with the caseworker the practical problems and uncertainties involved in such a plan, the emotional hazards for the baby and herself, and the possible alternatives. She had a stable school history and was well motivated to take responsibility for her child. After each interview she discussed the problems and potentialities with her aunt, who had reared her since her mother's death six years earlier. After a series of interviews, she and the caseworker worked out a plan whereby the mother and the baby would live with the aunt, who would care for the baby until the mother was able to assume care independently. In order to carry out this plan, the agency undertook responsibility for supervision and for financial subsidy to augment the aunt's limited income. Casework and agency support of the plan were indicated on the basis of these combined considerations: a) the mother's promising potential for adequate parenting; b) the availability of a stable plan; c) a social environment in which the child and the mother would have a reasonable opportunity for growth and security.

THE BORDEN CASE

A twenty-six-year-old white unwed mother requested adoptive placement for her baby. The mother was intelligent, had well developed job skills, and a stable employment history. She was emancipated from her family, but, had her family known of her pregnancy, they and she would have been profoundly disturbed socially and psychologically. Before delivery she went through a stage of indecision about relinquishing the baby for adoption, but she could not discuss the reason. It was observed that she seemed to be in a precarious psychological state which she tried to conceal. After the birth of her baby girl, she again wavered and deferred a decision about adoption. She was withdrawn and depressed. She wanted more time to reach a decision, although she was aware that she could not provide directly for the baby's care and did not express any wish to do so.

In view of the mother's precarious emotional state, she was supported in her wish to take more time to resolve her conflicting feelings about the plan, and it was agreed that she would be referred to a psychiatrist for help; the baby would be placed temporarily in a foster home. Shortly thereafter, the mother was hospitalized with a severe depression. The baby was then transferred to a foster home in which she could be reared as long as care was needed and adopted in the event that this would become possible. After the mother's discharge from the hospital she sought private psychiatric help. For two years, in response to the agency's continuing efforts to keep in touch with her, she wrote saying that she did not want an appointment; she was not ready to face the decision about the baby; her therapist knew the situation and they were working on it.

With her permission, the caseworker and the psychiatrist agreed that the decision would be postponed until a time when the psychiatrist thought the mother would be able to manage the stress involved in the final decision. During this time she was employed in a responsible job and maintained a stable life. As it became increasingly apparent from her letters that she was strong enough to tolerate some pressure in the interest of the child's welfare, the agency pressed her therapist and the mother, directly, for a decision. She carried out the legal relinquishment of the child, although she would not discuss the matter with anyone other than the therapist.

This was a delicate, precarious, and long-range operation. The mother's mental health and the child's welfare were both in the balance. Both could be served only through case management carefully attuned to the diagnostic perception and anticipation of the course of the mother's emotional illness.

In this type of situation, critical factors in planning for the child are (a) the agency's consistency in pursuing the desired goal and (b) securing foster parents who are able to provide permanent care and at the same time accept the child's uncertain status. The fact that the foster parents are potentially able to adopt the child is desirable, but of secondary importance. Of primary importance is the willingness to rear the child as a member of the family. Foster parents can best do this when they and the agency have a mutual goal of permanent placement. An early decision on the agency's part to make a commitment to the desired goal is one of the critical elements in reducing uncertainty for the family and, consequently, for the child. The element of uncertainty is compounded when the mother is unable to make a final decision and the agency is unwilling to commit itself to the goal of permanence in the event that the mother relinquishes the child.

Married couples who present similar problems in diagnosis, decision-making, and goals are not uncommon. Two contrasting cases illustrate differences in the clients' situation, the agency's approach, and the immediate outcome.

THE CORWIN CASE

Mr. and Mrs. Corwin, a white couple in their mid-twenties, applied for foster home care for their four-year-old son. In a brief study it was learned that the mother had placed the child in a private foster home, shortly after his birth.

The mother, who talked unreservedly, revealed a long history of severe personality disorganization. There appeared to have been no stable periods in her life in any area of functioning. She had been reared in an institution and at the age of thirteen had made several suicide attempts. Her subsequent life-pattern was marked by self-destructiveness. She was intelligent and artistic and wanted to pursue artistic interests but had not been able to do so with any consistency.

The father was emotionally more stable, but he suffered from a disabling cardiac ailment. Both reported almost constant discord between them which centered on all of the important aspects of their life together, including the child.

The mother had been erratic in visiting the child in the private foster home. She visited, accompanied by casual men friends, at odd hours. She repeatedly insisted on taking the child for outings, returning him after he was overly fatigued, unkempt, and in tears. The foster mother, who was genuinely attached to the child and gave him good care, decided that she could not continue care because the mother's behavior was too disturbing to her and the child. The mother, in her request for agency foster care, insisted that she would abide by the agency's visiting regulations, but it was apparent that she could not see the rationale for them. The child was found to be somewhat withdrawn but not seriously disturbed, and had been able to respond well to the good care he had received.

The mother's lifelong instability, her emotional exploitation of the child, and her lack of interest in making a home, combined with the father's terminal illness and his wish to provide permanent protection for the child, strongly contraindicated a foster care plan. The parents were told that the agency could not offer foster care; the reasons were carefully explained; the stated wishes of both parents for the child to have an opportunity to grow-up in a stable home were supported; and the caseworker proposed that the parents consider a plan to provide the child with a permanent home through legal adoption. The mother, as expected, at first rejected the plan, but she agreed to think about it. The father was encouraged to talk it over with his parents.

For a few weeks the mother aimlessly tried to make other plans for the child's care. The father's parents, aware of his cardiac condition and unable to offer a permanent home to their grandson, agreed to care for him temporarily but supported the proposal of adoption through the agency. Both parents later agreed to the child's adoption.

In this case, it was apparent that the child was not in danger of serious neglect, and that no real emergency required foster care as an interim plan. The request for foster care by parents who have had no important relationship with the child and have little motivation or capacity to make a home for him in the future usually reflects a maladaptive pattern of meeting problems by avoidance and denial. The provision of foster care for these parents who have such a life pattern enables them to continue to evade facing the real issues, much to the detriment of the child and with no benefit for themselves in the long run. However, if the child is in danger of physical harm or serious neglect, and the parent is unable to decide in favor of permanent placement, the agency must give priority to the child's need for protection and accept the risk that the desirable goal of legal adoption may be indefinitely postponed.

THE DANIELS CASE

This contrasting case illustrates factors that may operate in this kind of situation. The parents, a married couple of mixed Jewish and Protestant faiths, in their early thirties, applied for foster care for their eighteen-month-old son. They wanted him placed immediately because they feared that the father, in a fit of rage, would injure him. Both parents expressed hatred and rejection of the child. They said, unreservedly, that they had never loved or enjoyed him because they had not wanted him. The pregnancy occurred a few months after their marriage and they felt cheated of their freedom. They did not falter in their verbalized rejection of the child. His day-care had been entrusted to a neighbor since shortly after his birth. The mother took him to the neighbor's home each morning and picked him up each evening. The mother mentioned that they probably would want to consider permanent relinquishment in a year or two. The father refused to discuss this. They had no family resources for their child; they were alienated from both sets of grandparents.

It became apparent that the application for placement had been triggered by the father's unstable emotional condition. He had become severely depressed and agitated following his expulsion from graduate school after involvement in a student protest demonstration. He had always resented the child's demands and now found the child's presence intolerable. At the same time he was unable to tolerate any exploration of his future goals for the family. He was aware of his wife's wish to give up the child but he became agitated and explosive when the caseworker attempted to engage him in any considerations beyond his request for immediate foster care. He talked about Jewish values of family life. He had sought psychiatric help and gave permission for the caseworker to talk with his therapist. The therapist confirmed the potential danger to the child, although the father had not abused the child physically in the past. He could shed no light on the father's inability to consider permanent plans for the child in the light of his apparent rejection.

Further exploratory sessions with the mother confirmed a lack of maternal feeling for the child. The day-care "mother" had provided good care and confirmed that the baby had been normal and healthy from birth.

This case differs from the previous one in three important respects. First, and of transcending importance, the parents' fear of harming the child, in itself, signalizes an emotional climate that is untenable for the child and the parents. Second, there were no family resources for the child's protection. Third, the father's inability to move beyond his initial request was not a reflection of an identifiable pattern of denial and avoidance requiring external limits and structure, but rather it stemmed from an acute internal conflict. Although all of the known facts pointed to adoption of the child as the desirable goal, the circumstances required that the agency offer foster care as a temporary means of alleviating the crisis. The purposes were twofold: to protect the child and to provide an opportunity for the father to recover from his acute depressive reaction and work out a solution to his conflict about the child.

In one respect, this situation parallels the Borden case. In both, the parents' psychological conflict interfered with the immediate decision in favor of the best plan. In such situations, the constructive use of foster care and achievement of adoption as the long-range goal may depend wholly on the agency's initiative in pursuing a parental decision, with attention to the development of a positive working relationship and appropriate timing.

LONG-TERM FOSTER CARE

It has long been a stated and strongly held belief that foster care must not be a way of life for children, but rather that it is intended as a short-term treatment measure which, for the children's welfare, must eventuate in their return to their parents or in legal adoption. During the past few years it has been generally recognized that the experience of foster care agencies does not support this belief. In an important number of cases these goals are either unattainable or undesirable. The "either-or" approach failed to take into consideration the range of interrelated social and psychological factors that cause long-term placement and those that indicate the need for continuance of the plan until the child reaches a stage of relative or complete self reliance. Interestingly enough, the opposition to long-term foster care paralleled the free use of place-

ment as a time-limited treatment measure to provide relief from intense problems and stresses in parent-child relationships. Foster
care for the child, accompanied by casework service to parent and
child, was often the treatment of choice for families who, today,
would be offered some form of treatment short of placement. With
greatly increased knowledge about children's reactions to placement and the specific therapeutic advantages to child and parent
of working out family problems within the framework of the family, placement has become the treatment of choice only when it is
clear that other less drastic measures cannot be used effectively.
The use of expanded techniques for prevention of placement—
family therapy, crisis intervention, reaching-out techniques—has
demonstrated that under certain conditions family disintegration
can be arrested and rehabilitative processes set in motion before
the situation deteriorates to the point of requiring placement of the
children. It is now recognized that, in the main, if a family is sufficiently stable to be reconstituted after a predictable period of
placement of the child, it is sufficiently stable to be helped without
removal of the child. As a result of this change in the approach to
the use of placement as treatment, the parents who now need foster care services have a great variety of problems that interfere
with realistic future planning.

In some cases the defined goals of the parents may be unrealistic, in part, because the factors involved in anticipating the duration of placement are exceedingly complex; they embrace potential
changes in each parent's future psychological condition and life
situation; developmental changes in the child, and changes that
take place in the interpersonal relationships among family members. In other cases, ego disintegration is so severe that the parent
is totally unable to consider the goal of placement, as illustrated in
the Bryant case.[2] These parents' wishes, plans, hopes, or fantasies
cannot provide even a clue to what is possible in the future. The
lack of ability to plan realistically or to carry out plans is one of
the symptoms of the major disturbance that caused the placement.

[2] See pp. 23–30.

Consequently, when the circumstances are such that the child's return cannot be anticipated and planned in advance (as in the well-defined need for temporary care), rehabilitation of the family can be tentatively planned in only limited kinds of situations. Foremost in this category of cases is that of the child who comes from an organized family unit and needs treatment for emotional problems. The parents are able to maintain a stable home, are free from gross personality disturbance, and their goal is the return of the child to the family. In this group of cases are children who require in patient treatment in psychiatric units of hospitals or in residential treatment facilities of various types. The reasons these children cannot benefit from outpatient treatment may encompass conditions in the family, the community, and the child himself. In some families, a particular emotional disturbance in a child is so severe or the specific nature of the disturbance is so noxious in terms of the parents' vulnerabilities that the child's presence in the home produces intolerable stress. With the removal of the child to a suitable treatment facility, some parents are able to stabilize themselves psychologically and provide adequate parenting for the other children. In such cases the prognosis for the child's return to the family depends largely on the change that takes place in the child in the course of care and treatment and, to an important but usually a lesser extent, on modifications in the parents' feelings and ego tolerance. Changes in either the child, the parents, or both, may alter the quality of the relationship and the interpersonal interaction sufficiently for the child to be returned to his family. In some instances, however, failure to change sufficiently, in one or the other, may make it impossible for either the family or the child to manage the reunion during the child's developmental years.

Another type of case in which reconstitution of the family can be anticipated, although it cannot be planned, is the single-parent family in which the responsible parent to whom the child may be restored has had stabilized periods of adequate ego functioning in the past, and is strongly motivated to re-establish a home for the children. Demonstrated parental capacity and motivation point to the likelihood that this parent will create a new home either by remarriage or through other environmental arrangements. This likelihood can be taken into consideration in the selection of an appropriate facility for the child.

In an earlier publication (7), one of the authors identified and discussed a set of conditions that usually point to the need for long-term foster care in which restoration of the family cannot be anticipated and in which there is a strong likelihood that the child will grow up in foster care. In most cases a prediction can be made on the basis of the initial study even though some of the parents are unable to appraise the future realistically and some maintain a fantasy of a reunited family.

In indeterminate long-term foster care, in contrast to the findings of Sauber and Jenkins in relation to brief duration of placement, there is a multiplicity of contributory causes such as lack of strength in family relationships, the absence of organized family life, and identifiable precipitating causes which grew out of long-time, pre-existing severe problems. The conditions that characterized the long-term cases were described as follows:

First, a pattern of defective ego functioning can be seen in the past and current functioning of the parents. This is most commonly revealed in repetitive, unrealistic behavior and inability to learn from experience how to modify destructive modes of behavior.

Second, there is evidence in the parents' history that basic disturbance has affected their parental capacities so that in some, or all, of the developmental stages of the child the parents have been unable to meet his vital needs for care, affection, supervision, protection, or training.

Third, as a result of defective ego functioning and parental inadequacy the history of family functioning reveals long-standing chronic instability and the absence of stable family life to which the family might be restored.

Fourth, there are major developmental and/or psychological problems in the child, resulting from the interaction in the disturbed parent-child relationships, that require an indefinite period of corrective care and, possibly, treatment.

Fifth, there is an emotional involvement in the parent-child relationship, on the part of the parents, the child, or both, that demands a continuing relationship after placement for an indefinite period of time.

It should be noted in assessing the importance of each as a predictive factor that these conditions are interrelated and interdependent in their use. For example, we sometimes see cases in which severe, and even dramatic, social and psychological breakdown in the family necessitates placement of the child. However, the severity of the disturbance of the parent in itself does not indicate a need for long-term care; it is the duration of the problems, the timing and nature of the stresses that precipitate the crisis, and the degree and kind of damaging effects on the child that weigh heavily in predicting parental capacity to provide adequate care for the child in the foreseeable future (8).

PERMANENT FOSTER CARE [3]

Permanent foster care is designed primarily as a substitute for legal adoption under conditions that either preclude or contra-indicate adoption. In relatively few cases can this type of care be planned at the outset on the basis of the diagnostic study, although in some cases it can be tentatively anticipated as a long-range goal. The child's need for permanent foster care, rather than some other type of plan, is most clear-cut when, at the time of the intake study, a particular combination of factors prevails. First, the parents' legal rights are terminated (voluntarily or involuntarily) and, second, the child's psychological condition requires a prolonged period of treatment, beginning at an age that precludes the probability of a future adoption plan. In some extreme cases of parental disintegration, agencies or courts act to transfer legal guardianship from the parent to the court in order to protect the child and offer him necessary treatment even though it is clear that his condition precludes the possibility of adoption. For these children long-range

---

[3] Programs of permanent foster care, in some places, are based on the need for expanded resources rather than on diagnostic differentials. This type of program has been demonstrated in New York City, where the disastrous effects of shortage of adoptive families for black babies and young children is a serious problem.

planning for permanent foster care may include the use of one or several facilities. For example, the child may require treatment in an institutional facility followed by transfer to a foster home, or, depending on his age and the nature of his problems, he may benefit most from continuity of care in the single facility of his initial placement until he becomes independent.

Legal adoption by another family is contra-indicated for some children who are well-integrated emotionally into a stable foster home at the time the parents' legal rights are terminated. When the foster family provides good care and wants the child permanently, the damage that results from transfer to another family to effect a legal adoption may outweigh any potential advantages. The enormous benefit of the tentative anticipation of this outcome, based on the diagnostic study, is the agency's early commitment to a permanent plan if the parents do not remove the child. The Borden case illustrated one such situation.[4]

Long-term foster care may eventuate in fully defined permanent foster care in situations where the natural parents, while retaining a relationship with the child, are unable to make progress toward re-establishment of a home and come to accept the desirability of the foster care arrangement as a permanent one. The diagnostic clues to this potential outcome help not only in the selection of the facility but also in the total case management. Emphasis on the likelihood of outcome, as anticipated from the study and from subsequent observations of the parents, enables the caseworker to share the assessment with the surrogate parents, reinforcing their security and that of the child.

In all permanent foster family care, if the parents' legal rights have been terminated, the plan may change to adoption, by mutual consent of the foster family and the agency. When this potential outcome can be anticipated at the time of the initial placement, agencies often are able to find foster parents who give direct or indirect indications of potential interest in and capacity for becoming adoptive parents to the foster child. In fact, many of the most successful adoptions of older children are reached through

[4] See p. 46.

this route. The success lies in the fact that the adoption takes place at the mutual wish of child and foster parents after a substantial experience with a tested, well-established relationship.

In summary, the use of the initial study for prediction of the duration and outcome of placement requires that the study process be utilized not only for gathering and assessing information but, concomitantly, for helping the parents arrive at a suitable plan for the child. In some instances this approach leads to an early decision in favor of adoption; in some it leads to a tentative plan for return of the child to his family; in some the parents are unable to evaluate their situation realistically or use help to do so, and the agency is obligated to act on its own goals, relying on the working alliance and the helping process to enable the parents to cooperate with the plan that is best for the child. Plans for the outcome of placement begin in the intake process but the ultimate outcome often is determined by the agency's consistency in pursuing the treatment goals through continuity of casework service to the parents.

Selection of the Placement Facility

The selection of the placement facility, closely tied to the anticipated duration and outcome of placement, implies that there is knowledge about the child and his family that is used as a guide in choosing the environment that will most nearly approximate what the child needs for as long as he will need it, and that there are facilities from which a selection can be made (9). The term "placement of choice" has been used by some to designate the process of selection based on assessment of the child's needs. There has been considerable disillusionment in child welfare circles as surveys have revealed that this principle does not permeate placement practice. It is axiomatic that in the absence of a diagnostic evaluation selection is a matter of expediency and the outcome a matter of chance. Equally apparent to the experienced practitioner is the limited availability of resources which narrows and sometimes nullifies choices. However, the concept of choice is, at best, a relative one, since a number of coalescing conditions determine, at any given time, what facilities are available for use. These conditions include not only the range of facilities in a given community but also the ebb and flow of changing conditions within the facilities, within the community, or in the parent-child relationship. Limiting factors within the group facility may be: lack of vacancies to coincide with emerging needs (this sometimes may be a matter of timing rather than a general deficit in facilities); the composition and experience of the staff (or foster parents) or the current composition of the group which contra-indicate the use of this environment, at this time, for the particular child needing placement. Limiting factors in the community may range from the absence of special resources, such as a special school when needed, to attitudes temporarily crystallized in strong opposition to the presence of children with certain kinds of problems. In the parent-child relationship, either the parent or the child may be unable to accept a specific type of care because it represents a particular threat to the balance in their relationship. These examples of limiting factors are presented only to suggest the diversity of changing conditions that affect the availability and usefulness of existing resources, and the fluidity that characterizes the relationship of needs to any network of facilities.

At first glance, it may appear that the limits on the availability of resources negate the usefulness of the diagnostic study in planning. In practice, the opposite is true. The more fully the caseworker understands the child and his family, the better he is able to identify the qualities in existing facilities that are potentially able to meet essential maturational needs and the viable ways of compensating for important deficiencies. From a dynamic as well as a practical standpoint the central question in the selection of the facility is: What qualities in the environment are essential to provide an adequate opportunity for the maturation of a particular child, and where can these best be provided?

Controversies over the appropriate uses of foster family care versus institutional care have tended to create dichotomies and cleavages that exaggerate the problem of decision-making. The various approaches and guidelines set forth by experienced observers [5] do

---

[5] Burmeister, Glickman, Kline, Lippman, Matek, Meier, and others.

not coincide in all respects, but they define a span of observations which reflect the experiences of the writers. The diversity of observations, if based on evaluation of experience, suggests that there is a wider potential usefulness for both types of care than is commonly recognized. The experience of the authors in the interchangeable use of various types of facilities supports this view. It has been observed that the maturational needs of some children can be met in either a foster home or group setting.[6] For these children the essential qualities in the environment rather than its structure are of paramount importance. In contrast, some children cannot adapt to large, congregate institutions, nor can some institutions adapt the environment to the children's needs. Some of these same children can be offered an adequate maturational environment in small group settings, in which the groups are modeled along the lines of family life.

The attempt to classify children in accordance with the type of facility needed is productive only up to a point. In general terms, it is almost universally agreed that the preschool age child needs the quality of mothering, closeness, attention, and cohesiveness of the environment that would be found most readily in family life. At the other end of the maturational scale, adolescents, in the main, are likely to accept and adapt to a group facility in which: (a) the peer group shares in some of the decision-making processes; (b) general expectations and limits are applied to the group with impartiality and objectivity; (c) opportunities for close relationships with adults are available but not implicitly expected; and (d) the structured environment provides built-in ego supports. Theoretically, these qualities in a facility meet certain specific developmental reactions that are characteristic of adolescence: the ef-

[6] For the children whose maturation can proceed in either type of facility, agency philosophy plays a dominant role in determining choice. If it is believed, as the authors believe, that in a family-centered society the experience of family life is preferable for children who can use it, the foster care agency will make strong, creative, and continuous efforts to expand foster home resources which meet qualitative requirements for an adequate environment. At the same time, such an agency will not hesitate to develop or use existing group facilities, which are qualitatively adequate, to augment the available foster homes. The absence of a sufficient range of facilities is the chief cause of using those which do not meet the needs of children.

forts at emancipation from parents; the concomitant rebellion against authority; the increased need for privacy; and the process of ego disintegration which is characteristic of this developmental stage.

These theoretical generalizations are supported by experience, but experience also demonstrates that the generalizations must be viewed with caution and cannot substitute for individual assessment of the child's needs and evaluation of the qualities actually provided in the facility under consideration. For the preschool child, the closeness, attention, and continuity that are essential may be better provided in group care that approximates these goals than through a series of foster homes that fail. For children between the ages of six months and approximately three years the issue of anticipated continuity weighs heavily as one factor in the decision since the child is most vulnerable to loss and change in this stage of development.

An adolescent may express a preference for a foster family. This preference may or may not be realistic in terms of his current adaptive patterns, or in terms of available facilities, but exploration of his wishes may be highly productive in illuminating the decision-making process, and the helping process in the use of a facility which is available.

The choice between the two categories of care—foster family and group care—is influenced by the choices available within each of the two categories. With this orientation, a systematic approach to the decision-making process may be carried out along these lines:

1) What experiences and qualities in the environment are most needed for the child's continuing maturation?

2) Of these needed experiences, what can the child accept and adapt to at the time of placement?

3) What qualities and characteristics in the child or in the parent-child relationship preclude the use of a specific resource?

4) Which available resource can best provide the experiences the child needs and can use?

5) What services can the agency offer or obtain in the community to augment the environment, compensate for important defi-

cits, or modify the conditions that would interfere with the use of a given resource?

This approach requires the marshaling and ordering of general knowledge about the needs of children in successive maturational stages and the assessment of the developmental and psychological status of the individual child, as well as the nature of the parent-child relationship. It requires familiarity with the current conditions in existing facilities, and demands that the agency review its own resources for providing the needed supportive services at each point in time.

Generalizations about selection of the placement facility must be viewed with caution. They serve a useful purpose as a guide to a wide range of possibilities. They cannot substitute for individualized, case-by-case decision-making and painstaking prediction of the probable duration of care. The tasks inherent in the diagnostic study and decision-making processes are not and cannot be the responsibility of the caseworker alone. They involve specialized knowledge, diagnostic skill, and administrative planning. Nowhere is collaborative staff effort and coordinated planning more specifically needed than in the process of the diagnostic intake study and the decision-making steps that lead to placement.

REFERENCES

1. Gordon Hamilton, *Theory and Practice of Social Casework*, Second Revised Edition, Columbia University Press, New York, 1951, pp. 147–213. Esther Glickman, *Child Placement Through Clinically Oriented Casework*, Columbia University Press, New York, 1957, pp. 3–22. Draza Kline, "Differential Diagnosis in Planning Placements for Children," in *Selected Papers in Casework*, 1952, National Conference of Social Work, Columbia University Press, New York.
2. Therese Benedek, M.D., "The Family as a Psychological Field," in: James Anthony and Therese Benedek, *Parenthood*, Little, Brown and Co., Inc., Boston, 1970, pp. 109–35. Nathan W. Ackerman, M.D., *The Psychodynamics of Family Life*, Basic Books, Inc., New York, 1958, pp. 15–80.

3. For detailed presentations of deviations from normal development see: Anna Freud, *Normality and Pathology in Childhood: Assessments of Development*, International Universities Press, Inc., New York, 1965. O. Spurgeon English, M.D., and Gerald H. J. Pearson, M.D., *Emotional Problems of Living*, W. W. Norton & Company, Inc., New York, 1945.
4. Selma H. Fraiberg, *Psychoanalytic Principles in Casework with Children*, Family Service Association of America, New York.
5. Shirley Jenkins and Mignon Sauber, *Paths to Child Placement*, Research Department, The Community Council of Greater New York, 1966.
6. *Ibid.*, pp. 85–86.
7. Draza Kline, "The Validity of Long-Term Foster Care," *Social Work Practice*, Columbia University Press, New York, 1964.
8. *Ibid.*, pp. 184–85.
9. Esther Glickman, *Child Placement Through Clinically Oriented Casework*, Columbia University Press, New York, 1957, pp. 64–101. Draza Kline, "Understanding and Evaluating a Foster Family's Capacity to Meet the Needs of an Individual Child," *The Social Service Review*, Vol. XXIV, no. 2, June 1960. Ord Matek, "Differential Diagnosis for Differential Placement of Children," *Child Welfare*, Vol. XLIII, No. 7, 1964. Elizabeth G. Meier, "Foster Care for Children," *Social Work Year Book*, Russell Sage Foundation, New York, 1960.

CHAPTER III

THE CHILD

The Psychological Situation of the Placed Child

The practitioner who would understand the placed child and aim to provide for him in the foster care environment needs both a background of theoretical knowledge of personality development and experience that leads to an empathic understanding of how the child experiences the events and relationships involved in the foster care situation. Since separation is one of the universal human experiences that cause anxiety, the ability to meet the child's feelings with strength and with a minimum of anxiety and guilt about his placement does not spring full-blown from the caseworker's intent and wishes; it comes gradually, with theoretical knowledge, self-knowledge, and the intellectual and emotional integration of what is learned from practice.

A telescopic view of early childhood development will be presented to provide a suggestive approach to some of the connections between this development, typical problems of children in the placement experience, and therapeutically oriented [1] approaches necessary for meeting these problems in the foster care environment.

[1] The term "therapeutically oriented environment" will be used here to denote one in which meeting the normal needs of the child in daily life is augmented by understanding his special needs and by modifications in his care which are adapted to this understanding.

DEVELOPMENTAL NEEDS

What one sees in the placed child is understandable only in the light of understanding the normal maturational needs of the infant and young child [2] and the tendency for characteristic behavior and needs of these early stages to reappear later as a defensive reaction to stress.

Winnicott observed that in planning for children in foster care a great deal can be learned about what the child needs from what the healthy mother gives intuitively to her child from infancy onward:

Continuity of the human environment, and likewise the nonhuman environment, which helps with the integration of the individual personality;

Reliability, which makes the mother's behavior predictable;

Graduated adaptation to the changing and expanding needs of the child, whose growth processes impel him or her toward independence and adventure;

Provision for realizing the child's creative impulse (1).

These provisions might well be called the watchwords for agencies engaged in the foster care of children, in families or group facilities of any kind.

Most of the children who need placement through social agencies have experienced, before placement, some degree of maladaptive care which has interfered with or distorted the normal maturational processes in varying stages of development and varying degrees of severity. Some children have been separated from the mother, father, or other child-caring adult and have been shifted about in the stages of infancy and early childhood when continuity and reliability of the mother [3] are most critical for early

[2] The term "infancy" is used here to refer to the period from birth to six months, and "early childhood" designates the next sequential period, up to about two years.

[3] The word "mother" is being used to describe the person(s) who carries out the mothering functions, whether mother, grandmother, father, foster parent, or others.

development. Some have remained with their mothers but have experienced serious deficits in the quality or quantity of care necessary for meeting developmental needs. Some have experienced sudden, traumatic loss of one or both parents. Often agency placement is a culmination of a prolonged period of disturbed, unstable family life that has not offered the minimal conditions necessary for continuity of age-related emotional growth and socialization.

Of the various mental functions of the child, his adaptive capacities [4] (ego strength) when he comes to the placement experience are a major determinant of how he responds and what he needs in the new environment to facilitate the maturational processes. There are wide variations in age, maturational stage, and the environmental conditions of the children who are placed. Each of these factors influences ego functioning. Normally under adequate environmental conditions the child develops an increasing ability to handle stress and new situations, and there is a rough comparability between age and the capacity to cope with loss and strangeness. In general, the older the child the better he is able to tolerate the loss and the strangeness involved in placement. However, the older child who suffered from traumatic separation earlier in life may experience this separation as though it were a repetition of the life-threatening loss in the early stages of dependency on the mother. Ego-functioning is adversely affected by feelings of panic reactivated from the earlier traumatic experience. Although no longer realistic to the child's current age and situation, these feelings are very much a part of his internal reality and his resulting reaction to the current separation.

Translating the needs of all children, as defined by Winnicott (2), into the needs of children in the foster care system, agencies should aim to provide:

1) An environment in which the child can experience stability; that is, a group and a place (family or other facility) where he knows he can live as long as he needs that particular environment.

---

[4] A child's ego strength depends on such factors as his heredity, his preceding caretaking experience (both positive and negative), and his age. The building blocks for ego strength consist of his successful experiences in mastering each step of developmental growth.

This parallels the needed continuity that furthers the integration of the personality of the young child.

2) Adults (surrogate parents and agency) on whom the child can learn to rely, to parallel the early childhood need to be able to trust the mother.

3) Adaptive responsiveness by the environment to the child's growth processes, his increasing capacities for self-help, and movement toward independence, which go on throughout his growing-up years.

4) Opportunities for playing, learning skills, expanding and enriching his sphere of imaginative or creative self-expression, and for contributing something to the life of the family or group which is needed and valued by them. Opportunities for play are not luxuries, as has sometimes been thought; they are essential to the maturational processes.

5) Adaptation of the environment, casework, and other agency help to the special needs of the child, needs that are related to his life situation or to internal conflicts that interfere with the growth processes.

6) Avoidance of elective replacement of a child between the ages of six months and two to three years, if the child is in an adequate, stable situation.

The environmental conditions at the time of placement that affect ego-functioning relate to the situation that causes the placement, the degree of family disorganization or trauma that precedes placement, the presence or absence of supportive participation by parents, and, likewise, the degree of supportive help provided by the caseworker (agency) and the prospective parent-surrogates, preceding, during, and after placement.

The provisions made in the new environment are predicated not only on the child's previous developmental status but also on the many ways in which the inner drive for growth and the fluid personality of childhood are open to the influences of the changed human environment and all that it includes.

Within the framework of psychoanalytic theory of personality development, Winnicott divided the emotional growth of children into three stages from dependence to independence (3). This classification lends itself well to a generalized view of the connections between early development and placement reactions. The three stages are absolute dependence, relative dependence, and toward independence. Progression through these stages is, within broad limits, age related. The stage of absolute dependence covers about the first six months of life, in which the mother-child unity (symbiosis) is essential to the baby, who is still too young to perceive any differentiation between the self and the mother as separate persons. Advancement of his internal maturational potential is absolutely dependent on the human environment—the mother's provision of what he needs. Physically, the baby's life is endangered in the absence of sufficient care. Psychologically, his progression from absolute to relative dependence depends in part on how well the mother meets his needs for holding, feeding, changing, protection from external impingements and discontinuity of care, and on how able the mother is to offer this care in ways that the child can utilize.

At about six months of age the child, moving into the stage of relative dependence, begins to perceive the mother as a person separate from himself.[5] The sense of self develops slowly as the child makes the differentiation between self and mother and gradually learns that he can rely on this separate person to meet his needs.

The well-known attachment of infants and young children to an inanimate object in the environment occurs between the age of about six months and a year. The object—soft toy, pillow, baby blanket, or whatever the child chooses—assumes great importance and if, for any reason, the object is unavailable or is changed, the child is in distress. Winnicott (4) identified this as a transitional object which represents an aspect of progression in development from the symbiotic stage to that of object relationship. Normally, the infant outgrows the attachment to the original object, but later it may be used again as a regressive defense against anxiety. Chil-

[5] It is suggested by some authors that this can occur much earlier but is only apparent to the observer at six months.

dren under stress, when lonely, depressed, or anxious have been known to cling to the original soft toy, or blanket, or some other object.[6]

It has been observed that in the period of differentiation, the baby, between about six months and two years, suffers intensely from the mother's absences if they exceed his gradually increasing tolerance. This period is characterized by developmental ambivalence: the need for the mother versus the rage against the mother that accompanies the frustrating awareness that she is a separate and relatively noncontrollable person with a separate life which includes the father (the world outside the mother-infant couple). If all goes well, developmentally, the rage against the mother (love object) subsides with the establishment of confidence that the mother will meet his needs.

With the increasing growth in ego strength and ego functions, which include mobility, speech, memory, and reality testing, around the age of eighteen months to two years, the acute need for the mother begins to subside and the child enters the stage of moving toward independence, which continues in maturational phases until he enters adulthood. Developmentally, these new trends enable him to begin to cope with separation. They include his sense of an ongoing self, which is strengthened by the ego functions and the gradual internalization of the image of the mother as an external love object. At approximately eighteen months of age, the child who has had a sufficiently good relationship with his mother has built up in his mind a series of mental memory traces or mental representations of his mother. When enough of these memory traces have been established, he is able to be away from her and still realize that she exists. This stage of "object constancy" allows the child to separate from his mother without panic or undue anxiety. Mahler observed that "normal symbiosis paves the way for the

[6] Freud and Burlingham observed this phenomenon, in extreme form, in some of the children evacuated from London during the war, and noted that the gradual relinquishment of the object, brought with them from home, was the first sign that the child had overcome the shock of separation and had found new living objects for his affection. See Chapter reference no. 6

separation-individuation phase (from the age of twelve to eighteen months on)," and emphasized that as the infant develops into a toddler, and can move away from the mother by way of his own mobility, but still in the presence of the mother, the "developmental process is characterized by predominance of the child's pleasure in independent functioning" (5). In contrast to traumatic separation experience, Mahler emphasized that this normal individuation-separation phase can take place only in the presence of the mother.

Socialization begins only after the ego functions of speech, memory, and reality testing have been well developed. The accomplishment of socialization, however, is further dependent on the quality of the relationship with the parents, which enables the child to accept and ultimately internalize, their social ideals and also enables him to develop object relationships with others.

In the maturational processes, the child's innate anxieties and developmental anxieties change. The innate, or archaic, anxieties include fear of disintegration and lack of survival, fear of separation, falling, strange people and places, darkness, and loud, sudden noises. These anxieties dissipate as the ego grows. But it must be kept in mind that early ego growth is absolutely dependent on the quality of mothering: the adaptation of the mother to the child's needs, and the consistency with which she provides an auxiliary ego, which enables him to cope with these innate anxieties. The primitive anxieties may persist in overt form to the extent that ego growth (reality testing) is stunted if there is insufficient or traumatic care. Normally, the primitive anxieties become covered over but may reappear from time to time throughout childhood and into adulthood if the individual is exposed to sufficient stress. Normal developmental anxieties, as differentiated from archaic anxieties, appear in connection with internal conflicts characteristic of the maturational stages.[7] The early fear of physical separation from the mother is succeeded by rage and fear of loss of the mother's love as she is recognized as a separate individual not under the child's

[7] Developmental conflicts refer to basic psychoanalytic theory of personality development and the major developmental phases.

control. This fear is partly or wholly resolved or is fixed, depending on the degree of reliability and continuity and the quality of the mothering and fathering relationships.

Any of the feelings or behavior that characterize the various developmental phases and developmental conflicts may reappear in later stages, either as transitory means of handling normal stress or in persistent regressions in reaction to traumatic situations. Just as psychological maturation can be interrupted by stress, socialization, too, can be interrupted by sudden separation from the parenting adults with whom the child has identified.

THE MAJOR CHANGES AND THEIR EFFECTS ON THE CHILD IN PLACEMENT

The adaptive tasks that confront the child in the placement experience are contained in three major elements of change and in his ability to deal with his feelings about them:

1) Loss of the family and extended environment (persons and places).

2) Introduction of the agency and its personnel (strange persons and places) to assume responsibility for planning, securing direct care, and providing other services normally provided by family members.

3) Introduction to a new family or group facility and extended environment.

The stress of the loss, combined with the anxiety introduced by strangeness, is likely to reduce the child's capacity to cope, regardless of his age or the ego strength he has achieved. He is confronted with adaptive tasks which, at best, can be integrated only very slowly, in part, and with help. The chief aims of the placement procedures and the subsequent services are to help the child deal with his feelings about the changes in order to reduce the traumatic effects of the placement experience to their minimal level; to prevent massive, fixed regression (as differentiated from temporary regressions, which serve the cause of health); to initiate and maintain new relationships that will create optimal conditions for recovery and growth. These aims can rarely be achieved wholly; but with adequate help they are likely to be attained substantially with significant benefit to the child. Ideally, the help offered the child in the initial stage of placement should come from three sources: the parent he is leaving, the caseworker in the foster care agency, and the parent surrogates who are prepared to accept him.[8]

LOSS OF THE FAMILY AND
EXTENDED ENVIRONMENT

It has been well established by research and empirical clinical evidence that young children react to periods of separation from the parent which exceed their developmental capacity for tolerance with feelings of rejection, worthlessness, and reactive depression (6). In the separation created by placement, the degree and kind of traumatic impact on development and the prognosis for recovery of previous functioning levels are dependent on several variables: (a) the child's unique constitutional endowment and age and stage of development; (b) his internal conflicts; (c) the conditions surrounding the loss; (d) the human environment in which the loss occurs; (e) the kind of help he is offered in this crisis and thereafter.

These variables, in combination, can be illustrated by two contrasting, hypothetical situations.

A relatively healthy child, who has resolved the acute stages of developmental ambivalence and achieved object constancy, is left by the death of a parent in a stable family with the remaining nuclear family and is helped and sustained by an important adult. This child is likely to suffer the least trauma and have the best potential for recovering from the loss without fixed interference in the maturational processes.

At the other end of the scale, the most damaging circumstances of loss are those in which the child is deserted by the care-taking parent (willfully, as the child sees it) when he has not developed

[8] The effectiveness of the help offered by the parents and surrogates usually depends in part on their capacities and in part on the support and guidance offered them by the caseworker.

sufficient ego strength to cope with his feelings or with his physical environment, and when he is left in an unstable, disorganized situation, without environmental continuity, and without help.

Obviously, there are unlimited variations between these two extremes and each factor influences the child's response, positively or negatively, in some area of his development.

Usually the child does not perceive his parents as "bad" or his care and nurture as inadequate to meet his inner maturational drives. He may appear depressed or unhappy, but he may not be aware of his feelings. He may be observed to be anxious and worried, but usually he is not conscious of his anxiety. When he is angry he may entertain fantasies of running away or of getting rid of his parents. This is the negative side of normal, developmental ambivalence. However, the child's ability to integrate the hostility is related to its intensity, any previous conflicts about hostile feelings, and his current ego strength. The latter, in turn, is related in part to the actual deprivation and to the unreliability he has experienced in the relationship with the parents. The overwhelming rage, guilt, and fear create the conflict that interferes with the child's capacity to make normal separations, to come to terms with the drastic separation involved in placement, and to make relationships with substitute parents.

Regardless of how good or how bad his environment is for him, the child usually leaves his nuclear family against his will and thus feels a quality of helplessness that may be reminiscent of the helplessness of early childhood and the fear of nonsurvival.

In this experience, the child suffers other kinds of loss. He leaves his customary ways of finding comfort, of turning to some familiar person, place, or object for reassurance. In the Bryant family,[9] during the caseworker's visit and in the face of the threat of placement, both boys, although scolded and threatened by the grandmother, sought comfort through physical contact with her. They sat close to her on the sofa; patting her arm, and they were patted in response. When threatened by Ted's teasing, Dick crawled be-

[9] See pp. 25–28.

hind the sofa; in his present environment this represented a place that offered some protection and comfort.

Any aspect of the human and the nonhuman environment in which the child experienced continuity is lost when the child leaves it. The nuclear family as a unit, its ways, its customs, its dynamic system, of which he has been a part, have also been a part of him, his equilibrium, and his sense of identity. Each relationship within the family has had its place, whether primarily positive or negative, in his psychic equilibrium. Having a younger sibling to envy, tease, hug, or push around, or one close in age to play with, quarrel with, and use as a companion in mischief or in loneliness, or a big brother or sister to turn to for help or to envy, provoke, or emulate, or a younger child in the family to mother—all have their place in the child's inner life as well as in his social relationships.

The familiarity of his home, the place he sleeps, his friends, his school, and the neighborhood to which he is accustomed have special meaning in the child's experiencing of his world and his place in it. The neighborhood may be deteriorated, the friends few and even undesirable, the educational opportunities inferior—but these are adult reactions. The child himself does not feel this way. To him they are known and familiar, and hold aspects of cherished intimacy which he has made privately his own. All of the small mysteries and rituals of a child and his absorbing feelings about these activities are a part of his life in a specific environment; they are his ways of gaining comfort and gratification, his ways of solving some of his problems of living.

What the placed child misses most is in part age-stage related. For the young child it is the mother, primarily, but also the father, and the more dependent he is the more is he damaged by the loss. For the school-age child, in addition to his parents and siblings, his peers are of great importance. It is in this period that he begins to rely heavily on the companionship of his friends and his interests in his activities outside his home. For the adolescent, there is also his special chum, who shares with him the turbulence of the adolescent revival of earlier developmental conflicts and the new developments of approaching adulthood (7), (8).

In brief, removal from his family and community includes loss and change in all of the important spheres of a child's life.

INTRODUCTION OF THE AGENCY'S SERVICE

In considering the introduction of the foster care agency's service into the child's life, it is well to see both the helping role and the meaning of strangeness to the child, in connection with the integrative tasks that confront him (9).

The sources of normal anxiety, as discussed earlier, are both innate and developmental. Strange persons and places create some degree of anxiety in most normal, healthy individuals, but ordinarily this anxiety is actively mastered by the ego. Beyond early childhood, the degree of anxiety aroused by strange places and strange persons is determined in part by what is feared, what is at stake, what one expects or is expected by others to achieve, and what impact the outcome has on one's welfare.

For adults, a change in job is one of the normal life situations that creates an emotional crisis calling for a high order of adaptive and problem-solving techniques. One needs only to view the normal reactions of adults to such ordinary life situations to gain some appreciation of the relative anxiety mobilized in a child when he faces the strangeness of a social agency and its personnel, and their purpose in his life, under circumstances that are acutely stressful. The child cannot tell the caseworker what he is experiencing; his reactions are usually revealed indirectly, nonverbally, and by symptomatic behavior. A child's mastery of anxiety depends on his age, his ego strength, and the ego support provided in the environment.

Usually the child's first awareness of the agency reaches him through some communication from parents or parent surrogates. However, clinical evidence suggests that often the possibility of placement becomes a reality to the child only when it confronts him in the form of the first direct contact with the foster care agency and the caseworker. Thus, the caseworker and other agency personnel are at once a potential threat and a potential aid in his extreme need. It is somewhat of a dilemma that the child's greatest need for strong ego support from the caseworker occurs at the beginning stage of service (which includes the preplacement, placement, and immediate post-placement periods), because in many cases there is relatively limited time in which to develop this relationship. Consequently, the facilitation of its development at the outset of service is one of the highly important skills of the foster care practitioner.[10]

Initially, the child's task in relation to the caseworker and the agency is to master, to some extent, the anxiety that the experience arouses. Subsequently, his tasks will include a gradual integration of the new pattern of role relationships that constitute the foster care system, which includes the transfer of many parental responsibilities to the agency. Ultimately, it is here that he must gain a sense of trust and continuity before he can feel confident about his future care, since the agency now has primary responsibility for deciding where he is to live and what kind of life he is to have. In providing service to the child the caseworker confronts him with adaptive tasks that can be accomplished only in small steps and then only to the degree that the services are offered in the context of a carefully nurtured, reliable, ego-supportive relationship, unified into a coherent, consistent whole by the caseworker with whom that relationship exists.

THE NEW ENVIRONMENT

Whether the facility selected for the child's care is a foster home or a group care setting, the "human and nonhuman environment" [11] is strange to him in ways that are illuminated beyond previous understanding by the relatively recent studies of family and group dynamics. In either the foster family or the institution the Gestalt is altered by the introduction of a new member into its dynamic system. By the same token, the child entering the new setting is introduced not only into new individual relationships but also into a new pattern of organization and a different

[10] See pp. 82–92 for detailed discussion of this point.

[11] D. W. Winnicott uses this phrase, with emphasis on the importance of continuity in the total environment.

life style. The new environment is, objectively, superior to the one he has left in its capacity to meet his essential needs, but before he can accept the care that is offered he must have the opportunity to develop some trust and some comfort in individual relationships and in the strange environment. This trust and comfort is likely to come slowly and unevenly, with periods of growth and periods of regression. "Homesickness," a condition common to children and adults alike, often is composed of both a longing for the familiar and discomfort with the strange and new. The strangeness of the new environment, however, is only one aspect of the problem. The other side of the problem is that the child is strange to the people around him.

The issue of ego identity emerges fully in the situation in which continuity and stability of the child's sense of self and sense of "who he is" in the eyes of those around him are broken off. To whatever extent the child has achieved it, his sense of personal identity is under heavy siege in these circumstances. Erikson has observed that ". . . a young individual must learn to be most himself where he means most to others—those others, to be sure, who have come to mean most to him" and that ". . . the term identity . . . connotes both a persistent sameness within oneself . . . and a persistent sharing of some kind of essential character with others" (10).

For the child in the process of placement there is neither sameness within himself nor in what he means to others. The former remains to be restored and the latter to be achieved. Ultimately, in his adult life, the placed child may always carry within him a specific vulnerability to separations and to strangeness. How he manages these stresses—by repetition-compulsion, by avoidance, or by active mastery—will depend to some extent on the help he receives in the placement experience and the capacity of his ego to master the accompanying anxiety (11).

In the light of these three major aspects of change (loss of the family, the child's introduction to the agency, and introduction into the new environment), and their effects on the child, guidelines can be developed for the preventive and therapeutic measures needed in each step of the total placement process. Also, a perspective can be gained of the length of time involved in the child's recovery from placement shock and his readiness for continued growth. It is essential for the caseworker to attain this perspective and to share it with the other persons involved in the child's care.

POST-PLACEMENT REACTIONS

The most common general reactions in the post-placement stage include regression, pseudo-adaptive denial and repression of anxiety, and testing behavior as differentiated from other forms of ego defenses. These are discussed separately here, but in practice they usually are mixed and may occur simultaneously.

Regression

How the child gets through the preplacement and placement procedures influences his adjustment in the immediate post-placement stage. The degree of ego mastery he achieves before placement decreases to some extent the severity of the reactions after placement. In general, the placement experience is met with ego regression. For the experienced foster care practitioner the overt evidences of regression are so familiar that it has become almost routine practice to prepare the prospective surrogate parents for some forms of potential regression.

The areas of regression depend to some extent on the age-related developmental stage of the child. The child who has relatively recently achieved bowel or bladder control is the most likely to regress temporarily in these areas. The child who is in the process of mastering speech may suffer a temporary or prolonged interruption in speech development. Regression in some areas, such as fear of the dark, fear of being alone, disturbances in eating and sleeping, shortened attention span, agitation, and destructiveness, may occur at any age and may represent a recurrence of archaic anxiety, developmental anxiety, or both.

Other regressive symptoms commonly observed in children during or immediately following placement are crying, whining, clinging, demanding behavior, temper tantrums, disobedience, defiance, intense anxiety over brief separations, withdrawal, and isolation, or anti-social behavior such as stealing. In brief, any of the behaviors typical of the normal phases and stages of development, after having been outgrown, may reappear as regressive phenomena under the stress of placement. The regression may be minor, circumscribed, and relatively transitory, or it may be massive and severe, and recovery may be comparably difficult to achieve.

In evaluating these regressions one must keep in mind that transitory regressive phenomena bring gratification and comfort and serve the purpose of psychic recovery. Persons who have lived with or observed normal young children are familiar with these transitory regressions. When a young child is tired or ill one sees him revert to earlier forms of behavior, such as thumb-sucking, clinging to a transitional object, messing with his food, fretting or crying, or wanting to be taken up and held more than is typical of his current daily behavior when he is not under stress.

A significant aspect of the appearance of these regressive phenomena is the child's reactions to them and their potential as a secondary source of infection, so to speak. A persistent symptom may represent a narcissistic injury to the child, or it may take on secondary gratifications that help to entrench it. For example, in the first instance, if the child has stabilized bowel and bladder control and has incorporated a parental attitude of shame, disgust, or strong disapproval, the symptom may bring shame, embarrassment, fear, humiliation, or expectation of punishment. Or, in the second instance, if the child regresses in his eating or sleeping habits, satisfactions unconsciously derived from the response of adults may serve to perpetuate the regression beyond what is necessary.

It is important to differentiate regressive phenomena that occur in reaction to the stresses of placement from symptoms of disturbances that have been present previously. An assessment of the child's developmental status before placement is the basis for the differential diagnosis. The implications can be seen in a commonplace example. If it is known that a three-year-old child has not yet fully achieved nighttime bladder control, it can be anticipated that the completion of this task may be delayed by the timing of the placement. Since this is a borderline age for the achievement of full bladder control, it may take a prolonged period of time after placement to determine whether the development will proceed or whether a pre-existent problem will interfere with completion of this developmental task. If it is known that a four-year-old child has achieved a stabilized stage of full bladder control, the occurrence of night wetting can be clearly identified as a regressive phenomenon. If it is known that a five-year-old child has never achieved full bladder control, there is a signal of some earlier interference in the developmental process which will need future diagnosis and, possibly, treatment.

Recoverability from regression, as noted earlier, varies according to the stabilized level of development, the ego maturity the child has achieved, the intensity of the trauma of the separation and its surrounding circumstances, and the kind and quality of help the child receives in coping with the changes.

Repression of Anxiety and
Pseudo-Adaptive Behavior

Some children, in direct contrast to those who react to placement with overt disturbance, present a superficial picture of adaptation to the entire placement experience, with a notable absence of the kinds of behavior that make adults uncomfortable. Even symptoms known to exist before placement may suddenly disappear. This phase has sometimes been called the "honeymoon" period. It may last for a few weeks or a few months. It is reassuring to the adults involved to see the child accept the loss of his previous environment without overt distress and take on the new environment with apparent ease. It is difficult to hold diagnostic judgment in abeyance, and it is exceedingly tempting to accept the child's behavior as a reflection of true adaptation. In most instances, however, the initial conforming adjustment is not a reflection of adaptation; on the contrary, it may reflect a degree of anxiety that the child cannot master except by total repression and denial. Only as he becomes increasingly safe in the new situation can he tolerate the anxieties that threaten him; then the pseudomaturity may break down into symptomatic behavior, sometimes after weeks or months of placement. For example, a severely disturbed seven-year-old boy who had already experienced several losses of adoptive homes, seemed to adjust well in a foster home for eight months before he felt safe enough to begin to feel and express the intense anxiety and rage that he had successfully repressed. He then reacted to all limits with severe screaming, kicking, temper tantrums, and many other evidences of former pathological development. The foster parents, typically, reacted by feeling both responsible and disappointed.

Child care workers and foster parents alike are susceptible to a sense of personal failure and disappointment in the child when his defenses are such that he makes an initially "good adjustment" and then breaks down. A somewhat over-simplified but useful attitude for the practitioner is to assume that any marked degree of apparent maturity, beyond age-adequateness, or apparent stability that is unrealistic in the face of the inherent stresses of the placement experience (loss and strangeness) is pseudo-adaptive and contains a potential breakdown into some form of severe regression or, at least, reappearance of previous symptoms of known disturbance or substitute symptoms.

The preventive and therapeutic measures taken by the caseworker in the replacement and placement process, to be discussed in detail later, are designed to reduce this massive repression as much as possible. However, there is usually a rough correlation between the extent and duration of massive denial and repression and the severity of pathological functioning.

Testing Behavior

The phenomenon of testing behavior is familiar to all of the disciplines engaged in the care and treatment of children. In placement, it is a nearly universal phenomenon. However, the use of the term "testing" is subject to over-generalization. Vital understanding of a child's behavior may be lost in this undifferentiated diagnosis. The concept is most useful if limited in definition. The fact that children want and need to know the limits within which they are operating is highlighted in the strange situation of placement. Normal testing of a new environment can be described simply as a child's efforts to see how far he can go, what the adult will tolerate, and what controls and limits will be set. The child exploring his new human environment is, in a sense, establishing a kind of blueprint of its outer limits. This behavior, as differentiated from conflict-driven behavior, is usually provocative in quality. It takes such forms as disobedience, excessive demands for privileges, or other behavior that tests the limits set by adults up to the point of eliciting firm, consistent controls. Implicitly, the child is testing the ego integrity of the adults in his new environment. His own inner controls and his sense of identity and personal integrity are in a fluid, unsure state. In part, this fluidity may reflect a normal developmental stage, but in part, the placement experience erodes the feeling of ongoing personal identity, interferes with ego functioning, and increases the need to rely on external controls. Then it is important for the child to know how reliable is the ego integrity of the adults on whom he is expected to rely. This kind of testing is prominently highlighted by young children whose inner controls are not well established and by the adolescent when he enters a group setting that is new to him or when he experiences changes in the child care staff. The adolescent defies the rules, breaks curfew, overspends his allowance, and the like. In this way he finds out whether the adult is consistent in holding to reasonable standards and expectations. The adolescent may not meet these expectations, but he learns that he can rely on the consistency of the adults' standards and values. Behavior that reflects normal or deviant developmental conflicts can then be differentiated from testing behavior. (Normally the adolescent rebellion is against the parenting adult. It is part of the struggle for emancipation.) Meanwhile the demonstrated ego integrity of the adult provides a reliable object for identification, even while the young person is busy rebelling.

In placement, normal testing behavior may be easily confused with behavior that expresses more complex conflicts. A common example is the behavior of the child who has learned to defend himself from the trauma of rejection and loss by unconsciously trying to precipitate the dreaded event himself through behavior that is intolerable to the new substitute parents. Thus, the child seeks to control his own destiny. This behavior is different in cause (and in

needed therapeutic response) from that of the child whose unacceptable, provocative behavior serves the purpose of establishing
limits and testing adult reliability. In either case, the reliability is
essential, but when the provocative behavior is a defense against
the anxiety produced by an internal conflict, the child usually must
have some additional help directed toward modifying the defense.

The presentation that follows will deal with the caseworker's relationship with the child and the application of principles of psychological development to the pre-placement, placement, and
post-placement phases of service.

The Child and the Caseworker

The caseworker has special importance to the child in foster
care. The child in his own home looks to his family to provide for
his needs and to secure for him the services he needs from others.
When the parental responsibility is transferred to a foster care
agency, it is the caseworker who makes the services concrete, real,
and understandable at either an emotional or an intellectual level,
or both, depending on the child's learning status. The agency as an
institution speaks through the caseworker. Unlike other casework
treatment relationships, this one involves the child's total life situation, and the caseworker has importance to the child in relation to
the complete spectrum of his past, present, and future life. As
pointed out earlier, in foster care, more than in other social services, the agency has a commitment for continuity of service related to the child's need for care, and consequently there is a reciprocal investment between client and agency, represented in the
person of the caseworker, that transcends the usual limits of commitment for treatment in which day-by-day care is not involved.

The concept of the agency as a "parental force," developed first
by Robinson and elaborated by Barnes, illuminates the essential
agency role as an institution on which the child can rely for his future care, regardless of the other changes that occur in his life.
Barnes, paraphrasing Robinson, described the "parental force" role

of the agency as "a responsible, conscientious, and emotionally involved . . . guardian" (12).

In practice, the child can experience this quality of agency involvement only to the extent that someone in the agency, like a good parent, knows what the child needs at all times and wants to provide it for him. Beyond the caseworker, key administrative personnel who participate in major decision-making carry responsibility not only for supporting plans made for the child but also for insuring continuity when staff changes occur. The child's awareness of the backing of the agency fortifies and strengthens his sense of the reliability of an ongoing "parental force" in his life. It is equally true that agency limitations which lead to persistent denial of needed services amount to de facto neglect that the most meticulous reliability on the part of the caseworker cannot significantly diminish. Deprivation of needed services has a simple definition to the placed child: it means neglect, through passive indifference or active rejection. As Barnes aptly noted, "negligent state guardianship is no better than negligent parental guardianship" (13).

The cultivation and promotion of trust is the transcendent therapeutic goal of placement because the capacity to trust the caretaking adult is the essential soil for genuine maturation and ego growth. The placed child may have developed some degree of basic trust during infancy and early childhood, but usually he has experienced some deficits or traumata in the early environment which make him excessively vulnerable to later experiences. Placement is usually experienced as a rejection and as confirmation that adults cannot be relied on. The caseworker can safely assume that the child in placement is normally distrustful because of his preceding experiences, whether or not he evidences the distrust. The beginning of trust in the placement system is a fragile thing, and its nurturing requires special and continuous attention.

The development of the child's trust in the caseworker and his confidence in the agency as a parental force begins with the initiation of service. The pre-placement, placement, and beginning post-placement experiences are the critical demonstration of the agency's capacity for continuity in its conscientious involvement.

During this process, the child is the most helpless and the most vulnerable. The treatment approach is specific: a carefully defined, continuously confirmed reliability in the casework relationship, which, in turn, represents the agency's parental role. The object is to make reliability clearly visible to the child—that is, to make him consciously aware of the issue of trust, through verbalization and through action. For this therapeutic purpose, the meticulous reliability of the caseworker goes beyond ordinary reliability. The child needs the opportunity to learn that the caseworker's actions and commitments are in his interest, and, concomitantly, that no commitments will be made that are either unrealistic or undesirable, either implicitly or explicitly.

This point may appear obvious and simplistic. It is neither, as experienced practitioners can testify. Meticulous reliability includes both major and minor actions. It includes the thoughtful preparation of the child for the experience that lies immediately ahead; the prompt and timely administration of concrete services; the structuring of appointments and routine promptness in appearing for those appointments; availability for needed help; and the like. Administration of tangible services, integral parts of the foster care system, is the axis around which the relationship develops. Empathy and emotional support, while essential, are actually misleading and seductive if the important concrete services are unduly delayed or neglected. It does little good, for example, to support and reassure a child about his new school if, at the same time, the practical arrangements for his school transfer are overlooked so that delay causes added problems and anxiety. It is worse than useless to assure a child of support if appointments are not met promptly or the child is left in a state of uncertainty about matters important to him. Any of these events can occur when the caseworker is under work pressure and not fully cognizant of the reasons for priorities in this area of responsibility.

A similarly important issue is in the setting of limits and making of promises and commitments. It is natural for an adult to want to comfort a suffering child by acquiescing to his demands with promises that appear to offer immediate solace. It is only later that one sees, in some instances, that the commitment was not in the child's best interest. When one gets caught up by the child or by his own feelings and is trapped into violating a commitment to reliability, acknowledgement of the error is a further step in crystallizing the issue of trust. The practitioner does not advance the cause of trust by reliably carrying out an ill-advised promise; being human, he can make mistakes, give the matter further thought, reach a different conclusion, and accept the child's reactive hostility or disappointment. He does not always have to be right; he does always have to be thoughtful in relation to the child's needs. The placed child needs not only a visible demonstration of reliability but, equally important, continuous evidence that he is valued by those responsible for his care. Thoughtfulness about him and his needs is such evidence. Thus, one offers him both of the essential components for promoting trust and growth: (a) the provision of what he needs in an emotional climate of empathy and thoughtful concern, and (b) firm, defined limits in denying what is either undesirable or not feasible.

It has often been observed that some placed children continue long after placement to distrust and fear the caseworker responsible for their placement. From this the inference has sometimes been drawn that the participation of the caseworker in the child's life interferes with adaptation and that it is better for the caseworker to withdraw and to make only those contacts that are administratively required. This inference rests on an incomplete understanding of the child in the dynamics of the foster care system. In a relationship as important to the child's life as this one, avoidance serves to perpetuate and reinforce maladaptive defenses. In the service of establishing trust it is essential to understand and work with the problem, if it persists beyond the early post-placement period.

The child who relies on the caseworker for help in a painful situation may experience both positive and negative feelings in this relationship. Characteristics of the psychotherapeutic relationship illuminate the nature of this foster-care relationship. In psychotherapy, in the course of receiving help with problems that have painful associations, the child may develop both positive and negative feelings toward the therapist. The negative feelings have to be recognized, dealt with, or otherwise worked out in order to maintain the positive feelings as a constructive force for growth. If the psychotherapist were to withdraw in order to avoid the discomfort of the child's anxiety or hostility, he would leave the child without needed help and, further, would confirm the child's unrealistic fears and anxieties. So it is with the placement caseworker.

Other causes of persistent fear or anger that may contribute to the negative aspect of the child's feelings may lie in some combination of the following conditions:

1) The child may have identified with a parent's defense of projecting onto the agency the responsibility for the child's placement, or, more simply, he may have relied on the parent's interpretation of events because his own ego development was not sufficient to enable him to perceive reality independently.

2) The child may use projection and displacement as characteristic defense mechanisms. In this situation the defenses serve to avoid the pain of recognizing feelings of rejection, anger, and guilt in the relationship with the parents.

3) The child may fear and intensely distrust all adults, with a feeling generalized from a basically poor relationship with the parents.

4) The persistent reactions of fear may be responsive to the absence of appropriate supportive and therapeutic measures in the placement process and thereafter.

5) The child may be reflecting problematic attitudes in the surrogate parents if they originate or reinforce negative feelings.

In brief, intensity and persistence of predominantly negative feelings encountered in the child reflect either a realistic reaction to the environment or internal maladaptive defenses which require a therapeutic resolution.

Perhaps, in some instances, the foster care practitioner is especially vulnerable to the manifestation of such feelings because of some persistent doubt of his own about placement as a treatment measure. It should be recognized, however, that the child's total or relative dependence on the agency holds a high potential not only for regression and the use of pathological defenses but also for correction of earlier problems and the promotion of the maturational processes. With proper therapeutic management, the child in placement is usually able to work out a relationship with the caseworker in which the essential elements of trust are developed.

In the successive stages of placement, the caseworker's role in the direct relationship with the child is altered in specific ways. In the pre-placement and placement process the caseworker functions primarily as an auxiliary ego for the child. Immediately following placement, some of these functions are transferred to the surrogate parents, and other functions involving continuity with the past and communication and support in adaptation to the new environment become transcendent. Subsequently, when the child is settled and relative stabilization of the placement is achieved, the caseworker's role and functions are further modified and individualized to fit into the ongoing situation. The caseworker continues to carry responsibility for the child's ongoing involvements with his past and for continuity in providing needed services. In addition, maturational and environmental crises occur in the course of long-term care and emerge as important focal points of preventive and therapeutic intervention. Ultimately, the caseworker's functions are focused on the approaching termination of placement as the child either returns to his family or approaches independence. If the agency has established and maintained itself as a reliable parental force, the caseworker's activity in each of these stages is responsive to specific needs as they emerge.

The Placement Process

THE CASEWORKER AS AUXILIARY EGO

Because of his dependence on adults and his critical situation, the child needs the caseworker to serve as an auxiliary ego in the placement process (14). In order to provide the needed support, it is necessary to establish as much trust and confidence as the child (and the environment) will allow through a series of direct contacts before placement. The caseworker's function as an auxiliary ego includes helping the child with reality perception and reality testing and, by his presence, providing support and assuming the active functions that are beyond the child's capabilities. In application, this role is both therapeutic and preventive. Its purposes are to relieve anxiety, to enable the child to experience to a masterable degree some portion of the feelings generated by the situation, and to give the support necessary to prevent unnecessary trauma. In the presence of a relationship with a perceptive, supportive adult, the child is not likely to experience the traumatizing terror that comes with total helplessness. Serving the child as an auxiliary ego is not the totality, but it is the crux of the treatment approach in the placement process. Because of his age and stage of development, and the complexity and emotional meaning of what is taking place in his environment (the one he is leaving and the one he is entering), the child cannot perceive correctly what is happening to him. Ego functioning is invariably impaired by the impact of the experience. Helping the child by serving as an auxiliary ego may reach into all aspects of the caseworker's activity in the placement process.

For the child to perceive the caseworker's role, it must be explained in words, as well as demonstrated in action. The reality of the casework relationship begins with the identity of the caseworker and his function. The caseworker's confidence and clarity, communicated at both the conscious and unconscious levels, act on the child's anxiety at both levels. Since the period immediately preceding and during the placement process sees the child at the height of his anxiety, it is important that the practitioner responsible for service during this period should have sufficient training and experience with children to feel comfortable in his role of helping the child and his parents. The caseworker's feelings are of the utmost importance, since the usefulness of the technical approaches is largely determined by the emotional atmosphere in which they are carried out. It is a well-known therapeutic principle that an anxious client is helped as much, perhaps, by the practitioner's calmness and relaxation regarding the anxiety-laden content of information as by the technical approaches to the content. Familiarity with the agency and its procedures and knowledge about the child, his family, the placement facility, and the details of the placement process contribute significantly to the practitioner's sense of self-confidence and capacity to absorb the anxieties of the child and his parents at this critical period.

To state this principle in another fashion, the practitioner can serve best as an auxiliary ego for the child when his own ego is free from undue stress and able to absorb the added tasks implicit in this stage of foster care service.

In the beginning relationship with the child, the details of explaining the function of the agency and of the caseworker are adapted to the child's age and ability to understand. Even for the very young child at a preverbal stage, the caseworker's focus on his purpose through simple words, along with a gentle, confident attitude, creates a supportive emotional climate, important in itself and in counterpoint to the emotional climate created by the anxious, ambivalent parent.

Communication with the older, verbal child should allow for the child's expression of his questions, his conscious fantasies and fears, and his wishes. His anxieties are usually revealed indirectly in unconscious ways. His self-expression derives its initial focus from the caseworker's identification of his function and his purposive structuring of the procedures for carrying out this function. Identifying this function includes, importantly, his relationship with the responsible or important adults in the child's life: his parents or surrogates acting on his behalf. Structuring the subsequent relationship includes the purposes, the mechanics (time, place, frequency of contacts), and the patterning of the practitioner's approaches that characterize his intentions. For the child embarking on this experience, advance preparation for the various activities that involve him is a vital aspect of ego support, or what might more accurately be termed "ego protection." The purpose is to protect the functioning ego and its adaptive capacity, to the greatest possible degree, from experiences that drastically assault the ego and impair its functioning.

Erickson illuminates this ego state as follows:

In childhood, of course, fear and anxiety are so close to one another that they are indistinguishable, and this for the reason that the child because of his immature equipment, has no way of differentiating between inner and outer, real and imagined, dangers; he has yet to learn this, and while he learns, he needs the adult's reassuring instruction. In so far as the child fails to be convinced by the adult's reasoning and especially when he perceives instead the adult's latent horror and bewilderment, a panicky sense of vague catastrophe remains as an ever ready potentiality (15).

If this applies to the normal child, in the normal family situation, it can be seen readily how the placement situation heightens and intensifies the child's vulnerability and his need for "the adult's reassuring instruction" as a cushion against the sudden shock of discontinuity in his environment, as well as for guidance in distinguishing the real from the unreal.

The optimal maintenance of the child's existing capacity to perceive and cope with reality and the strengthening and growth of reality testing are advanced by appropriate preparation, opportunity to react, clarification of incorrect perceptions, and direct help with accompanying fear and anxiety. The child's preparation for placement should include: (a) the opportunity to develop sufficient relationship with the caseworker to enable him to accompany the caseworker without overwhelming anxiety; (b) support from the parents or parent surrogates responsible for his care before placement, to whatever extent they are able to participate constructively; (c) opportunity to become acquainted with the oncoming parent surrogates and other family or group members and the new physical environment before placement.

The content of the caseworker's specific preparation of the child for placement is flexibly adapted to the child's age and total situation, but it should reflect back to the child, to the extent that the information is available, the caseworker's firsthand knowledge of the child's present living situation, his parents, and the new situation awaiting him. If the case is a collaborative one, in which the service to the parents or placement facility is provided by a different caseworker, or if there has been a transfer of caseworkers, or under various other circumstances, meeting this requirement may call for special arrangements to visit the foster home or institution and to schedule a special appointment with the responsible parent. These practical steps provide one of the means through which the caseworker achieves integration of the current situation and continuity between the immediate past, present, and future for the child.

Ordinarily, it would be preferable to have from three to six weeks after the decision for placement in which to develop a relationship, prepare the child, and carry out the pre-placement visits with the prospective surrogate parents. Within this available time a caseworker can make choices in the timing and spacing of contacts with the child. In many cases preschool children require three or four contacts with the caseworker at one-to-three-day intervals before they are comfortable about leaving the parent or parent surrogate and accompanying the caseworker, knowing that they will be brought back after a walk in the neighborhood, or the like. Older children show discomfort in other ways: their lack of freedom to accompany the caseworker to an interviewing room or their inhibition of verbalized expression within the interview. The older child, having a better time sense, carries over the relationship response for longer intervals. Therefore, frequency of contacts can be related in part to the child's age.

However, time, a vital factor in the establishment of the child's feeling of comfort with the caseworker, often is strictly limited by circumstances. Such a limitation is sometimes unrealistically imposed by a sense of urgency on the part of parents or referral sources or by undesirable interagency procedures. Recognition of the damage wrought by precipitous or unnecessary emergency placements is gradually making inroads on detrimental practices. On the other hand, there are situations that realistically require emergency action and others in which the practitioner has little choice as a result of the operational practices of courts and agencies in the community network of services. The work that needs to be done to affect modification in these practices is another subject. Meanwhile, the child must be served as effectively as possible under existing conditions. This requires the optimal use of placement skills within the limits permitted by the circumstances, compressing into a short time the procedures that are optimally effective in a longer time span.

When an emergency placement precludes adequate planning, the ingenuity and flexibility of the practitioner allows for application of the principles for the establishment of a supportive relationship. In an emergency, it helps the child if he can have at least one contact with the caseworker before he is taken from one setting to another, even if both events occur on the same day. It helps him to see this person, to be told who the caseworker is and why he is there. It helps him to have an opportunity to ask questions and to know what to expect. Preparation means, in part, that the child has an opportunity for the strangeness to wear off and time in which to "get used" to the expected changes. To the extent that this can be accomplished in emergency placements, the shock of discontinuity is reduced.

The highlights of a series of interviews with a five-and-a-half-year-old boy show the dynamic interplay of the major typical reactions to placement and the details of the helping process.

THE DEAN CASE

Briefly, this was the presenting situation: Mrs. Dean, aged twenty-seven, the white Protestant mother of Tom, aged five-and-a-half, and Barbara, aged two-and-a-half, was divorced from the fathers of the two children. Her first marriage lasted for two years, the second for only a few months. The whereabouts of Tom's father was unknown. Barbara's father had been in a state mental hospital in another part of the country for some time. The children had no contact with either father. The mother had been variously employed as a waitress, receptionist, and call girl. She had left all of her jobs because of "fights with the boss." She left the children with a "sitter," a divorced woman who had teenage children of her own. The mother took Tom home at night when she wasn't working, but left Barbara at the sitter's. This arrangement had existed since Barbara was seven months old and Tom was three years old.

Mrs. Dean had been unemployed and received public welfare assistance intermittently. She was subject to periods of acute anxiety and depression during which she felt as though she were "going to pieces." There were indications of periodic alcoholism and suspicion of the use of drugs. She had had no stability in her childhood or adulthood, appeared disorganized, and was overtly hostile, accusing, and distrustful. She slept with Tom and she said that she had taught him about sex differences by bathing with him in the tub. She had gone to several social agencies in the past to make plans for the children, but fled when the issue of court custody was raised.

The precipitating causes of her application for placement of the children were seen in a cyclical exacerbation of the mother's mental illness, new problems with the sitter in reaction to the mother's behavior, Tom's reactive disturbance, and complaints from the neighbors. Tom's age and increased perceptions made the mother's promiscuity increasingly unmanageable for her, and her guilt about the unstable, inadequate care of the children became more intense. There were no relatives or close friends, as the mother had severed her relationships with the various adoptive and foster parents who had reared her.

In her sessions with the caseworker she at times followed her violent, verbally abusive outbursts by a semi-apology, saying, "Don't take me too seriously when I blow up." She appeared to be intelligent, verbalized well, and was aware of her problems. But she would not undertake a course of treatment for herself.

Both children were found to be physically healthy and intelligent. Although functioning at age level, they were showing evidences of emotional disturbance. Initially the mother requested placement of the children "for about a year." She greatly feared losing the children, but with extensive support recognized that the duration of their placement was not predictable. An indeterminate long-term placement was planned in view of her chronic, severe mental and emotional illness, the absence of previous periods of adequate parenting, and the apparent lack of capacity to benefit from treatment of any kind. A male caseworker was assigned to the children because of the mother's intense rivalry with women who shared responsibility for the children.

Interviewer's Notes, May 14 to July 9.
There were seven sessions and two cancellations.

5/14 I had been introduced to Tom in the waiting room by mother's caseworker on 5/7 when I had met mother for a prelimi-

*nary interview. Tom is a sturdy, appealing youngster of about av-
erage size. He seemed to have a cold. He related quickly (too
quickly, I thought) and accompanied me willingly to my office. He
asked a number of testing questions. Exploration brought out that
he knew his mother came here "on account of finding a place for
him and Barbara to stay." He described how the "sitter" yells, that
she is so bad that her own daughter ran away. I found that Tom
knew his mother doesn't like her job as a waitress and wants to
study to be a nurse. I explained that Mrs. Sanders, his mother's
caseworker, and I will be working together to help him and his
mother and Barbara have good care and that this is the agency's
work, to help parents take care of children when they need help.
He nodded, but had no questions. I told him he and I would get
together this way every week for an hour, for the next few weeks,
to get acquainted. We can talk about anything that is on his mind.
The toys are for him to play with if he wishes while he is here; he
can help himself to the candy in the jar. (The quantity available
was limited to what he would be allowed.) He can ask me any
questions and I will always try to answer them. If I don't know
the answers I will tell him so. I will always tell him in advance
about any plans or changes so he will know what to expect.*

*Tom said, in response to all this, that wherever he goes to live
would have to be near his present school because he likes the
teacher. He wanted me to go see the teacher. I agreed that I
wished it could be there since he has a teacher he likes, but that
the agency has no foster homes near his present school and we do
not now know where it will be. As soon as we do, he and I will
talk about it. I told him I knew from Mrs. Sander's talks with his
mother and the school that he does very good work in school and
that the teacher likes him. Wherever he lives, it will be near a
good school. He talked of having visited a battleship recently with
mother and her boy friend. He could not elaborate. He asked me
to go home with him today, as his mother was not working. I clarified again the purpose of my seeing him in the office. This reminded me that he had spent only part of each day with his
mother, sleeping at home when she does not work at night and
Barbara sleeps at the sitter's house. He confirmed this. I explained*

that when he moves to a foster family, there will be two parents, and also that he will stay day and night; and that this will be different for him. He was not ready to talk about this. He made several comments as he played, stating tentatively that mother will be worrying about where he is. I acknowledged this worry mother and he would have at times, and again told him the identity of the persons who would be available to help. When I offered to help him with scotch tape he was using, he said he didn't want my help; he could take care of himself. He said he brought his own scissors and he was glad he did. He then asked if I would go upstairs now and get Barbie, but he seemed pleased when I focused on him and limited this hour for his use alone. I explained that I would see and get acquainted with Barbara separately.

There was some procrastination about termination, and on the way upstairs he asked if I was married. I told him "yes." He agreed to come to see me next week at the same time as his mother comes to see Mrs. Sanders.

5/21 Tom was somewhat defensive today, involving himself in much play activity. At times he wasn't sure what he should do. When I gave permission for him to keep himself busy as he wished, he drew a house. I picked up on our discussion of the last hour. He had no further comment or questions about moving, but he seemed willing for us to continue thinking about it. Since he has had no experience in normal family life, either at home or with the sitter, I offered to tell him about how families live when there are both a mother and a father in the home. I explained about daily routines and roles, when the mother remains at home and looks after the house and family and the father goes to work. He listened, but made no verbal response.

He wanted to bring water into the office; he asserted that the scissors in the desk drawer were really his. (He had not brought his today.) As I set limits and held to reality, he ate a piece of candy, and said that he had a toothache, that he had told mother, but she refused to take him to the dentist. He said his mother doesn't want him to eat candy, and I should not tell her. I told him his mother had given permission when I talked with her. I would ask her again if he wished. (I had learned from Mrs. Sanders that Tom had upset his mother by telling her he had secrets with me.)

I had to tell him several times during the hour that the scissors and other play materials belonged here, and were for his use while here, but that I could not let him take them home. I had the feeling throughout that he was unconsciously trying to provoke rejection.

5/28   Appointment canceled by mother.

6/4   *Tom was brought in fifteen minutes late. I told him I was glad to see him and talked about the interview he missed last week because his mother was ill. I mentioned the letter I had written to him and he acknowledged that he had received it.*

Sequence of this session was approximately as follows: I had the drawing of a house Tom had started in the previous session. He wasn't able to fantasy about it except that it was the sort of house he would like to live in. We talked further about the kind of families who are foster parents for the agency, married couples who have children of their own and know how to take care of children; about specifics regarding father's working and being at home with the family evenings and on weekends; about the mother's cooking and taking care of the house and the children; about the family's doing things together; and so on. Tom thought a foster home was a very big place, but was vague about it. I thought probably in his mind the change was a big one, and for most children it was scary at first because of all the changes and uncertainty. He said it should be near his present school, and it should have animals if they are allowed. Tom likes parakeets and he likes to go fishing. I said I was glad he told me. When we have the home that seems right for him and Barbie, I will tell him all about it, as will his mother. I will take them to see it; he will meet the family, and I will help him, step by step, in making the change. He cut out folded paper, making abstract designs, saying he learned this in school, but could say no more. As he copied and threw away various designs, I talked more about the uncertainty and worry boys and girls feel in wondering what it will be like. Maybe he has questions about how he would be taken care of, or when he will see his mother, and so on. As I talked in a slow, reflective manner to allow him to respond if he wished, he switched to playing with cowboys, then with soldiers. He was unable to respond to my wondering what they were up to, what was going on. He once mumbled something about, "Is there a war on? Why are there soldiers?" I talked further about maybe he didn't like leaving his mother and going to a new home. He ate some candy, took several pieces with him after asking permission, and gave one to Barbara in the waiting room.

6/11   Tom was fifteen minutes late. He did not want to come with me to my office. Mother stated that he did not want to, because there aren't enough toys there. She was not able to help him leave her, saying he didn't want to go today, but maybe would go to my office some other time. After mother left the waiting room with Mrs. Sanders, I tried to find out Tom's reason for not wanting to come to my office. He said he didn't want to. I talked with him in the waiting room, saying maybe he was telling me he didn't want to hear any more about a foster home; he didn't want to leave his mother and didn't want to go. Most children feel this way, so I wouldn't be surprised if he did. He said vehemently that his mother did not want him to go to a foster home. He agreed to my comment that he might be feeling that I am taking him away from his mother, right then and there. I said it was easier for him if he could pretend that his mother could take care of him. I reminded him of my promise that there would be no surprises, that both his mother and I would let him know in advance what was coming up, and suggested that he ask his mother to tell him again about her plans and the reasons. Tom still did not want to come. We remained in the waiting room, in a private corner where we could talk.

I talked to him about the appointment for next week for psychological tests. (By plan, his mother had already told him.) He listened closely while I explained where the tests would take place and told him that the tests were for the purpose of helping us understand him and how best to help him. There would be word games and stories about pictures and drawings. He said, "Like in school." He then accompanied me to the office and stuffed his pockets with candy. He was unable to stay in the room, but wanted to go for water and then back to the waiting room. I stayed with him and he asked again for the details about the procedures for next week.

Several times he went over to ask Barbara for some toys, then tried to grab them. When she defended herself, he switched to "sweet talk" and approached the receptionist to ask her to intervene.

6/18   Tom came to my office readily today, but had nothing to say. I talked about last week's visit and his worry that I wanted to take him away from his mother and take him to a foster home. I inquired whether he had had a chance to talk more with his mother about her wishes about a foster home for him and Barbara. He said he sort of talked with her, but could not remember what she said. I reviewed his mother's situation and the reasons she felt that he and Barbara needed a foster home where they could have better care. I said it was hard to think about it and put it into words. A lot of children go through this feeling that it isn't their parents who are doing this because they wish it wouldn't happen at all, and then they get frightened and mixed up. He looked at me, knowingly, and nodded. He worked with some clay, made a drawing, and became interested in my pen and pencil set. He expressed concern about where Barbara was, knowing she was with the psychologist, and asked to go and see. I took him to the outside of the testing room, but did not allow him to go in. He accepted this readily. I commented at one point that he has to find out for himself whether he can rely on what I tell him, and this is O.K. After we get better acquainted he will find he can trust me. During this session he was unable to participate in any further discussion of his feelings or thoughts about leaving his present environment or about the future.

6/25   Tom resisted coming with me. This time it was clear that his anxiety was in response to his mother's inability to separate from him. She held him on her lap, hugging and kissing him, saying he didn't have to go with me. Mrs. Sanders suggested that

*mother accompany her to her office and leave Tom in the waiting
room with me, which was done. I repeated some of the previously
given reassurances and awareness of his anxiety about leaving his
mother. He then repeated his insistence that mother was not send-
ing him and Barbara away. I said it was a hard thing for him to
think about. He didn't have to like it or be happy about it, but he
and I both had to face the fact that mother was bringing him here
for this purpose and no other because she thinks it is the best for
him. We agreed with her. I reviewed the reasons and said he needs
to get used to the idea that he is not alone in this, that I will help
him step by step. As he gradually relaxed I reviewed again the
steps in detail, such as a visit here in the office with the foster parents, getting acquainted by visiting their home, seeing his room,
playing with the other kids, seeing the yard, and having something
to eat. He then came to my office with me, very briefly, for some
candy, and wanted to see our medical clinic again. I explained
how he would have an examination here and introduced him to
the agency pediatrician, who responded in a warm, welcoming
manner.*

7/2   Interview canceled by mother.

7/9   *Tom came readily to the playroom. It developed that his
mother had told him yesterday the details about the new foster
home, which had been communicated to her by Mrs. Sanders. He
remembered all the details and from his attitude I was impressed
with how well his mother had prepared him. He wanted me to go
over the details with him again. I described the people in the family; why the parents wanted foster children; the home; pets; and
care of these by various members of the family; and something of
family routines. As Tom became fatigued and anxious, I talked
about this being a hard time for him. When his anxiety decreased,
he asked more questions and we reviewed the family members by
name and age and what each one does. He returned to his worry
about not being with his mother and when he would see her. I reminded him that he and Barbara would have regular visits with
his mother in our office and that his new family would bring him
here for the visits. At one point he laughed and said his mother got*

*caught in an elevator and couldn't get out. He could not elaborate.
I said she was probably scared and kids get scared of the things
that scare their parents, but he is to remember that Mrs. Sanders
will be helping his mother with her problems; mother has her job
to do, which is getting over her nervousness and getting a better
job, and he, Tom, has his job to do—getting acquainted with the
new family, and settling down to live there and go to school there.
I will be helping him and his foster parents with this part of the
job. We discussed the day and time when he would meet his prospective foster parents here in the office. I told him I would be
with him in the visit, then said I wanted to tell him about my talk
with them about him. He nodded. I related many of the details, including how he and Barbara and his mother managed in the past;
the fact that he didn't remember his father; the reasons his mother
could not take care of him and Barbara (her nervousness, the un-
satsifactory care of "sitters" while she worked, her wish for the
children to have better care); his wish for a pet; his good school
work and unhappiness about leaving his present school and his
home; the fact that he sometimes gets angry and breaks things; his
favorite foods; and the like. I said he and I would be talking together with them about these things, and he, too, can talk to them
about anything. I also told them about the problem he had recently, soiling his pants, and that this was because he had been
scared and unhappy.*

*Tom started to run around the room as I talked about this prob-
lem. I asked him to sit down and listen, and then told him that Mr.
and Mrs. Jameson said they were sorry he has been so unhappy;
they wanted to try to help him with these things and help him get
over it. I thought he might have been worried about what would
happen if he had an accident.*

*He seemed relieved and asked more questions about the Jame-
son's son, Terry. I reminded him that Terry was about his size but
that Terry would be allowed to do things that are right for a
seven-year-old boy and he (Tom) would be doing things that boys
his age do.*

*I then described the anticipated pre-placement and placement
sequence, discussing family members by their specific names. He
asked what he might call his foster parents, as his mother had*

raised questions about this. He had no preference. I said they would get to this, when they are acquainted and he feels more like a member of the family. Sometimes it takes a while; in the meantime he can call them Mr. and Mrs. Jameson, but after a while children usually like to call the grown-ups by the same names used by the other children in the family. (This had been handled similarly with his mother.)

I explained that I would take his mother for a visit to the foster home tomorrow; then Mrs. Jameson (foster mother) would come here the next day to meet Tom and Barbara. I will take him and Barbara to the foster home for a couple of visits, to get acquainted. I will tell him ahead of time the exact time, and I will also move them to the foster home.

I went over with him again that I will be coming to his foster home after he goes to live there, to talk to the Jamesons and to him. I reviewed how we worked together. He seemed to grasp quickly my explanation that the Jamesons, Mrs. Sanders, his mother, and I would be working together to take care of him and Barbara. I gave examples from what he had already experienced. I also explained again the role of the foster parents in taking care of the children, their school, clothes, meals, bedtime, and the like, just as with their own children, which would be different from the care given by the sitter when he went home at night and when his mother made these decisions.

Although this was a good deal of information, Tom was responsive, asking questions and hearing answers.

After the interview I introduced Tom to the clinic nurse and to Miss Breen, who would be our escort-driver during the pre-placement visits. He now knew the building well enough to playfully run ahead of me, hiding behind corners, and closing doors to keep me out. He smilingly responded to my interacting with him in this as a game, knocking on the door, saying "Who is there? May I come in? etc".

*Discussion of the Interviews: Common Emotional
Responses and Therapeutic Aims*

Analysis of the interviews shows something of the emotional responses common to children in various age groups when they are

faced with placement and of the common therapeutic aims of practitioners. Tom, because he was unusually intelligent, perceptive,
and verbal, and because sufficient time was allowed for observation of feelings as they emerged, makes visible the dynamics that
are often hidden either by the child's defenses or the lack of opportunity to observe the dynamic process in the child over a sufficient
span of time. The material suggests specific dynamics at various
levels of conscious and unconscious meaning; however, this discussion will be limited to those aspects of meaning and technical management that are generally pertinent in child placement.

At the beginning we see that this child relates quickly to the
caseworker, repressing his anxiety and maintaining distance with
good techniques for superficial relationship. Children who are less
able to contain their anxiety have been observed to use other defenses, such as withdrawal into relative silence or breaking into hyperactive, destructive behavior, verbally or physically. The caseworker's main objective in this contact is to find ways to begin to
establish himself with the child as a reliable, helpful adult. He can
be reliable and helpful in this specific function only to the degree
that he can establish who he is and why he is here. In this instance
the caseworker approached the issue first by tentative exploration
of what Tom already knew about his mother's plans and the reasons for them, then by confirmation and elaboration of the facts. It
can never be assumed that a child comprehends the reasons for
placement, regardless of what he has been told. He tends to deny
and repress this knowledge, and may need help with it from time
to time through his placement experience.

The caseworker next defined the purposes of the sessions and the
structure of the relationship: that is, the time, the place, and the
ground rules within which the relationship would operate. Clarity
in defining the reasons for placement, the caseworker's function,
and the relationship structure at the outset is an essential aspect of
defining the reality for the child and concomitantly providing ego
support.

The caseworker did not include the usual definition of confidentiality of the child's communications, as one would in structuring
interviews for a course of individual psychotherapy. Rather, the

open communication system was stressed, as part of the approach to the placement process. The purposes of this relationship, in their therapeutic and mental health aspects, require emphasis on open communication among all of the participants in the placement system. This does not preclude the possibility of treating appropriate communications of private feelings confidentially as the need arises. For example, if Tom were to reach the point of being able to verbalize his negative feelings toward his mother, such expression could be treated with confidentiality without interfering with the unifying aims of an open communication system. Or, if he were to ventilate negative feelings toward the prospective parent surrogates or others following a placement visit, his work on these feelings could be treated with the necessary confidentiality. However, the primary consideration here is the aim of helping the child gain confidence in the total foster care experience, the social environment which is new to him and within which he gradually gains confidence. An open communication system in relation to all of the items relevant to his welfare, between and among the individuals now vitally concerned with his welfare, is the central and focal procedure for achieving this unity on which confidence can rest. Within this framework, other therapeutic aims can be defined and achieved, as needed, including confidentiality restricted to defined purposes.

The assurance to the child that he will be told specifically and in advance what to expect is based on the fact that, in general, anxiety about unknown dangers is more difficult for the child to cope with than anxiety about known dangers. The assurance of preparation, however, must be followed by the actuality, since it is the actual preparation that is reassuring to the child, helps him differentiate the real from the unreal, and cushions him against the shock of discontinuity.

In the second session, the caseworker used his knowledge of the child's history to identify some of the major, concrete changes the child will experience. Knowing that Tom has never lived in a family with two parents, the caseworker knew that there would be a major change in a known way of life. Concomitantly, his knowledge of the details of school and home life enabled him to reflect back to Tom some comprehension of his identity and to explicate the threads of potential continuity.

Of comparable importance, Tom's testing behavior points up an avenue for the establishment of trust which has some implications for the concept of ego integrity. Can the child trust the ego integrity of the caseworker? His past environment is characterized by vacillating, unsure, unreliable adults. Both his mother and the sitter were easily manipulated and unpredictable. This is the characteristic environment of many children who need foster care. These children need speedy evidence of a steady and unshakable value system in the adults who assume their care.

In the face of firm limits on his actions, accompanied by acceptance of his feelings, Tom responded with complaints about his mother's neglect of his teeth and with an attempt to set up a triangular situation in which he and the caseworker would become accomplices in a forbidden pleasure (eating candy). The meaning of this response can be interpreted at various levels, but for present purposes it illustrates the need to view the open communication system and respect for the mother's role as key determinants in the caseworker's response. This is the safeguard against the pathological manifestations that would tend to set up nontherapeutic alignments in the casework relationship with the child and also to confound the positive use of the interrelationships in the foster care system.

The third session (6/4) followed a cancellation by the mother. Tom could take no initiative in considering the subject most important to him, but he could respond somewhat to the caseworker, telling what he wants and likes. The absence of questions suggests increasing anxiety and repression as he comes closer to the reality of placement. The caseworker chose to verbalize some of this anxiety, which was expressed only indirectly by silences, talk of war and soldiers, and clinging to his present school. It should be noted that the caseworker relied on four main approaches: acknowledging and encouraging the child's participation; giving him further information; identifying feelings of uncertainty and anxiety; and reaffirming the steps that will be taken to help him. The concerns that were suggested did not include concern about angry feelings.

While it is inevitable that hostility to the parent forms a part of the child's mixed reactions to the prospect of placement, facing these feelings may be the last thing that he can do, and then only after he has safely and firmly established himself in a stable relationship with parent surrogates or in the relationship with the caseworker. At this stage in the placement process he may need his defenses against recognizing his anger. He can be helped with his hostility only if he voluntarily and directly expresses it. Then acceptance and understanding by the caseworker will be of vital importance. Some children are not afraid of their hostility and its effects, but are afraid of their tender feelings. In such cases the hostility to the parent may flow freely. In either case it would be unwise for the caseworker to "take sides" with either aspect of the ambivalence, since usually one side is expressed but the other is present, consciously or unconsciously. The caseworker should be in the position of helping the child with either one by accepting both.

In the next session (6/11) we see Tom increasingly anxious and unable to accompany the caseworker to the office. An observation is made that his mother showed more than usual anxiety in parting from him. While the work that had been carried on with the mother is not reported here, it is important to know what is taking place. Another aspect of the increased anxiety of both is the increasing confrontation with the reality of placement. The child's tendency to deny that it is real often continues far into the initial stage of the process. Tom expressed his denial overtly by saying "My mother does *not* want me to go to a foster home." The caseworker inferred from this and from Tom's refusal to go to the interviewing room that he was unknowingly displacing onto the caseworker the responsibility for "taking him away" from his mother, as well as his hostility to his mother. This common phenomenon is the child's way of defending himself against a conflict that he seeks to avoid—the feeling that he is rejected and the reactive hostility and guilt that present him with internal dangers. The child displaces the responsibility elsewhere, as well as the hostility and distrust. At the same time, below the level of articulate awareness, he knows that this is not true and usually is accessible to help in tolerating the reality and clarifying the distortion. Increased tolerance for reality comes from specific treatment approaches by the caseworker and, to a significant degree, from the parent when the latter receives and is able to use the needed help.

In this case the caseworker brought out into the open the child's wish not to leave his mother and the displacement of responsibility for the decision. He universalized the feeling of not wanting to leave the mother and encouraged Tom to talk more with his mother about it. Working over the feelings and redefining the reality situation often will tend to reduce the anxiety and guilt felt by the child, making the conflict somewhat less threatening to him.

On 6/18, the fifth session, the anxiety is decreased and Tom accompanied the caseworker to his office. The caseworker pursued the same issues, and clarified again the mother's reasons for asking the agency to help with the care of the children.

One might well ask whether such clarification touches the unconscious conflict, and why it is helpful to the child. The answer lies in observations of each child's responses, but in general the process that seems to take place includes these dynamics: (a) Factual clarification tends to interfere with misunderstanding. Repetition by the caseworker and substantiation by the parent may help correct the child's assumption that the placement signalizes rejection arising from his own badness. (b) The concurrent support and guidance tend to strengthen the ego tolerance for anxiety. Consequently it becomes less necessary to repress all of the affect. (c) The active help and the demonstration of valuing the child's individuality, understanding his feelings, and accepting him as a worthwhile individual cut down on the feelings of helplessness, rage, and worthlessness, increasing his capacity to tolerate and deal with reality. All of these are ego-supportive and ego-strengthening techniques.

On 6/25 Tom again insisted that his mother did not want him to be placed, and clearly reflected the mother's anxiety. The work that had been going on with the mother in the interim is pertinent, since the potential availability of an appropriate foster home for the children had been under discussion in her most recent interview. Since this was an acting-out mother who functioned at a borderline psychotic level, it could be expected that her behavior would be at the mercy of her impulses, to some extent, in discussing placement with the children. The caseworker's insistence on the reality in the situation was the only available ballast for Tom's emotional equilibrium. The outcome of the work done with the mother, however, is evident in the subsequent session with Tom on 7/9.

The clarity of Tom's recollection of the details given by his mother and his capacity to ask for more information indicate the achievement of better ego integration, as contrasted to the earlier ego state, when he was overwhelmed by anxiety, evidenced by the blocking out of information and the avoidance of discussion in earlier interviews. Heightened anxiety and avoidance by running around the room appeared again when the caseworker introduced the subject of Tom's soiling. The importance of this aspect of preparation is seen in the sequence of, first, the appearance of acute anxiety when the subject is brought up and, then, immediate relief when he knows that his problems are known and accepted by both the caseworker and the prospective foster parents.

It is significant that the child's problems are included for discussion as one item within the context of the total picture of the child —his tastes, skills, likes, and dislikes—rather than as an isolated set of facts. Children tend to over-generalize their faults, to feel that the guilt or shame-laden behavior is the total self. The caseworker begins to work on correction of this distortion, indirectly but specifically, as he reflects back to the child in his various communications with him, not just the problems, but the total self. By the same token, omission of discussion of his known problems would leave the child in an emotional dilemma: Would he be accepted if his problems were known? What will happen to him when they are discovered? This anxiety and fear interfere with the beginning steps in the development of trust in the new relationships. However, sensitivity to the child's feelings of shame and guilt guides the timing and the handling of open discussion of problem areas. Although the matter-of-fact attitude of the adult goes far toward desensitizing the child's exaggerated feelings of shame about a given symptom, if the symptom is ego-alien, ill-timed discussion may bring a sense of intolerable shame and withdrawal from the relationship. This suggests that the child should be permitted to limit discussion of his problems to the minimal essentials, if he needs to do so, as demonstrated in the interview with Tom.

A routine part of the preparation includes specific information about the new environment. Physical descriptions of the persons in the family or group facility, as well as what they are like and what they do, have the purposes of introducing reality (as opposed to the child's fantasies, which flourish in the absence of facts), and of engaging the child's future participation in making his own observations for sharing and discussion. Are the surrogate parents tall or short, blonde or gray or brunette, fat or thin, stocky or wiry, fast or slow or average in speech, actions, and the like? Pictures of family members or child care staff are a desirable focus for a beginning introduction to a new environment. Ego mastery proceeds in small steps, with mastery of concrete details shared in advance and thereafter.

This approach also implicitly communicates to the child and the parent the fact that everyone cares. The prospective surrogate parents and the caseworker reveal, through their acts, a thoughtful investment in understanding the concerns and the meaning of this experience to the child as a unique individual. These acts are implicit communications of object-related concern; they set a tacit example of child-rearing attitudes; they form part of a pattern of a relationship that promotes trust and confidence.

The mother's role in telling the children the details about the forthcoming foster home before the caseworker's discussion with the child has equally important implications. This is a desirable procedure regardless of the child's age (adolescents as well as younger children) in all instances in which the parent is able to assume such responsibility. The procedure serves several useful purposes. It tends to counteract the child's tendency to displace responsibility for the separation; to dispel some of his feeling that the parent is rejecting all responsibility for him; to preserve some thread of continuity in the parental role; and to help prevent manipulative maneuvers in setting up destructive triangular situations. It demonstrates to the child from the outset the pattern of the agency's respect for the parent-child relationship and a beginning pattern for the interrelationships in the foster care system. When the parent is available but unable to carry out this responsibility, it is beneficial for the parent to participate by being present when the caseworker clarifies the facts with the child, wherein the parent can confirm and support the plan.

The preliminary visit of the parent to the selected foster home or institution has similar purposes. It is not for the purpose of parental participation in the selection of the foster home or facility (except in voluntary cases, in which group facilities are needed and the parent's decision-making participation is based in part on his own evaluation of the institution). It is for the purposes of building his working alliance with the agency; maintaining and promoting the parental capacity for appropriate, responsible participation in the child's changed life; engaging his collaborative efforts through participation; and maintaining his role with the child and his support of the child in the preparation for placement. There are, of course, some extremely disturbed parents who cannot utilize this experience constructively, but who can benefit from information about the facility and may, at some later time, need and be able to manage the experience.

Preplacement Introduction to the Foster Family: Summary and Discussion

On 7/11 Tom and Barbara met foster mother and her daughter, Dorothy, aged eighteen, in the office. Tom was shy, controlled, and unsure about relating to them. Barbara was more outgoing and readier to involve herself. We had crayons, paper, and scissors at hand and brought in refreshments (cookies, milk, and coffee). Tom responded with increased comfort as foster mother and Dorothy did not push him, but expressed interest and gradually reached out to him. He drew pictures, including a tree and a house. I used their content to verbalize simple questions. Foster mother picked up on these, describing their home, their family, what they do during the day, what they had to eat, etc. When foster mother talked about the family members, the home, and the animals it was notable that Tom remembered the details I had given him previously, and responded to the foster mother with elaborations of her comments.

We talked briefly together about the reasons the children's
mother needed a foster family for them, the plan for them to visit
with their mother in the office, and how they would live in their
foster home as members of the family. Foster mother and Dorothy
affirmed the family's wish to have them and reconfirmed plans for
their visit.

In two subsequent preplacement visits to the foster home, the
caseworker's observations included several fairly typical reactions
indicating, indirectly, the anxiety experienced by both children. In
the automobile, they required frequent limits in standing up, put-
ting hands out the windows, and climbing around. The ground
rules for car behavior were defined and repeated, in terms of
safety. The children were reassured about their safety, and assured
again about the purpose of the visits (to get acquainted) and the
return to meet their mother in the office. Verbalization of questions
was encouraged. Both children were able to accept reassurance, to
scribble on the drawing boards, and to look at pictures, although
in a somewhat distracted way.

It has been widely observed by practitioners that the anxiety experienced by children in the separation process is accompanied by
marked anxiety about transportation. Fear of accidents and injury
is highly mobilized and is expressed directly as well as indirectly
through verbalization of irrational fears and hyperactivity. It is a
period during which children need a calm, reassuring presence,
firm controls, and realistic reassurance. For the small child, the
physical closeness of being held may be the most comforting and
reassuring. Ordinarily, verbal restraint of undue physical activity is
sufficient, but in some instances stopping the car, augmenting verbal reassurance with a brief period free from fear of the moving
car, helps the child gain some mastery over his anxiety. Sometimes
breaking the trip with a stop for rest and refreshments acts as a
restorative and an opportunity to drain off anxiety through talk
and physical activity.

If these measures are ineffectual, it suggests that the child's pre-
placement preparation has been insufficient for his particular ego
state and internal stress. The child's ability to respond to realistic

reassurance is a further clue to his ego state and his underlying capacity to trust.

During the visits, the children met the family members. They were given a tour of the house and yard and spent some time in the bedrooms that were prepared for them. Tom rode Terry's bicycle in the yard; the two boys played together. Foster father showed them the pets, talked about how long they had had them, and explained the care given the dog and cat, and the places where they were fed, slept, and the like. Foster father reaffirmed the family's expectation that Tom and Barbara would live with their family and be like members of the family. He mentioned their mother and made explicit his understanding about visiting arrangements. Tom asked if he could go home for his birthday. The caseworker explained that he would have a visit with his mother in the office for his birthday, but the children would spend all of the holidays and birthdays in this home, like the other children in the family. The foster parents participated in the discussion, as did Terry and Dorothy. Tom said quickly, "Then I'll have two birthdays." The caseworker added, "You will also have two families; and this is the one you will live with."

The caseworker noted some shyness, hyperactivity, and bragging on Tom's part, in contrast to Barbara, who was uninhibited in playing with the paper dolls, jabbering about the animals, their names, and the like. She followed Dorothy to the kitchen to bring milk and cookies. Both children ate moderately, a further signal of a degree of psychological mastery of the experience.

During the second visit to the foster home Tom asked to be allowed to stay rather than return to his home. He bragged about his imaginary exploits with ships and airplanes, in which he reported phenomenal experiences of prowess in steering, climbing rails, and so on. At one point, the caseworker found a suitable occasion to inject a comment to Tom and the family that Tom likes to pretend these things, like pretending to be grown-up. (This pattern of defense had been apparent in his initial interviews, at which time his response to the caseworker's handling confirmed that he was well aware that this was pretending.)

All of this information is included here to illustrate a differential diagnosis in the meaning of the child's request to stay in the foster home or group facility where he is making a preliminary visit. Under some circumstances, the child's request reflects true readiness for this step. Under others, when the request occurs during the first or second visit, it is usually accompanied by some clue to the fact that the request is another unconscious defensive maneuver to get it over with. Plunging into the dangerous situation is a common defense that can be mistaken for mastery. In this case, Tom's bragging was the clue to his feeling of helplessness.

After the second visit, an interview with Tom enabled him to talk over some of his feelings. For example, he asked the caseworker not to tell his mother he rode the bicycle; she would be angry. This led to a discussion about the foster parents' responsibility for permitting or limiting his everyday activities, his mother's agreement with this, and Mrs. Sander's (mother's caseworker) role in working out these matters with his mother. The issue of divided loyalties was taken up; permission to like many people at the same time—relatives, friends, parents and foster parents—was communicated to him. These are some of the common areas of conflict in placed children, highlighted by this child's verbalization of what bothered him.

Conflict about authority, values, loyalties, and roles seems to characterize the child whose parents are confused and in conflict in these same areas. Another common problem is the role confusion in which the child feels responsible for his parent. This often is a defense against the child's inner feelings of helplessness regarding his parents' actions. Sometimes it derives, in part, from the child's guilt toward the parent, but it is most likely to take this form in situations where the immature parent has used the child as an object for emotional dependency, implicitly assigning this role to him in subtle or overt ways. For these children, it is important to know that the agency is providing the help needed by the parents. The caseworker can offer further correction through verbal clarification of roles. This is supported and made more real through the actual behavior of the adults: caseworkers, foster parents, and others in these roles. Many children respond gradually to these approaches because of the fluidity of the childhood personality structure. When the conflict is deeply internalized and nonresponsive to these approaches, it may become necessary to institute a supplementary course of intensive psychotherapy geared to dealing with intrapsychic conflicts.

The importance of the concomitant work with the parent during this process is highlighted again here. The child's anxieties are in part his own, but in part they mirror the messages that are being transmitted to him from the parent, either overtly or by contagion. In the process of decreasing anxiety and increasing ego mastery, one hopes that the parent's tempo of progress can be maintained at least one step ahead of the child's, to enable the parent to communicate less by contagion and to give overt support to the child. This goal is not always attainable because the parent may be less amenable to help than the child. Tom's mother, it was known, was struggling with her wish to retain some form of control over the children's day to day activities and with her jealousy of the potential parenting relationship of the foster parents. Tom's concerns reflected this with some precision. The caseworker's effectiveness in helping Tom was increased by awareness of the family interaction. When more than one caseworker is involved, effective collaboration includes sharing of detailed information, and the fullest use of the open communication system mentioned above.

It should be noted that this case illustration is not intended to serve as a model for the specific structure of the service, but rather to illustrate the distinctly individualized features of case management that arise from the diagnosis of the parents, the circumstances of the foster family, and the assessment of the children.

The use of two caseworkers, one to work only with Tom's mother, was based on a combination of problems in the mother. Early in the study, her disorganization, her unrealistic, hostile, verbally abusive testing behavior in the casework relationship, and her intense jealousy of Tom's relationship with other women, suggested that the psychological burden on her and the impact on the caseworker would be more manageable if the direct service to the children and the foster parents was carried by another staff member. This is a departure from the more usual use of a single caseworker in the initial study and placement procedures, which enables the caseworker to coordinate and integrate all aspects of the service. Such a departure from routine practice, however, should be possible when factors in the situation indicate the need for it.[12]

The introduction of the children to the foster mother in the agency's office is also an elective procedure, related to the individual case. The office meeting was utilized in this instance, because it appeared that for Tom this step would be more masterable than the larger step involved in a home visit. Ideally, the caseworker would have liked both foster parents to participate in this visit, but since the foster father could not be available, the next best plan was utilized. It has been observed, in the placement of children in foster homes, residential treatment facility, or other group facility, that if the child has had an opportunity to become acquainted with the caseworker and is somewhat familiar with the surroundings of the office, a preliminary meeting in this environment is helpful. It is a means of partializing the steps in the change, mitigating the total strangeness of the new environment, and giving the child a greater sense of confidence about the first pre-placement visit. It also strengthens the sense of the agency's role in the total relationship system.

PLACEMENT

Many practical questions of case management arise in connection with the transfer of children into and out of placement facilities. The caseworker is confronted with a series of tasks that overlap or must be carried on simultaneously. These tasks combine both the management of the physical aspects of the move and the response to the psychological needs of the various participants: child, parent, and foster parent or child care staff.

To illustrate, Tom and Barbara were given the necessary complete physical examination several days before placement in order

[12] There is evidence that the integrative capacity of practitioners cannot encompass the transactional complexities and range of emotional demands that are inherent in serving all of the participants in each individual placement system. It is probable that this factor is one of the major causes of the absence of service to parents. Consideration should be given to further use of collaborative teams for this reason.

to avoid the emotional stress of undergoing those procedures on the day of placement. Forty-eight hours prior to placement, they were given a benign, superficial check-up to rule out the presence of contagious illness. Immunization procedures were postponed until after their placement. Since most children are afraid of skin punctures, such medical procedures should be carried out when the child feels reasonably secure in his environment.

On the day of placement, the caseworker, accompanied by a driver, arrived at the home, by plan, at mid-morning. Knowing the mother's disorganized functioning, it was anticipated that the children's clothing and personal belongings might not be ready at the appointed time. Extra time was allowed for helping with the completion of these tasks, if necessary, and for the kinds of verbal support and clarification the mother and children would need at this parting. In actuality, most of the packing had been completed, but the final organization of toys and shopping bags was accomplished with the caseworker's help, and some packing supplies (bags and boxes) were provided from the trunk of the caseworker's car.

The mother's tendency to cling to Tom and to make unrealistic promises could be anticipated also. The caseworker becomes the auxiliary ego for all of the family members at this juncture in the process. For the emotionally unstable, disorganized parent, as well as for the self-contained parent under stress, the caseworker's matter-of-fact attitude and use of structure cuts down on the anxiety of parents and other family members.

The structure, on this day of the move, included the review of the day's time table and the reaffirmation of the appointment time and place for the first visit with the mother. The mother wept and talked unrealistically about telephoning the children daily, taking them home in a year, and the like. The caseworker intervened with realistic limits and reassurance. He told them that they would all feel better soon; the matter of telephone calls would be talked over after everyone had settled down; and he intervened directly in the mother's impulsive promise to take the children home in a year. He explained to all of them together that the mother and the children were feeling sad today, and the mother was saying this to try to make them all feel better, but it is natural and all right to feel sad and cry. He reminded them that they had all talked about this plan many times. This brought the mother back to the realities of planning which had been worked out with her in her interviews with Mrs. Sanders and with him on the day he accompanied her on the visit to the foster home.

The allowance for extra time in departing from the home made it possible to arrive at the foster home relatively early in the day, thus permitting the children to have an opportunity to explore the physical environment again and to have enough time with family members to take the edge off the initial feeling of strangeness before bedtime.

Meanwhile, information that had been transmitted to the foster family about the details of the children's routines provided links of continuity. Barbara's doll and her familiar robe and pajamas were unpacked and placed on her bed. Her usual nap time was observed. Tom's routine of changing into his dungarees and the custom of both children of having a mid-afternoon snack of milk and ginger snaps were carried out.

These are small examples of the use of information about customary and familiar routines, activities, tastes, and stages of self-help prevalent at the time of the transfer of young children from a known to an unknown environment. They suggest some of the practical ways of cushioning the psychological shock of discontinuity in the environment and preserving as much continuity as possible to protect ego identity and ego functioning.

THE PRESCHOOL CHILD

For purposes of simplification, the focus in this case has been limited to the details of the work with the five-and-a-half-year-old boy. The considerations given to the case management with the younger child, Barbara, are also pertinent, as they are related to age and stage of development, assessment of psychological status, and relationship to the nuclear family. First, the time span for the preparation of the younger child is usually shorter than for the school-age child and the contacts are spaced closer together. The preschool child has little time sense and more need for repetition of the contacts at close intervals (a day or two) if they are to be supportive and comforting during the actual process of physical transfer to the new environment. Management of the simultaneous preparation of preschool and school-age siblings is complicated by these differences in capacity for mastery of time and tolerance for anxiety.

Second, the pattern of the child's reactions to separation is a further guide in case management. The normal preschool child gradually achieves increasing capacity to separate from the mother for short periods of time, as the tasks of early development proceed through the successive developmental levels.

What then, is involved in the placement of the preschool child? (16) Barbara, at aged two-and-one-half, has already been partially separated from the mother since the age of seven months. She evidences no marked anxiety when separated from the mother or foster mother (sitter) who has provided for her care for nearly two years. Her calmness suggests that she has already developed some internal mechanisms for coping with her separation experiences in ways that, on the surface, may appear to be adaptive, but are so extremely unrealistic for a child this age that they are clearly pathological. It must be anticipated, then, that these mechanisms are likely to interfere with healthy personality development in ways that will emerge as she moves on through childhood and adolescence.

A healthier two-to-three-year-old child, with better capacity for relationship, would tend to show more open evidence of anxiety, fear, and possibly sadness. The child's capacity to be in touch with his feelings enables adults to offer comfort for those feelings.

When the feelings are almost completely repressed and covered by superficially good adaptations, the helping and care-taking adults are limited to those measures that are generally recognized as cushioning the experience and protecting the child against unnecessary trauma.

The recognition of inappropriate composure as a covert symptom in reaction to stressful experience is just as important as the recognition of overtly disturbed reactions. Barbara, for example, made this move without overt evidence of severe anxiety or resistance. This alerts the practitioner to the need to observe the child's future development carefully in order to offer the guidance needed by the surrogate parents and direct psychotherapeutic help to the child, if necessary.

THE ADOLESCENT

Procedures for the placement of adolescent children require age-appropriate adaptations of the principles already discussed, but include other considerations in the decision-making process. Children in this age range are capable of and usually need a greater degree of participation in various aspects of the process. Literally, the young adolescent cannot make the decision about placement any more than the younger child can, for the reality situation that requires his placement usually is such that he cannot alter it and he is not ready for full independence.[13] But some viability of plans, presented in ways that provide for choices, within reality limits, and a relationship that reflects respect for his autonomy, his level of independence, and his capacity to participate, are of great importance in preserving and promoting his ego functioning and safeguarding against his acting out by running away, etc. An illustration follows.

Peter, aged fourteen, an eighth-grade student living temporarily in the home of one of his friends, was referred to a foster care agency by the principal of his school. The report stated that he had lived with several different families in the community for the past year, since a serious quarrel with his mother. The mother, who worked in a tavern and was known to be alcoholic and negligent, had taken little recent responsibility and showed only sporadic interest in Peter. There was no father in the family. Peter was a moderately good student in the eighth-grade and was approaching graduation. He was liked and respected by his teachers, who reported good peer relationships and social standards.

[13] The older adolescent, if maturation has proceeded reasonably well, may assume a large degree of responsibility for the decision about where he lives until he becomes fully independent.

Several interviews with Peter revealed a fairly stable youngster, who had maintained himself for a year by living with the families of various friends and earning his clothing and incidental expenses by working at odd jobs on weekends. He was bitter about his mother's lack of interest in him, but at the same time revealed a strong wish for her interest. He did not remember his father, who, he reported, deserted his mother when he was about two years old. At that time his mother arranged with a "sitter" to provide his full-time care. This was an elderly widow who died about two years ago and who had apparently given him adequate care. Peter then returned to live with his mother and her then current husband. He stayed there for close to a year but was unhappy over the brutal quarreling. He left after an unusually cruel fight in which, he said, his mother nearly strangled him.

He respected and liked the school principal and his teachers; he wanted to remain in this neighborhood and transfer to the high school where his current friends would be. He came to the agency only because the school principal wanted him to do so. He admitted he was tired of moving around and did not like the uncertainty of his future situation, but would accept no plan unless he could live in the present neighborhood, attend the school of his choice, and have the freedom he felt was important to him. He asserted several times that he could and would take care of himself.

This pseudo-independence, while not a reflection of true maturity, encompassed effective skills for living which he had learned through necessity. This was a critical juncture in Peter's life. He was open to a further identification with constructive social values, and the promotion of adolescent development along the lines of growth and maturity if the stability he had found for himself could be preserved and if new channels of self-expression, autonomy, and identification could be found and established. He was also open to turning against himself and society if the environment in his adolescent years could not provide the opportunity to complete the tasks of adolescent development, correct some of the malaise that had already set in, and offer opportunity and support to achieve his conscious aims.

The issue of the adolescent's need to participate in the plans for his future is highlighted by this boy, whose social and psychological situation made it possible for him to openly verbalize and insist on this prerogative. This participation is essential to the self-esteem and growth of the adolescent. Peter, for example, was given information about the agency's services and facilities, and several sessions with the caseworker were spent examining the available alternatives. The agency's group facility for adolescent boys was not located in the district of the high school he wanted to enter. Whether he would be accepted in a school outside the district of his residence could not be determined at the time. Consequently, no commitment could be made even though it was desirable to meet this request, if possible, and give Peter continuity in his social environment, which was a constructive one.

Another problem was in the level of autonomy Peter had reached in making his own decisions. He was wary of entering an environment that would limit what he called his "freedom." The program of the group home, the privileges, expectations, and the responsibilities and limits regarding daily routines, hours, education, social activities, financial management, and the like were described to him. He had many objections, especially as to "coming and going as I like." He was offered the opportunity to consider the realities, to express his feelings about them, to consider the alternatives, and to weigh them in relation to each other. His strengths were supported, his wishes and feelings respected, and reality pointed out in connection with unrealistic aspects of his proposals. Ultimately, he decided to accept the risk involved in the school districting problem, knowing that efforts were underway to resolve the question. Concomitantly, as he was given explanations he gained awareness of the issue of absolute self-determination versus roles of adults and teenagers in decision-making in a family or institution in which responsibilities are appropriately understood and undertaken.

The role of the natural parent in the agency's service to an adolescent can be a confusing issue. From the outset, Peter was told that efforts would be made to locate his mother, that plans would be talked over with her, and that necessary legal action would be taken for transfer of guardianship. His response was an indirect revelation of the conflict, typical of other children in such situations, but usually hidden. He said, "I would want the agency to have my guardianship. My mother won't interfere. She couldn't care less." He later revealed intense interest in every step of the agency's contact with her. When he was told that she would be taken for a visit to the group home prior to his admission, he shrugged it off, saying it wouldn't matter. Later he inquired, "Did my mother like the home?" He was keenly disappointed when told that she had not kept the appointment for the visit. The mixed feelings of hostility over the rejection and longing for signs that the parent cares often persist long after placement, and the child or adolescent may need continuous help with them.

Despite the mother's unreliability and negligence, Peter, like others, was better able to enter into a placement plan with the agency when he knew that his mother had been brought into the planning, not just on the basis of legal necessity (which, of course, was acknowledged) but also on the basis of the agency's recognition that he had some importance for her and she for him, despite her lack of capacity for adequate parenthood and the negative aspects of his feelings, which were wholly accepted.

There are adolescents in need of placement whose acting out against authority by delinquency, running away, physical assault, and the like, has reached such proportions and become so entrenched that they are not able to utilize the opportunity for participation to reach a mutual, reasonable decision that they can carry out. In such instances, planning breaks down, interrupted by behavior such as running away or severe delinquency that moves the youngster toward enforced detention of some type. When it is known in advance that enforced detention in a hospital or a closed facility is needed, participation is approached at a different level, and in some instances it is not feasible.

PLACEMENT IN SPECIALIZED GROUP CARE FACILITIES

The preparation of a child for admission to a group care facility is governed by the same principles as the general preparation for placement already discussed. There are in addition some technical features of the preparation and process of placement that arise from the purposes of the group facility and its aims and program structure. This discussion will be focused primarily on the self-contained residential treatment facility for emotionally disturbed children, since this type of facility lies at the opposite end of the spectrum from foster family care in its use and way of life. Other types of group facilities fall somewhere in between these two in their uses, programs, and impact on the child and his family. Principles regarding preparation of the child for admission to other types of group facilities can be modified and adapted to the specific distinguishing features of each.

The residential treatment facility, whether small or large, self-contained or partially reliant on community institutions, is distinguished from other group care facilities by its primary therapeutic function. It is used selectively for the treatment of children with emotional disturbances so severe and pervasive that they are not amenable to outpatient treatment.

While each institution has its own procedures and requirements for the preparation of children for admission, there are two aspects of preparation that are inherently related to the selection and use of this specialized facility. These are: (a) the child's need for intellectual insight in connection with understanding the reasons for placement in a treatment facility, and (b) the unique social structure of the institution, which is essentially alien to the child's previous experiences.

CONSCIOUS SICKNESS INSIGHT

Children placed in residential treatment settings come by many routes. Some come from wholly or partially intact families, through the voluntary application of the parents, based on their awareness of the child's severe emotional disturbance. In these instances, one of the caseworker's aims with the parents is to gain their optimal participation in clarifying with the child the reasons and purposes of his placement in a residential treatment facility. Some parents, with help, are able to include not only the causes that are within the child but also, to some extent, their recognition of some aspect of their own part in the problems. Such preparation by the parents is essential but, even at its best, it is insufficient. Ordinarily there remains a good deal of vagueness, misunderstanding, and misinterpretation in the child's mind, and sometimes almost complete repression and denial of the nature of his problems.

Other children do not come by this direct route to the residential treatment facility. They come from disrupted families by way of foster care agencies, courts, and other community referral sources in which a diagnostic study of the child indicates the need for this type of treatment. These children, for the most part, are almost wholly unaware of their condition and needs. Thus, regardless of the way the child comes, a vital part of his preparation by the caseworker is the clarification of the reasons for the selection of this facility. This aspect of preparation serves the same purposes as those defined earlier, in connection with foster family care, but its content is specifically related to the nature of the institution. It defines reality for the child; it provides opportunity for participation through expressing questions and positive and negative feelings; it sets up some of the primary conditions for the establishment of trust; and in addition it begins to define a focus for his treatment.

Helping a child gain awareness of his problems and his responses to them may take many forms, depending on the nature of the problems and the child's defenses. Some examples will show some of the common variations among children.

Jim, aged eight, was removed from a foster home to a residential treatment facility. His overt symptoms were: school failure as a result of inability to learn at the first- and second-grade levels; stealing parts from cars in company with a group of delinquent neighborhood children; uncommunicativeness in relationships with adults. These problems were apparent to him; he knew that he was in trouble—in school, at home, and in the neighborhood. A comprehensive personality study revealed a depressed child with severe internalized psychological problems. Sickness insight, however, usually includes the identification of only those problems that make sense to the child—that is, that he is consciously aware that they exist and is able to see that they are his problems. The inclusion of others serves to bewilder him. In Jim's situation, the overt problems were apparent to him and he was aware of his unhappiness. He had sufficient ego capacity to accept the fact that the problems were in him. He recognized that he needed help of the kind that was available in the facility to which he was going. The special aspects of the institution discussed with him included the school program designed to help children overcome learning disabilities; a staff that would give the guidance and control he needed to help him stay out of trouble while he learned better ways of living, having fun, and growing up; and individual treatment to help him understand himself and what was causing him to have these troubles. He was relieved to know that the help he needed was available despite the fact that his distrust of adults, his poor self-esteem, and his depression made him feel hopeless about the outcome.

This degree of available insight, however, is unusual. Many children with manifest, severe symptoms tend to deny, repress, or project responsibility for them. Herbert, a nine-year-old boy, shows some of the common resistances of children to sickness insight. His parents applied for his admission to a residential treatment facility. He was like Jim in some of his overt symptoms, but unlike him in other important ways. He could not be contained in school because of his rebellious, destructive, hyperactive behavior; he had no internalized learning disability, as such. He had a slight physical handicap, in the form of a limp. His peer relationships, like Jim's, were based on group delinquency, but he reacted to the slightest provocation with violent, destructive rage, which he attributed to provocations from other children about his physical disability. When the manifest reasons for his proposed care in a residential treatment facility were discussed with him, he revealed awareness of unhappiness and discomfort, but felt that others were to blame for his troubles or exaggerated their importance. If they would behave differently he would be all right.

Herbert's inability to accept any awareness that his troubles were a part of him rather than the exclusive responsibility of the world around him was partly a reflection of a defense borrowed from his mother. She, too, blamed the outside world for his problems, and was ambivalent about his need for residential treatment. It was only with the insistence of the school and the stepfather, who recognized the inability of the parents to help him at home, that the mother had brought herself to apply for his admission.

A somewhat different type of problem of sickness insight is seen in Linda, a bright, borderline psychotic, seven-year-old girl. She was unaware, consciously, of her illness and her need for treatment. She was the eldest of three girls of mentally ill parents. Before her placement, her mother had been committed to a state mental hospital and her father had disappeared. The mother had seen no problems in Linda's development; the problems were too like her own. Linda was quiet, withdrawn, conforming, and unable to relate to other children and adults. A pervasive inability to concentrate in school was the only problem that could be made visible to her. Since she was a bright child and liked to learn, the school problem caused her a great deal of concern, which could be utilized as a motivation for treatment. This type of child needs sickness insight in the form of an anodyne. In the context of empathic understanding, the total situation was approached on the basis that all that happened in her family would make any child feel confused and unhappy and that all children in this situation needed special help to recover and to sort out and understand what it was all about. She was especially able to respond to the opportunity to have help in school.

These examples illustrate some of the common reactions of children to sickness insight in preparation for placement in a treatment facility.

When overt symptoms are brought to the child's attention, as part of his preparation, they still may not be acknowledged by him. In brief, children vary widely in their reactions. Some children are aware of their problems and are able to gain intellectual awareness of their need for help. Others are aware of their problems but deny them verbally for self-protection, and may continue to do so long after their placement. Some children are unaware, consciously, of their problems and their unconscious awareness cannot be utilized explicitly in preparation for placement. These differences do not negate, but sharpen, the importance of this aspect of preparation for placement. It is the first step in the long process of establishing trust, defining reality, and relating the process to long range treatment goals.

The issue of sickness insight troubles some parents and inexperienced child care workers. They feel that open acknowledgment of the problems and the need for treatment injures the self-esteem of an already troubled, vulnerable child. It has been found, however, that although children may deny or repress awareness of their problems, they feel a measure of relief that adults are not taken in and that help is at hand. The child's self-esteem may appear to be injured, but at a deeper level the child always unconsciously knows the problems are there; he is an unhappy child and the presence of the problems and his associated suffering without hope for change is the most malignant force operating against the development of self-esteem. The investment of interested, nonpunitive adults in helping him overcome his problems and their hope for his future gradually convey to him a sense of being personally valued. In addition, the subculture of the institution is based on recognition of personal problems. All the children are there for treatment, and all of the staff are there not only to take care of the children, but also to help them overcome the problems that brought them there. The extent to which this recognition permeates the treatment institution is sometimes verbalized by the children after a period of residence that allows for the integration of this characteristic of the environment. One unhappy child was overheard telling another, who was newly admitted: "It's not bad here. They try to help you with your problems instead of blaming you." In another instance, a fourteen-year-old boy, after several years of treatment, while urging a ten-year-old girl to come down off a fire escape, said, "Laurie, when you grow up, you'll look back and see how sick you were. You'll never believe the things you did." Such insight comes hard for some children, and even then it is revealed only indirectly to those who most want to hear it.

THE UNIQUE SOCIAL STRUCTURE OF THE
TREATMENT INSTITUTION

Children who have had experience with family life, regardless of how poor or inadequate, have some familiarity with its social structure. When placed in a foster home, even though it may differ markedly from what they have known, as with Tom and Barbara, most children find elements of familiarity in the structure, organization, and roles. The group facility, whether small or large, is different (17). The initial strangeness is greater because of the physical structure, composition of the population, numbers of children and adults, differential adult roles, value systems, life style, and group dynamics. These very differences are, in many ways, a relief to the child for whom family life has become an intolerable threat, and they are designed for his ultimate therapeutic benefit. But at the outset one of the chief tasks to be accomplished in the placement process is to break down this massively strange experience into small segments of masterable, sequential experiences. We rarely know from the child what frightening fantasies fill his mind before he sees the institution. One eight-year-old girl, after her first visit, confided that she had been afraid it was going to be like the detention home where she had once been admitted temporarily for emergency care.

Disturbed parents, after visiting the treatment facilities and feeling reassured, sometimes reveal their own frightened fantasies, which include the expectations that the institution would be like a jail, a state mental hospital, or some other institution that they recalled with abhorrence. The anxiety surrounding such fantasies is communicated to the child, directly or indirectly. Seeing the place and the key staff members is the chief procedure for dealing with the anxiety. Reality provides a degree of reassurance against frightening fantasies. Pictures, available in advance, are an aid in preparation. In the actual experience, the gradual introduction of various persons and places, over a period of several visits, is the most desirable procedure. The objective is to familiarize the child first with the chief adults who will be responsible for his care. This is

sometimes carried out by way of an initial visit with the director of
the institution when this type of preliminary interview is built into
the diagnostic procedure as a part of admissions policies. This is
followed by a visit with the child care staff member who will be
responsible for the child's care. When it is feasible for the admissions process to be carried out in several visits, it is usually advan-
tageous to limit the child's initial visit to the key adults and to introduce the children in the unit in a subsequent visit. It is
important for the child to see and spend some time in his room, see
his bed, identify his place in the dining room, and become acquainted with his peers in his unit.

Some circumstances, such as long-distance placements, may realistically preclude the step-by-step procedures that familiarize the
child with placement, but the cost to the child should not be minimized. When placements are made without due regard to the
child's tempo of mastery, an added trauma is inflicted by the
placement procedure itself. The length of time required for recovery from the traumatic effects of placement is extended, and the
experience at the time of admission may remain with the child as
an intolerably painful and overwhelming one. That this is often repressed and not apparent to the observer is attested to by numerous cases in which a long period of intensive psychotherapy precedes the recollection and verbalization of anxieties attendant on
the admission procedures.

After Placement

"When will I get to feel like myself again? How long will it
take? I feel so strange since leaving Evanston."

In these words, a twelve-year-old girl expressed the feeling of
loss of identity common to children who have left their familiar environment to live in a strange one. In the period immediately following placement, strangeness is the dominant theme: strangeness
within and strangeness outside. Usually the ego of a child cannot
tolerate facing the inner feelings connected with separation until
the strangeness subsides and is replaced by some feeling of safety

in a supportive environment. The sense of an ongoing self, the ego identity, so closely tied to the auxiliary ego provided by the mothering person in infancy and early childhood, is again dependent for its restoration and growth on the external environment and the ways in which it sets about to meet the child's needs in this crisis of placement. It takes time for the child to recover sufficiently from the initial psychological shock of the change to be able to use the environment for growth. In an examination of a cross section of cases of children of both sexes who varied in age, race, background, preparation for the change, and agency setting, the authors found that the observed signs of integration into the new environment tended to appear after four to six months, and in some instances after as long as twelve months. The raw edges of anxiety apparent in the first few days tend to give way to regressive defenses, accompanied or followed by testing behavior during which the child engages in active exploration of the environment, what it will do to him and for him, what is expected from him. When these trends subside, the placement settles into relative stabilization, when developmental maturational processes (and pre-established maladaptive patterns) re-emerge and move along in response to the opportunities for growth offered in the environment. This process is illustrated in the cases of a little girl (Diane) placed in early childhood and a boy (Kenneth) placed in early latency. A third case illustrating reactions that led to repeated failures in placement, will be discussed separately.

DIANE

Diane, the youngest of five siblings, was placed in a long-term foster home at the age of two years and four months. The youngest of five siblings, she had lived with her family for the first eighteen months of her life. The mother then made a series of temporary-care arrangements that lasted for six months. At this time the father was admitted to a state psychiatric hospital and the mother was found to be suffering from an ambulatory mental illness. Diane was placed by the juvenile court in a temporary foster home, where she remained for three months before her transfer to a long-term foster home. Two teen-age siblings were placed in a group care facility by the juvenile court. Two others, then of school age, were placed in separate foster homes. The mother visited the teen-age children regularly, but resisted visits with the younger children. Diane had not seen her for several months at the time of her transfer from temporary court care to long-term agency care.

Developmentally, Diane showed no problems other than in reaction to separation and strange persons and places. Toilet training had been completed for both bowel and bladder control. Speech development was adequate. Physical health was good. No problems in eating or sleeping were reported. The caseworker found Diane extremely fearful. She clung to the temporary care foster mother during the caseworker's initial visits. After five visits with the caseworker in the foster home, Diane accompanied the caseworker willingly on a visit to the agency office. Following this there were two visits to the new foster home before placement. A report of her reactions to placement follows.

January 19

When I arrived at the court foster home to pick up Diane for the placement, she was extremely cheerful. She was playing happily but she knew where we were going and what was happening. She did not cry as she had on the previous occasions when we left the foster home for the pre-placement visits. In the car she played with her toys and announced, "Going to new home now." She ate cookies and sucked lollipops almost constantly. During the trip she wanted to be held and reassured. Her attention span was longer than on previous trips. She played with the tea set during the entire hour rather than changing back and forth every few minutes as she had done before. She went through the process of pretending to wash and dry the dishes. Her ability to ask for and accept reassurance and physical comforting during this contact was in marked contrast to her early reluctance to let me support her in any way. She also seemed at ease with the driver, although she paid little attention to him.

When we went into the house Diane seemed comfortable with

Mr. and Mrs. Henderson, easily allowing foster mother to help remove her coat and boots. There were no signs of the crying and fussing seen earlier. She remembered the layout of the house, made numerous trips by herself to the bedroom to get toys, asked Mrs. Henderson to play with her. She refused milk and cookies. Both foster parents were sensitive to her need to relate through playing games.

We reviewed together that she was going to live here now and I would leave and come back to visit in two days. She seemed to understand and was quite involved in play but waved and said goodbye when I left.

January 20

Telephoned Mrs. Henderson to see how Diane was doing since her placement yesterday. She said Diane played happily until about 4:00 p.m. She then got cranky and if things didn't go right she cried. She did not want her nap. Mrs. Henderson felt that she was missing the family in the temporary care foster home. At dinner time she did not want to feed herself, but accepted foster mother's offer to feed her and she ate moderately well. At bedtime she became quite fearful. Mrs. Henderson held her, read to her, and tried to soothe her. Later she put her in bed and sat beside her, holding her hand until she fell asleep. Diane slept through the night and woke up very cheerfully this morning. Foster mother observed that she becomes terrified with each change that is introduced, such as going to the table for a meal or going to bed.

This morning she ate toast and drank her juice, feeding herself, but wanted foster mother to sit close to her. She refused cereal. She ate lunch well. She was contented until nap time, when she cried and fussed. Foster mother again held her and read to her and she fell asleep shortly.

During the first three months of placement, the pattern that emerged in the first few days continued in modified form. Diane accepted and used the care, support, and affection of the family. She was extremely conforming and self-contained except at meal time, bedtime, and in the presence of strangers, when she became agitated and at times cried with a feeling of desperate panic. She gradually accepted conforting from Mr. Henderson. She reacted to the caseworker's visits with mixed eagerness and anxiety.

At the end of six months the caseworker made the following observations:

Diane is a pretty little girl. Her eyes are expressive and give her the apparance of being a twinkling, bubbly child. She smiles readily and is warm and affectionate with those she knows well and feels secure with. She is no longer the shy, conforming child of three months ago. She is beginning to play with other children on a sharing, participating basis. She loves and is very protective of the family's dog. She likes to be read to, plays imaginative games with her dolls, is just beginning to watch some children's programs on television. She plays in the sandbox, and enjoys riding her tricycle in the yard.

Her health and general development seem to be within the normal range. In the problem area, the fear of change in ordinary routine has diminished, but she still needs closeness and support from her foster parents at mealtime and bedtime. She is extremely frightened of strangers, clinic visits, or other changes. She clings to Mrs. Henderson in a desperate, panicky fashion. She cries easily when denied some request. The foster parents have not attempted to leave her with a sitter, as they feel she is still too frightened. She still becomes anxious on the days of my visits, but seems eager to have me come.

Six months later, the caseworker's summary, after Diane had been with the Hendersons for a year, included these observations:

Diane, aged three years, four months, is bright, verbal and well developed. The foster parents feel that she is their child and she reciprocates this feeling. Neither of her natural parents has been accessible; she has had no contact with them. Her mother refuses to discuss permanent relinquishment and the legal situation resulting from her father's commitment to the state psychiatric hospital blocks this possibility at present.

In personali*t*y, Diane is verbal, active, and open. She has mastered the changes in routine and needs no special care at mealtime and bedtime. Her appetite has improved and she sleeps well. She still becomes shy and clinging in the presence of strangers. She was terrified by a trip to see Santa Claus and also on a short train trip with the Hendersons. They still feel that they cannot leave her with anyone except a close friend who knows her well, and then only for a short time.

Diane does not seem to be fearful in her relationships with the foster parents. She fights back when they place firm limits on her. Recently when they restricted the quantity of candy she was eating, she stamped her feet, saying, "I wish I hadn't come to live with you because you won't give me any candy." They remained firm, telling her they knew she was angry but she didn't really mean it. She quickly changed her mind and settled down. Her emerging willfulness, wish for independence, and demandingness seem now to reflect security in her relationship with the parents.

Diane continues to be frightened of me. She cries when she first sees me, and then quickly warms up. Mrs. Henderson observed that Diane looks forward all day to my visits, and then, upon first sight of me, becomes panicky. This response has improved in the last couple of months since I have talked with her about her fear and reassured her about what to expect. She initiates games such as "hide and seek" or games with hiding themes. There are now clues that she may confuse me with her natural family and thinks her two older siblings are my children. I have planned with Mrs. Henderson to spend some sessions with Diane to clear up some of her confusion about me and her family.

KENNETH

Kenneth, aged six, was transferred from his mother's home after four pre-placement sessions with the caseworker and three visits with the foster parents, one of which included their two daughters, aged eight and eleven. Ken, unlike Diane, showed no fear of the caseworker; on the contrary, he was overly friendly and wooing from the time of their first meeting. His mother had participated in

preparing him for placement and he had protested openly. He
knew the plan for future visits with his mother.

Ken's early childhood history was free from separations from his
mother, but he had experienced the losses of his father and a stepfather, both of whom deserted the mother and the children. The
developmental picture was within the normal range. He had managed school attendance with no undue anxiety. His placement was
necessitated by the stepfather's desertion and the mother's reactive
emotional breakdown.

March 29

*The first day following placement, I telephoned Mrs. Black (fos-
ter mother) as planned with her and Ken. She reported that he was
being very good. She was a little worried because he wanted to do
nothing but eat all day. We discussed this as a transitory reaction
to change. We discussed the advisability of entering him in school
on Monday and decided to proceed, since he expressed anxiety
about his new school and it was thought he would be relieved to
get into it.*

*I talked with Ken. He demanded to know why I wasn't out there
to talk with him like I promised. I reminded him of the plan for
me to come on Monday, in two more days. I talked about his feeling up in the air because he hadn't been there very long. He said,
"Call me up tomorrow." I agreed, saying I'd keep in close touch to
help him over the first few days when he was just getting acquainted.*

April 1

*Foster home visit. Mr. and Mrs. Black were present for this ses-
sion and Ken was in and out. He was wound up, tense, giggling,
and running about a good deal. In general, the Blacks were enthu-
siastic about Ken. They freely discussed the problems they had observed in the three days since his arrival: 1) He wet his pants
while playing outdoors. 2) He was upset and angry about getting
no mail and would not explain, but when given a piece of advertis-
ing mail to play with he pretended it was a letter from his mother.
3) He was hyperactive, anxious, and giggly. 4) He came into the*

parents' bedroom at 5:00 o'clock in the morning, wanted to get into foster mother's bed, and said he always did this at home because his mother wanted him to get into bed with her. 5) He was compulsively clean in eating and caring for his clothes.

Mr. and Mrs. Black had been permissive in everything except the sleeping episode. Before placement, we had discussed his mother's seductiveness and his pattern of awakening early and going to his mother's room. Mrs. Black had taken him back to his bedroom, spent a few minutes with him, and told him that if he awoke early he could play quietly in his room. When this behavior was repeated the third time, she had told him firmly that he was not to awaken anyone, but that he could remain in his room and play and they would all get up at their usual time.

While we were talking the telephone rang. Ken ran in, asked permission, then answered the phone. The conversation went something like this: "Hello." Pause. "Oh, hello Mommy. I'm so glad you called. Oh, Mommy, I miss you so much. How are Janey and Tommie? What are they doing now? When am I going to see you? Oh, Mommy, I'm so frightened." It was apparent that this was not his mother and Ken was pretending. Mrs. Black took the telephone from him and I took him by the hand and went into the sun room. I said I knew he was upset. Was he wondering if he really would see his mother again? He nodded. We then reviewed in detail the plans for his visit with his mother, sister, and brother. After more talk about his pretending, we returned to the living room to reaffirm the visiting arrangements with Mr. and Mrs. Black. After this Ken calmed down and went out to play. Mrs. Black was somewhat puzzled and shaken by Ken's behavior, which we discussed at length.

Mrs. Black had observed that Ken was extremely anxious and tense about my impending visit. She thought he was afraid she was going to "tell on him." She reassured him directly that my coming was to help them, not to move him again.

April 5

Visit with Mrs. Black. Ken was at school during this session, but he returned in time to see me, as planned. Mrs. Black reported that

Ken had no trouble learning his way to school and said he liked his teacher. He wet and soiled his pants yesterday. He said he had "accidents," but was responsive to being reminded to go to the bathroom. As we talked, Mrs. Black thought they could remind him before he went out to play in the period between school and dinner, as this is when the accidents occur.

She thought that Ken was loosening up, was less meticulously clean about eating and care of clothing, had become very demanding for material things, was eating more reasonably. She found him in Nancy's bed yesterday morning. He seems so much younger than six years that the girls treat him like a three- or four-year-old. Mrs. Black explained to both girls and to Ken (as we had discussed earlier) that he is now old enough to sleep by himself, and this is what boys his age are supposed to do. She repeated her instructions to all of them that when he awakens early he cannot awaken anyone else; he is to stay in his room and play. She is confident that since she has spoken to the girls they will set the limits.

When Ken came from school, he spoke to me briefly and went to Mrs. Black immediately to show her some things he had brought from school. He participated with her in getting a snack and seemed much more settled and relaxed than in my previous visit. He again asked about his family. He wanted to know exactly what they were doing. He was confused about the number of days before the planned visit, and I counted them out for him.

April 15

In this period there have been two visits, one in the foster home and one with Ken and his natural family in the office. The Blacks reported that Ken's symptoms of wetting, soiling, and making excessive demands had disappeared. He became more natural, somewhat sloppy about his clothes, and less anxious to please. His teacher said that his initial shyness wore off within a week. She thinks he seems immature in some of his babyish ways and his wooing of adults. He learns quickly and is interested in the work.

In the visit with his family he was extremely affectionate with his mother and seemed pseudo-mature. He inquired about her work and health. He insisted that the details about the visiting plan be reviewed and asked innumerable questions about the apartment and what each one was doing. He continually forgot that Janey and Tommie were not living with their mother, and talked as though the home was still just as it had been before his move. It is not always apparent when Ken is pretending and when he is really confused.

COMPARISON OF THE TWO CASES

In these two children the similarities and differences in reaction to placement are typically a reflection of their ages and stage of development, their earlier histories, and the circumstances of placement. Both children evidenced healthy development in their capacity to accept and use the ego support of the caseworker and of the foster parents after having an opportunity to overcome their initial fear of these strange persons. Both were able to explore the new environment actively, and gradually to master the external details of the strange place. The capacity to accept and respond to the care, support, and reassurance of the foster parents then became apparent. It is this capacity, based in early personality development, that gives promise for continuing maturation when the child's environment is sufficiently adapted to his needs.

Both children regressed in certain developmental areas, including eating, sleeping, clinging, and, for Kenneth, bowel and bladder control. Both children showed confusion about other persons and acute fear of separation, but the fear of separation for Kenneth held a totally different quality from the agitation and panic experienced by Diane. The reasons are readily discernible. Kenneth, at the age of six, was well past the stage of total or relative dependence on the mother. He had experienced no traumatic separation during that critical period of his life. He was old enough to understand that there were reasons for his placement. He was assured of continuing contact with his mother, in part because he had learned in the past that he could expect it and in part because he had been given assurance verbally and could call for repetition of it when his anxiety surfaced. Consequently, his regressions, which were reactive to severe ego stress, were transitory. The opportunity to maintain continuity with his past through regular contacts with his family was important in restoring a sense of inner sameness and ego identity.

Diane, in contrast, showed good recoverability in all areas except the reactions to loss and strangeness. Her separation from her mother and the mother's total disappearance from her life came at the most vulnerable age and stage of development and no adequate substitute had been provided. Her intransigent reaction to change, loss, and strangeness persisted despite her healthy growth in other areas of development. The quality of her anxiety suggests Winnicott's descriptive phrase, "unthinkable anxiety," which the child in the stage of relative dependence experiences beyond what he can tolerate when separated from the mother. Superimposed on the initial trauma, Diane experienced added losses that she was too young to understand.

In the immediate post-placement reactions, the responses of the environment are of critical importance. Surrogate parents and caseworker are in a position similar to that of the mother who provides the maturative environment in infancy and early childhood. Sensitivity to the child's needs and willingness to give priority to meeting these needs provides the climate in which the child can most readily recover from the placement shock. Continuity, availability, and offering help in ways that the child can use are the benchmarks of a therapeutic environmental response. Meeting the needs differentially, in age-appropriate forms, is demonstrated in meeting the needs of Diane and Kenneth. Both regressed to early developmental levels. Diane's need to be held, comforted, fed, and accompanied to bed could be met directly, due to her age, without jeopardizing maturational strivings. Kenneth's needs for holding, comforting, and feeding could be met indirectly on a more mature level. Special attention was given to his food, but he was not fed; his regression to wetting and soiling was handled with the acceptance ordinarily given a younger child, but he was expected to cooperate in active measures to overcome it; his need for physical closeness was handled by substituting verbal and physical affection appropriate to his age. Since he had learned some inappropriate behavior in his relationship with his mother, it was important to avoid support of the maladaptive behavior, while at the same time meeting his needs for closeness. This is characteristic of the situation of the placed child, since he commonly brings with him from earlier developmental levels many needs which should be met, as well as some undesirable ways of seeking what he needs. These must be dealt with through direct intervention and substitution of healthy ways of relating.

Whether Diane, or any child, will need individual psychotherapy for the treatment of deeply entrenched problems depends on the response to environmental approaches and the persistence of problems that interfere seriously with development.

PLACEMENT FAILURE

A retrospective analysis of the experience of a third child, based on two years of casework treatment, illustrates the trauma of object loss which interfered with the maturational processes and with the beneficial use of foster care. This is an example of the child who does not get through the early post-placement phase successfully and is transferred to successive new placements, each of which is maladaptive in relation to the critical, specific needs of a particular child. This case was selected because it represents a familiar problem in foster care. The therapeutic measures taken, although belated, point up the child's need in this type of situation and the follow-up work shows the outcome through the period of emancipation of the young adult.

MARY

Mary, aged thirteen, and her brother Steven, aged eleven, were placed in the agency's receiving home on an emergency basis when their mother was hospitalized with terminal cancer. Their father had deserted the family just before Steven's birth and had never reappeared. Two older siblings, now emancipated, had helped rear the younger children. Two months after the placement of the children, the mother died. After four months in the receiving home, Mary and Steven were transferred to a foster home. Mary had six subsequent transfers between the ages of thirteen and sixteen. When she was a junior in high school she was placed in a therapeutically oriented girls' club which made a concerted effort to contain and sustain adolescent girls whose problems precluded foster family care.

A brief summary of Mary's initial reactions to placement in the receiving home stated that she vacillated between two extremes: she was either cooperative, overly compliant, and outwardly cheerful or was severely depressed and defiant, refused to attend to her school or home tasks, and interfered in the house mother's handling of younger children. She visited her mother regularly in the hospital and talked longingly about missing and needing her. After her mother's death she stopped talking about her and expressed no feeling about her death. During this time no direct casework help was available to her.

When arrangements were made for Mary's transfer to a foster home, she was resistive and did not want to go. Subsequently she was moved six times in a period of three years. It was noted that Mary's foster home failures resulted from aloofness, withdrawal, intense rivalry with younger children, and hostile criticism of other teenagers.[14] Despite severe emotional trauma, Mary had been a good student and had maintained excellent grades until her junior year in the new high school, when she entered the club. At the beginning of her senior year, when she was failing and in danger of losing her place in the girls' club, the agency provided a casework therapist for her.

Excerpts from the caseworker's interview notes illuminate the developmental conflicts and the reactions to object loss and placement experiences.

Eight-Week Summary: October–November

In the first sessions Mary appeared quiet and depressed. However, she accepted the offer of weekly appointments. She seemed superficially at ease except when finances were discussed. She then

---

[14] In this period of the agency's history, available foster families were not suitable for this type of problem and adequate help was not available to the foster parents or to the child.

became hostile, depressed, and withdrawn, insisting that nothing mattered.

During this period, Mary avoided discussions of her relationships with adults—housemother, teacher, or caseworker. She focused on the problems in her school adjustment, dating, and finances. In school she was failing in chemistry, shorthand, and history. She was in danger of failing to graduate with her class, but she could take no initiative in talking with her division teacher or seeking help.

With Mary's agreement, and in response to a letter from the school, a visit was made. The teacher, Miss M., went over the school record, pointing out that Mary had an excellent record in grammar school and her first two years in high school, but had done poorly after her move to the club and transfer to the present high school. Consequently, the school had made allowances for her poor work in her junior year, thinking she would be able to catch up later. However, currently her teachers reported that she did not concentrate and she stared out the window as though in a day dream. Her failure in chemistry was serious in relation to her ambition to become a nurse.

Miss M. was eager to help Mary and undertook to rearrange her classes and provide special help to enable her to graduate. She asked me to assure Mary of this. In the interviews, Mary's response was positive. She was relieved that she could drop chemistry and substitute a job-experience class. She was eager to improve the school situation. However, she did not follow through. It was pointed out to her that she wanted to graduate but for some reason found it hard to take the necessary action even though it was an easy thing to do; something was stopping her. She did not want to discuss this further, but the following day she made the necessary arrangements at school.

Her discussion of her dates centered around sorting out the qualities she preferred in boys, the behavior that is acceptable and unacceptable, and the like.

There was a good deal of discussion about her financial situation. She usually became depressed in this connection, emphasizing her wish to be independent and simultaneously expressing hos-

*tility because she could not have everything she wanted. She was
angry because the agency's October check was mistakenly sent to
the wrong place, but she postponed having the error corrected for
over a week. She resented having her check sent to her housemother and blamed the previous caseworker for carelessness and
indifference. (Later she used almost the same words in discussing
her mother.) She expressed fear that the agency would not let her
be independent and manage her own money. She used lunch
money to have her watch repaired, but did not mention it until she
was completely without funds. I approached this initially in a
practical manner to remove realistic reasons for her complaints.
We reviewed her budget, and made a clear plan, which included
the use of her monthly earnings and made adequate allowance for
the level of spending prevalent in a working girls' club.*

*Mary kept her appointments regularly, but in this two-month pe-
riod she avoided any reference to her feelings and could not tolerate any exploration. She gained some ego support and functioned
better in school.*

Eight-Week Summary: December–January

*Early in this period we discussed the school problem further.
Mary now admitted that she did not want to ask for a change in
her history class because she was afraid Miss M. would think she
was dumb and incapable of doing the work. She said she wanted
to manage for herself and thought she could if she did not think
too much about the past. (This was her first mention of the past.)
She wanted to become completely independent and try a new start
when she was eighteen. After that she did not want to think about
the past at all. Exploration brought out that this referred to the
time her mother died and the terrible things that happened after
this. She blocked and could explain no further, saying it would do
no good to discuss the things that happened. I commented that she
was unable to stop thinking about her past experiences; she spent
her energy trying not to think of the past, whereas if she could
think and talk with me about it she might find it would be easier
to work out the present problems. She denied this, became upset,
put on her coat, and said it was time to leave. I said that her wish*

to run away from her feelings was understandable, and that she did not have to talk about these things, but when she started to talk about her mother and then pulled back, it seemed that she really wanted help in this, but was still afraid. She asked anxiously if I would be here to see her the following week, even though she knew she had an appointment.

Following this she asked for help in discussing the history class with Miss M. She followed through, discussed her difficulty openly, and then began to put real effort into mastering the course content. She reported later that the history teacher had been calling on her in class and although she became confused once or twice she was able to give the correct answers most of the time.

The following week she introduced the subject of her adjustment in the club and asked for help in figuring out better ways to get along with her housemother and the girls. She was hostile to the housemother for "snooping around the house," coming into her room without knocking, and accusing her of neglect in housekeeping matters involving the kitchen, bathroom, etc. She was able to figure out some ways of handling these problems differently and volunteered that she felt better after discussing them.

I had the impression that this spurt forward was in part a determined effort to solve her problems without resorting to reliving the painful experience with her mother, even though she is apparently preoccupied with this a good deal. She also uses very actively the support she receives and seems to rely on the relationship, even though she is afraid of it. Her capacity to take responsibility for her relationships at the club seems related to her awareness that I respect her, and her self-esteem has been restored considerably.

Six-Months Summary

Mary continued to keep weekly appointments and focused on the same problems. Her school work continued to improve and she had no trouble graduating with her class. She felt that all of her teachers were sympathetic and approving. She had no trouble going to Miss M. for guidance. She decided to get a job and postpone nurse's training. She would take the required chemistry at a later time. She worked out a satisfactory solution to her problems at the club and handled those that came up directly with the person involved after discussing them first with me. She complained throughout about the inability of her boss to deal fairly with the girls who worked for her. In her relationship with me she showed increasing confidence. At times she was able to give indications that she was afraid of betrayal. She made several comments to the effect that she would go as far as she would be able to and if she was rebuffed she would withdraw immediately. She frequently discussed her need to belong somewhere and to rely on people. As I pointed this out, she could recognize that she would have to make some effort herself in working out relationships and would not necessarily be rebuffed, but might tend to feel so. She joined a church group and made some new friends. She sought out her relatives and visited them in another state after graduation.

During this period Mary began to show her reactions to my vacations or other absences. She admitted that she was unable to plan while I was gone. She changed jobs, and felt hostile to her relatives. She began to see the connections between these reactions and her feelings about my absence. She expressed jealousy of other clients and acknowledged that she had done so well with help that she was now afraid something would go wrong. She admitted her past anger at me for telling her she had been running away from the school and other problems.

In September, when it was necessary for me to change an appointment, Mary reacted by canceling the substitute appointment. She was vague and confused about time and thought it wasn't too important if she saw me. I gave her another appointment and insisted that she keep it. We then discussed for the first time her disappointment, anger, and feelings of worthlessness. After this she again kept her appointments. When she received a salary increase, she came in and noted that she had no self-confidence on the job and this was inconsistent with the salary increase; there must be a reason. I agreed that there was and that perhaps we could begin to try to understand it. She thought she would see first if her lack of confidence cleared up; if it didn't we should try to understand the cause.

This was followed by a period of coming late for appointments.

Then one day she came early and I was not in my office. She went to the washroom and came back late. She seemed scared. We discussed her anxiety, but she ran away from this into a discussion about her work. She then wondered why she was seeing me. We reviewed the reasons. She said she is afraid to talk because people will find out how dumb she is. We discussed her fear of not being liked and the feeling that something is wrong with her. She then talked about all of her foster homes, in which she had tried hard but could not please the foster mothers. No matter how she tried, she still had to move. She began to think there was something in herself that was wrong. In the last home, she knew immediately that she was not accepted because the foster mother continued to show interest in a former foster daughter. She knew one reason this didn't work out was because she "kept her distance." She must have appeared cold and unaccepting. She expected them not to like her, and then a vicious circle started. She wanted very much to have this work out but it could not because she had no one to talk to. Miss Anderson (caseworker) moved her without talking to her about it or about the reason. She liked Miss Anderson but she always seemed tired and unhappy and she knew she didn't understand her. At least her mother did that for her. Her mother accepted her and listened to her when she had troubles. She could not understand her mother and the things that went on at home. She was sure her mother must have neglected the younger children because two of them died, one from pneumonia and one from being hit by a car. They would not have died if they had been properly watched and given medical care. She said she was told that her older brother hated her; he pulled her off the bed and threw her on the floor when she was a baby. She was lucky to be alive. She acknowledged her attachment to her mother and her confusion and guilt about being the favored child, as well as fear about the deaths of younger children.

In the following session Mary seemed unusually happy and relaxed on the surface, but she was preoccupied with anxiety about hospital insurance and fear of cancer. She thought her fear realistic because of her mother's illness and death. She remembered it as being the unhappiest year of her life. When her mother went to the hospital permanently, Mary had to visit every day. Her mother insisted that everyone else leave and then talked to her about her pain and fear. She was so frightened that she was relieved when her mother died. She thought it was wrong to feel relieved, but she had been so scared. She was afraid to go to the funeral, but the family insisted and she hated them for it.

We discussed some of her feelings of loss, anger, and guilt. I pointed out that she was too young to handle all this alone; that she had come through a bad time with no one to help her understand her feelings, but, like most youngsters, she blamed herself for feeling relieved, for not wanting to go, etc. After this discussion she said she could never remember much about what their life was like earlier because whenever she thought about her mother all that came back was that awful year and all the pain.

After this she talked about her own health as being very good, and she seemed surprised. She thought her mother must have given her good care or she wouldn't be in such good health. We could then discuss the ways her mother showed her love for Mary and the ways her mother's dependence on her was too much for her at her age.

During this period, Mary continued to remember details of incidents and feelings connected with her mother's illness and death. She wept as she had not done during the actual experience. She was able to make the connection between her aloofness and distrust of foster mothers and her reactions to her mother's death.

Following this critical series of interviews, Mary continued her treatment for a year. She became stabilized in all areas of her life. She subsequently secured admission to nursing school, worked her way through, and became a nurse. She broadened her social and cultural interests and enjoyed her activities. When she was last in touch with the caseworker, she had terminated a long engagement with a young man whose family ties interfered in their relationship. She continued to be subject to intermittent periods of depression, but she was successful in her work and had established warm relationships with a few colleagues and friends and re-established her relationship with her younger brother.

This case is similar to many foster care cases in which failure to provide the services needed by the child and the surrogate parents in the initial, critical phase of placement leads to a succession of repeated failures and continued erosion of the child's self-esteem and use of his capabilities. One such failure may result from an insufficient understanding of the child, but this is a signal of the need for a careful examination of the causes, which usually are as fully apparent in the first placement as in subsequent ones.

SUMMARY

The foregoing cases have illustrated some typical reactions of children in the beginning phase after placement and some aspects of environmental help provided, responsively, by the surrogate parents and the caseworker. The major task of the environment is to provide the time and the necessary conditions for the child to master the initial strangeness and to restore the child to his former ego-functioning level. The environmental help needed by children of all ages in this stage of placement can be organized in broad categories. Within a stable climate of adult warmth and patience, children in placement need:

1) Structure and reliability.

2) Planned contact with the caseworker and important parent figures from the past.

3) Continuity of important, familiar possessions and useful activities and routines (toys, clothing, food, use of skills, sleeping and waking hours).

4) Support of adaptive behavior and nonsupport of maladaptive behavior. (Ken's sleeping behavior is an example.)

5) Provision for meeting regressed emotional needs translated into age-appropriate terms.

Many of the ego-supportive functions performed by the caseworker during the placement process are transferred to the surrogate parents whose role includes the provision of emotional support in connection with the details of daily living, as seen in the immediate post-placement situations of Kenneth and Diane. The caseworker retains major responsibility for certain ego supports that are connected, not with daily care, but with the foster care system. As seen in these cases, the caseworker's specific activities depend in part on the child's age and manifest needs. For the pre-verbal child, appropriate activities foster the transition from the old to the new by such activities as visiting frequently at short intervals, accompanying the child and surrogate parent to the clinic or elsewhere for any necessary procedures, maintaining the child's contacts with important adults, and the like. In the cases cited, one sees graphic illustrations of the child's need for continuity of contact with the caseworker immediately following placement. Beyond this, the child who is old enough to understand, experiences active ego support from a structure within which he knows: (a) when he will see the caseworker again (after the day of his placement), how often, for what purpose, and under what conditions; (b) when he will see or have information about his family members and under what conditions; (c) what arrangements are made for his entrance into school, his needed medical care, and the like; (d) the structure in which the child, surrogate parents, and caseworker will communicate and fit together; (e) the caseworker's availability to help him and with what, as differentiated from the role of the foster parents.

The child may have been told many of these things before and during the placement process, but he usually needs to have reconfirmation after placement.

The need for a course of psychotherapy, as differentiated from the preventive and therapeutic casework help which is an integral, routine part of foster care service, is a separate consideration. Determination of the need for treatment may be made in the course of the diagnostic evaluation or the need may become evident after placement. In either event, the timing of beginning psychotherapeutic help is an important factor in the child's ability to adapt to the new environment. This is illustrated in the cases of Diane and Mary. Both children, under totally different conditions and for different reasons, were traumatized by loss that set up emotionally crippling psychological reactions which might require psychotherapeutic intervention. Mary, however, needed this at a beginning, supportive level, immediately following placement, during the mother's terminal illness and thereafter. It was quickly apparent that without such help she was unable to accept a new environment. In contrast, Diane, although injured by early maternal loss, was able to accept and use the new environment for growth. Ordinarily the initiation of a course of psychotherapeutic treatment concurrent with the early stage of placement in a foster home is contra-indicated, except in those instances in which it is apparent that the child is unable to recover sufficiently to adapt to the new environment through the usual measures of casework and environmental help. In general, the beginning of treatment is a stressful experience, which arouses a great deal of anxiety in children and requires concomitant support and collaboration in the environment. Treatment should be undertaken only if it is clear that the child's maturational potential cannot be released and nurtured through the other therapeutically oriented approaches that the foster care system offers the child. Psychotherapy is not and cannot be a substitute for the various kinds of security and help that should be built into the foster care system.

The converse of this is also true. When the child needs direct psychotherapeutic help, as did Mary, to the extent that the environmental approaches are blocked and ineffectual, the provision of such help is the necessary measure to arrest the deteriorating ego integration. Many children, especially adolescents (18), are acutely in need of help, but are able to accept it only gradually after a relationship has been developed with the caseworker who is responsible for helping them with their total life situation. The caseworker's flexibility and skill in responding to the child's readiness and tolerance, moving at the child's pace, are often the key to furthering the psychological development of children who otherwise would accept no psychological help. Mary's resistance illustrates the fairly typical adolescent conflict between wanting and fearing help. Her use of help in areas inherent in the foster care system (living arrangements, school, financing, etc.) was the necessary proving ground for restoration of her earlier functioning level; for the greatly needed permission to grow up given by a woman with whom she was helped to develop a relationship; and, finally, for the gradual facing of some of her painful feelings of loss and guilt in relation to her mother.

The separation of functions between the foster care caseworker and the psychotherapist works to the advantage of some children, but to the great disadvantage of others. For those who cannot tolerate a formal psychotherapeutic structure, the building of confidence comes through the relationship established in relation to the functions of the caseworker which are an integral part of the foster care service.

Relative Stabilization of Placement and Direct Service to the Child

When the initial, critical phase of placement is worked out successfully by the child and surrogate parents, signs of the child's gradual integration into the environment begin to appear. One is likely to see increasing readiness in the child to accept offered help from surrogate parents, to turn to them for comfort, to share with them some of his daily experiences, to ask for what he wants. Agitated behavior, testing behavior, marked over-compliance, and other reactions to strangeness subside or appear only intermittently in response to a new stress, in contrast to the initial pervasiveness. Earlier levels of ego integration are recovered and pre-established patterns of behavior re-emerge. Participation in the family life and reciprocity in family relationships characterize the stage of relative stabilization.

Throughout his placement the child is subject to all the usual stresses of growing up, plus those specifically related to his life situation as a placed child. The term "relative stabilization" is used here to suggest the periods of equilibrium and disequilibrium common in the dynamics of family or group life and in the life of the foster child in response to inevitable environmental and maturational stresses. In this period of relative stabilization the child's need for direct help from the caseworker decreases and begins to fall into a pattern in which the caseworker performs only those services that cannot be absorbed appropriately by surrogate parents or others. Throughout placement, specific, direct casework services are needed by the child as distinguished from services on his behalf administered through surrogate parents, natural parents, or others (19). It is axiomatic that all direct help to the child is paralleled by and integrated with direct, ongoing work with the surrogate parents, and that individual or family group approaches, or both, are used selectively in response to the nature of the problem and the situation.

The areas in which the child needs ongoing direct service from the caseworker include:

1) The ongoing relationship with his family (whether present or absent).

2) Continuity in agency planning and services.

3) Crisis prevention and therapeutic intervention.

ONGOING RELATIONSHIP WITH THE NUCLEAR FAMILY [15]

Whether the parents are present or absent, the child needs to know about them and where he stands with them. Although the child may never verbalize this inherent need, the caseworker can safely assume that it exists. If the parent is absent, and the child is silent, there is a temptation to "let sleeping dogs lie." But the absent parent continues to hold an important place in the child's inner life (20, 21). Bringing him information about the absent parent opens the door to discussion and lets the child know that the subject is not forbidden. In some instances the caseworker may be unable to secure information; and even this is important to the child. Any family member who disappears from the child's life during his early childhood or beyond is a potential source of inner trouble for the child. In many instances, the trouble can be greatly modified and psychological crises averted by open discussion with

[15] The term "nuclear family" is used, despite the separation, to designate the family unit in which the child experienced his initial, important, parent-child relationships as differentiated from the foster family.

the caseworker, who is the valid link to the nuclear family. In some instances the disappearance of the child-caring parent has occurred at a time in the child's development and under such traumatizing circumstances that the developmental fixations cannot be resolved short of intensive psychotherapy, if at all. However, even in these cases the establishment of a climate for open discussion is the first step in learning how much help the child can use. The timing of the introduction of such information follows the same principles that govern general treatment approaches to subjects which are initiated by the caseworker (as distinct from responses to subjects initiated by the child). This means, always, that the caseworker looks for an appropriate opportunity within the context of an established relationship.

The active, visiting parents (and siblings) present the child with a different set of problems, which require the caseworker's participation and help. On the side of health, family visits preserve the positive ties, reassure the child that he is not totally rejected, and tend to prevent excessive repression of feelings and unrealistic destructive fantasies or idealization. At the same time, by virtue of the problems in the family that brought about the separation, the visits are likely to be characterized by interpersonal stress. Some children are overwhelmed by anxiety aroused by their inner conflicts each time they confront the parents. Some feel misled and betrayed by the parents' unrealistic promises. Some are distressed and burdened by the parents' unpredictable or disturbed behavior. In any of these situations the potential benefits of the contacts are not realized if the child is left to cope with them alone. The caseworker can provide vital help at various levels, through preparation of the child, support, clarification, correction of misconceptions, modifications in the structure of the visits if this is needed, or other treatment approaches. What each child needs is an individual matter calling for individualized observation and response, and for modifications in the nature of the casework participation in keeping with changes in the maturational stages and ego growth of the child.[16]

[16] For detailed discussion of family visits see Chapter IV.

In addition to information about or contact with his parents (and siblings, when indicated), the child intermittently needs information about his past life. He needs to know that the agency is the repository of such information and that the caseworker is available to answer his questions when they arise. Such information, like visits with family members, raises emotional responses and added questions with which the child will need help. The child's questions about his past life may be triggered by experiences from various sources. For example, many children are required to write an autobiography as a school assignment. Some who are sufficiently in touch with the caseworker, or with the guidance and support of the surrogate parents, turn to this source for information and concurrently are able to work out questions, confusion, and distortions that have lain silent and hidden. Others raise questions when inner stresses trigger off the need. The inner stresses may come with maturational changes or at other points of disequilibrium in the environment in relation to family, friends, school, or social groups.

These needs are directly related to the child's sense of identity and his integration of his past with his present and future life. They provide the opportunities to bring to the child the preventive and therapeutic help he needs as a concomitant to the foster care experience.

CONTINUITY IN AGENCY PLANNING AND SERVICES

In its role as the child's guardian and "parental force" the agency is responsible for an ongoing evaluation of the child's maturational status and his needs. The assurance to the child that there is reliable continuity within the agency in providing for his needs cannot be left solely in the hands of the surrogate parents. In some agencies, by plan, surrogate parents carry the responsibility for securing and implementing major auxiliary services—medical, psychological, educational, and recreational. In others, the caseworker is responsible for securing some or all of these services. However, in either case, since the formulation, authorization, and evaluation of auxiliary and special services are in the hands of the agency, direct communication between the caseworker and the child is essential to both. The child cannot have a realistic perception of the agency without direct communication, and the caseworker cannot evaluate fully the child's condition and responses to the services without firsthand observation.

The child's ongoing living arrangements, likewise, are the responsibility of the agency rather than of the surrogate parents. Should a change be indicated or necessary, the child who has no periodic contact with a caseworker is unlikely to feel the confidence and support he needs when this or any crisis arises in which he is dependent on agency action. Regardless of the problems presented by staff changes, the child can experience the continuity of the agency's involvement if the changes are discussed directly with him by both the outgoing and incoming caseworkers and the incoming caseworker demonstrates empathy with feelings of loss and familiarity with his past life, his current situation, and important plans that have been under way. It should be kept in mind, too, that the change of caseworkers may reawaken feelings about earlier important losses. The child may appear indifferent or rejecting or may show a temporary regression to symptomatic behavior in seemingly unrelated areas.

CRISIS PREVENTION AND INTERVENTION

The events that require preventive or therapeutic intervention in the course of placement include those related to inner problems and environmental problems. Any experience that is potentially damaging to the child properly claims the direct help of the caseworker. One of the common problems is reactivation of a separation conflict triggered by benign circumstances which, ordinarily, may not be anticipated as troublesome. In this connection, any situation that specifically signifies growing up may reactivate earlier, unresolved separation conflicts connected with the loss of dependency. Despite the conscious, positive wish to grow up, occasions such as birthdays, graduation from elementary or high school, or even marriage, may have an unconscious negative meaning. The reactions of the young person may appear to be wholly irrational and mystifying, so unrealistic are they in the current situation. Many other kinds of environmental experiences that are potentially damaging can be anticipated and the potential negative effects prevented or at least minimized. These experiences include such events as school failure, frightening or painful medical procedures, loss or serious illness or death of an important parent. An incident of school failure will illustrate the potential pattern of events and the thesis of prevention: a child threatened with school failure has to cope with damage to his self-esteem, negative attitudes of peers and adults, feelings of helplessness about the problem, and, ultimately, feelings of hopelessness. Failure to intervene may lead to secondary problems of either passive withdrawal or overt acting-out. The latter may take the form of truancy and concomitant minor delinquency, which in turn lead to serious problems in family and community relationships. The need for early, active intervention is manifest. The intervention may call for changes in the activity of the surrogate parents, such as an increase or a decrease in supervision of homework, provision of special help within the school, group or private tutoring, a special day school, psychotherapy, or some combination of these or other measures. The corrective measures operate at several levels against feelings of helplessness and worthlessness, and toward prevention of secondary symptoms; and they provide opportunities for the child to continue to learn. The process of deterioration is arrested and a process of growth re-established.

As another example, the death of a parent or parent surrogate is an experience of crisis with which any child needs help from an adult. For the placed child, in addition to the support available in the environment, help falls into the sphere of the caseworker by virtue of the fact that she is the central person in the network of foster care relationships, and the placed child has a pre-existing, known vulnerability to loss. The offer of help may be approached in various ways, depending on the child's age, adjustment, and the circumstances of the loss. The vital point is that help made immediately available in a suitable form is the essential characteristic of preventive mental health practice. It cannot be assumed that the child who shows no overt reaction when told about the death of a parent will have no severe internal reaction. Mary was a case in point. It will be recalled that after her mother's death, although she no longer mentioned her mother, her adjustment deteriorated swiftly. Experience with other children has demonstrated the value and importance of the caseworker's immediate participation. Some children who have been prepared by the caseworker for an impending death, when this was possible, and those who have been accompanied to the funeral services, when feasible, have been able to use the direct emotional support and the shared experience not only to tolerate anxiety but also to give some expression to their feelings. These children showed none of the later problems of major proportions that were associated with repression and distortion seen in other children given no immediate casework help. The caseworker's presence and participation not only give the child needed emotional support but also open the way to later help at a verbal level, should the child need it. Other experiences of loss of important persons, such as loss of a caseworker with whom the child has had a long relationship, or major changes in the child's environment, such as moving to a new community, may, for some children, reactivate a great deal of anxiety. The adaptation of some of the same approaches discussed in connection with the placement process are applicable and useful in preparing and helping the child through these experiences.

Other experiences of extreme stress, regardless of their nature or source, may be potentially damaging in unpredictable ways. One can be sure only that timely and appropriate use of the various helping approaches, built into the ongoing foster care service, is an essential aspect of prevention of crises that may cause lasting damage.

Inherent in this thesis regarding crisis prevention is the observation that in many instances the genesis of a crisis is remote in time and runs through the life fabric of the child's development. Appropriate intervention in situations that are known to be stressful beyond the child's existing capacity for active mastery is a preventive mental health measure.[17]

---

[17] For discussion of crisis intervention theory see pp. 271–74 and p. 285.

REFERENCES

1. D. W. Winnicott, M.D., *The Maturational Processes and the Facilitating Environment,* International Universities Press, Inc., New York, 1965, pp. 70–71.
2. *Ibid.*   3. *Ibid.,* pp. 84–89.
4. D. W. Winnicott, M.D., "Transitional Objects and Transitional Phenomena," *International Journal of Psychoanalysis, XXIV,* 1953.
5. Margaret S. Mahler, "Thoughts about Development and Individuation," *Psychoanalytic Study of the Child, XVIII,* International Universities Press, New York, 1963. "On Sadness and Grief in Infancy and Early Childhood," *Psychoanalytic Study of the Child,* International Universities Press, New York, XVI, 1961.
6. John Bowlby, M.D., "Grief and Mourning in Infancy and Early Childhood," *Psychoanalytic Study of the Child, XV,* International Universities Press, Inc., New York, 1960, pp. 9–52. John Bowlby, James Robertson, and Dina Rosenbluth, "A Two-Year-Old Goes to the Hospital," *The Psychoanalytic Study of the Child, VII,* International Universities Press, Inc., New York, pp. 82–94. Dorothy Burlinghan and Anna Freud, *Infants Without Families,* Allen and Unwin, London, 1944. Anna Freud and Dorothy Burlinghan, *War and Children,* International Universities Press, New York, 1943. Ner Littner, M.D., *Some Traumatic Effects of Separation and Placement,* Child Welfare League of America, Inc., New York, 1956.
7. For a detailed discussion of the changing meaning of peer relationships and the need for intimacy in latency and through adolescence, see Harry Stack Sullivan, M.D., *The Interpersonal Theory of Psychiatry,* W. W. Norton and Company, New York, 1953, chapters 15, 16, 17, 18.
8. Peter Blos, M.D., *On Adolescence,* The Free Press of Glencoe, a division of the Macmillan Company, New York, 1962. Helen Deutsch, M.D., *Selected Problems of Adolescence,* Monograph No. 3, Psychoanalytic Study of the Child, International Universities Press, New York. Irene Josselyn, M.D., *The Adolescent and His World,* Family Service Association of America, New York, 1952.
9. In connection with separation trauma, Littner, in "Traumatic Effects of Separation," discusses ways of helping the child master the placement process.
10. Erik H. Erikson, "Identity and the Life Cycle, Selected Papers," *Psychological Issues,* Vol. 1, no. 1, International Universities Press, New York.

11. For detailed discussion of the child's patterns of managing stress, see
    Ner Littner, M.D., "The Child's Need to Repeat His Past: Some Im-
    plications for Placement," *The Social Service Review*, Vol. XXXIV,
    No. 2, June 1960, or in *Changing Needs and Practices in Child
    Welfare, Seventy-Fifth Anniversary Papers of the Illinois Children's
    Home and Aid Society*, Child Welfare League of America, Inc.,
    New York, 1960.
12. Milford E. Barnes, Jr., "The Concept of 'Parental Force'," *Child
    Welfare*, Vol. XLVI, No. 2, p. 89. For original presentation, see J.
    Franklin Robinson, "Arranging Resident Psychiatric Treatment with
    Foster Children," *Quarterly Journal of Child Behavior*, II (1950),
    pp. 176–84.
13. Barnes, *Ibid.*, p. 91.
14. See Esther Glickman, *Child Placement Through Clinically Oriented
    Casework*, Columbia University Press, New York, 1957, pp. 102–51
    for discussion of steps in the placement process.
15. Erik H. Erikson, M.D., *Childhood and Society*, W. W. Norton &
    Company, New York, 1950, p. 364.
16. Rita Dukette and Margaret W. Gerard, M.D., "Techniques for Pre-
    venting Separation Trauma in Child Placement," *American Journal
    of Orthopsychiatry*, Vol. XXIV, No. 1, 1954, pp. 111–27. The
    authors describe the transition process in the placement of infants
    and pre-school children with emphasis on prevention of separation
    trauma.
17. For a description of the structure of the institution and a compre-
    hensive bibliography, see Morris F. Mayer, "Practice Theory and
    Practice in Institutions," *Foster Care in Question*, Child Welfare
    League of America, Inc., New York, 1970.
18. Irene M. Josselyn, "The Adolescent and His World," pp. 76–108.
19. For a detailed discussion of the provision of casework help to chil-
    dren after placement, see Glickman, pp. 243–331.
20. Draza Kline, "Services to Parents of Placed Children: Some Chang-
    ing Problems and Goals," *Changing Needs and Practices in Child
    Welfare*, Child Welfare League of America, June 1960, p. 36.
21. Almeda R. Jolowicz, "The Hidden Parent: Some Effects of the Con-
    cealment of Parents' Life Upon the Child's Use of a Foster Home,"
    New York: State Welfare Conference, 1946, mimeographed.

CHAPTER IV

HELPING THE NATURAL PARENT

The Parent as Agency Client

The parent of the placed child is a special kind of agency client with whom the development and maintenance of a working alliance holds an important priority during the intake process (or at the earliest time the parent is available) and, thereafter, throughout the period of service to the child. The helping approaches to the parent-client are determined by the nature of the parent's physical, psychological, and social condition. With the greatly increased emphasis on the prevention of placement and the use of supportive and preventive services, placement as a solution to the family's problems is increasingly limited to families who have reached a state of disorganization that requires protective intervention.

The parent who is sufficiently mature and integrated to seek placement and consciously to want help with his own part in the problem is the exception rather than the rule. The preponderance of the parents served in foster care agencies suffer from severe character disorders with overt evidences of personal and social disorganization. In many of their general social and psychological characteristics they are strikingly similar to each other:

1) They are overwhelmed by reality problems: economic need, poor housing, and often, poor health and inadequate health care.

2) They are either divorced or separated, or, if not, the marriage is characterized by strife and intermittent separations. Often, they

have made several unsuccessful marriages, and have never attained a stable period of family life which might be restored.

3) They tend to be self-defeating and self-destructive in their patterns of behavior in major life roles.

4) They distrust and fear the helping relationship which they so greatly need.

5) Their parenting roles are inevitably characterized by the excessive use of the children to meet their own psychological needs. Often, the children have been moved around a great deal and intermittently left with friends, neighbors or relatives.

The typical history of the parents reveals that in childhood they have had little experience in living in a stable family; they have had no model for adequate or pleasurable family life provided by parents or parent substitutes; they have had little, if any, opportunity to develop the skills necessary for meeting the demands of daily living in a family, and usually little preparation in learning job skills. More fundamentally, the lack of continuity in any relationship with an adequate adult accounts for the ego disfunction that occurs under the ordinary demands of living as a parent and a wage earner.

CHANGE IN PARENTAL ROLE

Once a decision is made that placement is needed,[1] the parent has a changed role in his relationship with the child and a new role in relation to the agency. He becomes a part of the new set of relationships that operate within the dynamic system of the service in some manner and degree, regardless of whether he is present or absent or whether or not the role relationships are well structured and defined by the agency. Unless the parent has permanently abandoned the child, the fact of agency placement creates at least some tacit changes in the practical and psychological situation of

---

[1] See Chapter II for detailed discussion of decision-making in the intake process. As noted, the referral to the placement agency following the child's removal from his home by a court action, does not obviate the agency's opportunity to make its own evaluation of the family and its recommendation for immediate restoration of the family, should this action be indicated.

the parent, including the absent parent. Often, the absent parent who has no contact with the agency continues to have a psychological involvement of some kind and a sense, no matter how vague, of a change in his current status and his potential parental role when he knows that the state has intervened and an agency has assumed responsibility for his child's care. Sustained absence cannot be interpreted to mean that the child's existence no longer has a place in the psychic life of the parent. This is amply demonstrated by the many parents who, after long absences, "whereabouts unknown," return and initiate contact with the child-caring agency. Consequently, the parent of every placed child whose guardianship has not been legally terminated is, and continues to be, either an active or a potential agency client.

This client role has several special components. The child is, of necessity, the primary client, and the parent as client is potentially both a cooperator on behalf of the child and a receiver of service. He may limit his client role to that of cooperator in relation to the child's care and treatment, or he may, in addition, receive service directly on his own behalf in his relationship with the placed child and in relation to other life roles. The agency, likewise, may limit the parent's role as client to a cooperative one by its limits on the services it offers. The cooperative role represents the primary, minimal agency goal with the parent-client.

While the goal of cooperation is designated as minimal, it is of paramount importance in its potential influence on the service to both child and parent. "Cooperation," by dictionary definition, means "a condition marked by working together or joint effort toward a common end" (1). The parent-client and the agency have the opportunity to work together in a cooperative effort for the child's welfare at many different levels and degrees of cooperation. Since active cooperation is an activity within a relationship that requires some degree of mature behavior, the achievement of a minimal degree of cooperation may represent a substantial therapeutic gain for some clients. The degree to which cooperation is achieved depends in part on the capacity and motivation of the parent and in part on the agency's attitudes, approaches, and procedures as represented by the caseworker.

Cooperation is viewed by some as an extremely limited objective in relation to treatment goals. Actually, within the placement system, it is a dynamic, necessary, and viable objective, and changes in the parent's capacity to carry out his role as cooperator are readily identifiable as an index to progress or regression. The achievement of cooperation with the agency and support of the child's placement, in accordance with his needs, may be far-reaching in the demands made on the parent for: (a) increased impulse control, (b) modifications of feeling and behavior in the relationship with the child, and (c) modifications in interpersonal relationships with adults as reflected in responses within the casework relationship or elsewhere in the foster care system. These modifications in the direction of improved functioning may lead to redefinition of goals and further treatment objectives.

The cooperative aspect of the client role may be viewed as a treatment objective rather than a role expectation, per se, when the parent's initial capacity and motivation are insufficient to enable him to carry out this aspect of the client role adequately. He then needs not only the opportunity to learn the new role, but also casework help to develop motivation and increase his capacity. To provide this service requires helping approaches that are not contained within the limits of any single casework treatment or psychotherapeutic model as such. It requires the flexible use of a wide range of helping activities, particularized in relation to the ego state of each parent-client (2).

In view of the unique nature of the parent-client's relationship with the agency, the term "treatment relationship" is not sufficiently broad to encompass the various approaches to cooperation and help that have been developed for this particular service. In many instances, the parent does not consciously want to enter into a treatment relationship, and would be greatly threatened by such an approach, but the various casework activities, purposively utilized, are intended to "influence him in a therapeutic direction" (3).

In the earlier chapters the term "working alliance" has been used to designate the relationship between caseworker and parent-client, within which the cooperative role of the parent can be nurtured and implemented. The achievement of a working alliance may come with relative ease, or, as indicated earlier, its achievement may be the initial therapeutic objective of the caseworker, and may call for the use of various reaching-out techniques and activities. To the degree that the parent is distrustful, afraid, and hostile in his relationships with adults who represent authority, his ability to enter into a working alliance is limited. The development of trust, as with children, is a slow process, and comes only with the opportunity to test and experience the attitudes and reliability of the caseworker (and agency) in the situations indigenous to the foster care system. The parents' common anxieties and fears in this relationship may include fear of disapproval, fear of losing the child, feeling of failure as a parent, expectation of rejection and blame by the person who represents authority, and fear of personal disintegration. The beginnings of trust, or at least the amelioration of active distrust, is nurtured in an atmosphere in which the client is neither neglected nor punished, and his provocations are not taken at face value. Concomitantly, the caseworker's ability to manage the relationship in ways that reflect a balance in his understanding and concern for both the parent-client and the child-client may be a critical factor in the parent's responses. This balanced approach is essential if the practitioner is to hear and understand what the parent communicates, and respond to it by moving into the areas of help the parent can use at any given time in the process.

Many of these points may be illustrated by the single interview which follows:

After four years in prison, the mother of a five-year-old girl appeared in an agency and demanded a visit with her child, who had been placed in a foster home at the age of one year. In the intervening four years there had been no communication between the mother and the agency. The caseworker, new to the agency, reacted inwardly with anxiety about the effect of the mother's arrival on the child and foster parents, who had formed deep attachments. At the same time she was aware that the mother had a legal right to visit the child.

The mother was demanding, hostile, and belligerent. She announced that she had just come out of prison and had a legal right to see her child. She asserted: "No one can take that away from me." She demanded the child's address. The caseworker reported later that her first inner reaction was one of anxiety and antagonism. The mother had been in prison following conviction in connection with the death of her second child. This, combined with her belligerent, demanding approach, set up the case worker's resistance and momentarily blocked understanding and compassion for the mother. Aware of her own feelings, the caseworker cautiously avoided a direct response to the mother's demand. She told the mother she was new in the agency and was not familiar with the situation. She asked more about it and then somewhat tentatively, said, "Then you haven't seen Linda since she was a baby?" Again the mother demanded to see her immediately, but this time she added, in the same aggressive tone: "She's all I have. I haven't even got a place to stay. At least I have a right to see my child." The caseworker affirmed her right to see her child and asked if she would like to hear about Linda first. The mother's belligerence subsided somewhat and she asked for and was given information. The caseworker picked up on the mother's statement that she had no place to stay. She learned that the mother was destitute. She literally had just come from prison and had used her funds for transportation. As the caseworker shifted focus from the mother's request to exploration of her immediate need and offered the agency's assistance in meeting this, the mother was able to talk realistically. The shift, however, had required that the caseworker feel empathy with the mother, which transcended her immediate antagonism and her anxiety about the child.

A summary of the subsequent course of the interview follows:

Mrs. M. seemed much less tense and belligerent after we arranged to provide funds for her long-distance telephone call to her father, a night's lodging, and meals and carfare to enable her to remain in the city for a day or two. I explained that a visit would work out best for Linda and Mrs. M. if Linda could be prepared for it, because she was so young when she was placed that she would not remember her mother. She agreed with this and then asked whether Linda had been adopted. After being assured that she was still legally Linda's mother, she was interested in knowing about Linda's relationship with the foster parents. She seemed to know before I told her that Linda thought of the foster family as her own and that she was treated as a part of the family. I told her that Linda has been told that her first mother had gone away when she was a baby and had not been able to take care of her.

'Maybe I could just go and see her once and they would not have to tell her who I am?'

'We can think some more about what would be best for you and Linda. Would you be willing to take some time to think about it and to talk to me again before you decide? It would be best from her standpoint if, when you see her, you have a notion about your future plans and where she will fit into them. It would be hard on her to be unsure about this, and perhaps it would make things harder for you, too, in the long run. Perhaps you've thought about this?'

'Yes, I thought a lot about it. I thought she might be better off adopted. If I stay with my father I can get a job, but I can't take care of her now.'

'Then would you want to stay here in the city for an extra day or two and take enough time to think and talk with me again about your plans and how things will work out best in the long run for both of you?'

Mrs. M. agreed. As she left, she said, gruffly, 'I didn't know I could get any help.'

The process of this interview shows, in a condensed fashion, the central elements in the reduction of distrust and the beginning of the working alliance that is essential to cooperation on behalf of the child. Mrs. M.'s provocative, belligerent, demanding approach is a typical defense against anxiety and fear, and sometimes may be a signal of desperation. If the caseworker's concern for the child or her own internal reaction to an aggressive defense leads her into opposition to the parent's demands, what ensues usually is a power struggle in which the parent clings to his position to exercise some degree of control over his own fate and to defend some remnant of personal integrity. When there has been no important parenting relationship with the child, the sudden appearance of a parent and the request to see the child often serves as a cover for a need which the parent is unable to reveal without sensitive, enabling help from the caseworker.

In this case the movement toward a common ground and a constructive resolution for parent and child was set in motion at the point when the caseworker was able to shift concern from the child to the mother and to see the mother's real, immediate needs, which were concealed by her request to see the child (4). It takes little imagination to see that a mother just out of prison and without funds or a home to return to may be in desperate need of human contact and support to re-establish herself in some nonalien environment. But it takes considerable self-awareness and the capacity to embrace the needs of both mother and child to use this imagination and to respond in ways that can help the parent move off the dead center of distrust into a constructive channel.

In this instance, the work eventuated in the mother's rehabilitation in the community of her family's residence and the child's adoption by the foster family. In this single interview, there were clues to the potential outcome, after the worker met the mother's need for emotional support and practical assistance at this time of crisis. These clues included her reference to her inability to take care of herself and her child; her acknowledgement that she had thought about adoption; and her expressed concern for the child's welfare.

This type of situation spotlights, also, the advisability of agency initiative in maintaining communication with the parent during the period of imprisonment or hospitalization. Ordinarily, the cooperative working alliance cannot be picked up so readily. But, once the agency's concern for the parent's welfare as well as the child's is established, the parent's re-entry into the child's life usually can be planned and carried out in an auspicious rather than a detrimental fashion.

Needless to say, the establishment of a working alliance fails with some parents, despite the caseworker's efforts to reach them. But there are relatively few such cases if the practitioner is willing to adapt his approaches to what the parent is able to use, whether working with voluntary or involuntary clients. The differences between the two, in situations and circumstances, are seen most clearly at the time of the parent's first contact with the agency. Among the voluntary clients there are some whose social and psychological stability is greater than that of involuntary clients. There are many others who are similar to the involuntary client in many respects.[2]

Development of the Working Alliance

THE INVOLUNTARY CLIENT

The development of a working alliance with the involuntary client calls for special approaches, sensitized to his practical and his psychological situation. The involuntary client is the parent whose child is removed from his care and custody through a legal action of a court when a child is found to be dependent or delinquent and the court determines that the home is not suitable for his care. There is a wide range of circumstances in which such action may be taken. The immediate, main reason for placement does not, in itself, signify conclusively the degree of seriousness of social and psychological disorganization of the parent or the more basic causes of the need for placement. Children may be left alone, unsupervised, when a mentally ill parent wanders away from home; or they may be abandoned for obscure reasons as a result of temporary breakdown in ego functioning; or neglect may be more generalized, involving a long history of inadequate physical care, protection, and supervision, which is brought into the open by some stress in the child or the parent, the last straw in a bad situation.

---

[2] When it is not possible to achieve a minimal essential working alliance with the parent, in some cases it may be necessary to utilize the legal authority of a court for the protection of the child.

Regardless of the specifics in each situation, the inability to participate in reaching a decision about the child's care reflects a state of
acute ego disfunction.

Some illustrative situations point up the extreme family disorganization and the range of differences within these families. Ra-
cial differences are not identified because they are not pertinent to
the points under discussion. The group, however, includes black,
white, and Mexican-American families.

1) A mother, recently widowed, was reported to the police by
neighbors, who stated that she left her six-year-old daughter alone
in the apartment while she visited neighborhood taverns, and that
she exposed the child to her sexual promiscuity, bringing home
men who stayed all night. The police raided the apartment when a
man was present and took the mother to jail and the child to the
detention home. The mother was given a substantial jail sentence.
It might not have been necessary, per se, to separate mother and
child, but once the mother was jailed, the child had to be placed.

2) A mother of two young children deserted the family after a
serious physical fight with the father. This had occurred twice in
the past. The father reported the mother's desertion to the juvenile
court and asked for care of the children, as he was unable to provide for their care. He was employed steadily, but feared that he
would lose his job under the emotional stress of the family responsibilities. The father refused homemaker service, as he could not
tolerate having the home maintained in this way. His own history
of parental instability precluded a voluntary placement arrangement and necessitated the transfer of custody through court action.

3) The court was called by neighbors to care for three children
who were left alone. The mother was found by police as she wandered about the streets, mentally ill. She was hospitalized. The father, with a history of hospitalizations for mental illness, had disappeared at the same time.

4) The need for protective care of four children was reported by
a visiting nurse. The children were ill, undernourished, and dirty;
they foraged for food in the neighborhood, and they were not sent
to school. The mother appeared to be mentally ill, sitting and star-
ing into space as these conditions surrounded her. The father, em-

ployed as a garbage collector, was away during the day. His own mental and emotional condition was such that he did not perceive that there was anything seriously wrong in his home. The extent of his disturbance precluded the use of homemaker service.

5) A seven-year-old girl was found hiding in a garbage can. She said her family had moved away and left her, that they drove off while she went back into the house to get her doll. She was unable to give sufficient identifying information for the court to locate the family. Later it was learned that her mother had been temporarily hospitalized. Her father, with his six other children, had moved; this child had wandered away, and no one looked for her. Her retardation in physical growth and intellectual development accounted, at least in part, for the father's outright rejection.

6) A child was taken into the custody of a court when the mother was arrested on a charge of breaking into a private home, in the company of a male companion, and stealing money, jewelry, and other valuables. The mother, unmarried, was sent to prison; the child was referred to a foster care agency for placement.

7) A mother took her two children to the juvenile court, asking for care for the children after her husband had deserted the family for the fourth time. She was without housing and had stayed at a shelter the previous few nights. She had been in a similar situation several times in the past four years, when she had sought help in community social agencies. But she had disappeared with the children, each time immediately after applying for help. She was at this time incapable of caring for herself and the children.

8) An eight-year-old boy was referred by the juvenile court for placement in a closed residential treatment facility. He was in detention for truanting, theft, and serious fire-setting. It was learned that three school-age siblings also were beginning to fail in school, truant, stealing, and setting fires. The mother, twice divorced, and with three preschool children, was overwhelmed with the problems of rearing the children, coping with poor housing, and existing on a subsistence budget.

In these capsule stories, one can see only the immediate causes of the court actions and the openly visible conditions that led to them. The variations, however, are relevant to family diagnosis, to the parents' feelings about the child's placement, to the type of plan needed, and to potential outcome. These parents, without exception, in the course of diagnostic studies, were found to be suffering from severe personality disturbances or mental illness. All of them were worried, ashamed, and guilty about the children.

In the course of subsequent service, three (1, 2, 7) out of the eight families re-established homes for the children after periods of placement ranging from three to six years, during which time they (the responsible parent) used the casework service of the agency in various ways. In one case (2) the parents reunited and used individual, intensive casework treatment provided by the foster care agency over a period of four years before they were strong enough to successfully absorb the responsibility for the children. In all three of these cases, the children were found to be able to use foster family care, and did so successfully. The parent(s) continued to need and use casework help immediately following the restoration of the children, and intermittently in times of crises thereafter.

In the other five cases, the parents maintained an active interest in the children, with a great deal of reciprocity in the need to maintain this relationship. However, the parents' disturbances were so pervasive that minimal stabilization on jobs and in their personal lives and cooperation in the children's placements were the optimal goals they could achieve. And this, for some of them, was only intermittent. In each of these families one or more of the children was found to be too seriously disturbed to use foster family care, and required residential treatment.[3]

INITIATING THE WORKING ALLIANCE

Ordinarily, the agency must take the initiative in contacting parents who are involuntary clients. Many can be located at the time of the court referral and before the agency acts beyond the point of

[3] These cases, selected at random to illustrate typical "immediate causes" of involuntary placements, support the general experience of the authors that when there is an identifiable relationship between extremely severe, long-standing disturbance in the parents and in the children, the chances of restoration of the family are slight.

a temporary plan, even though this may require visiting them in a hospital or a jail, writing to them in a prison, or searching for them through relatives, neighbors, employers, or previous addresses.[4] The omission of such action, for whatever reasons, suggests that social workers are sometimes subject to the same feelings of indignation and disapproval of a so-called neglectful parent as the lay public. Social work values, deeply rooted in a belief in the innate worth and dignity of each individual, are sorely strained when that individual is a parent who is seriously deficient in his capacity to function adequately in the parental role. The very use of the classification "the neglectful parent," common in social work parlance, reflects a social judgment that indicts the parent, over-simplifies the problems, and conceals the social and psychological illness of the adults who are consigned to this category.

This underlying rejection of the disturbed parent-client is also reflected obliquely when there is a general requirement or expectation, divorced from assessment of individual capacities as well as from the meaning of the relationship to parent and child, that these parents must either re-establish a home for the child or release him for legal adoption.[5] Such a requirement is, in its effect, punitive toward the parent who has had a substantial relationship with the child and does not want to lose it, but is incapable of re-establishing a home. Concomitantly, in many instances, it is a disservice to the child.

The timing of the agency's initiative in reaching out to the involuntary client is of dynamic importance in establishing the working alliance. The parent who has deserted the home is often the most disturbed in his feelings about the children's removal, the most vulnerable to any "neglect" he experiences at the hands of the agency, and the most extreme in his need to handle his shame, guilt, and hostility by blaming the agencies responsible for the children's protection and care (court and foster care agency). The

[4] In some cases, the first contact occurs at the court when a parent not previously accessible appears for the hearing.

[5] This philosophical stance is largely responsible for serious gaps in service to the children who require long-term foster care and who represent the largest number of children in placement.

mentally ill, hospitalized parent tends to react to the children's placement somewhat similarly. Usually, the greater the degree of nonparticipation in the placement, the more complex, hostile, and resistive is the parent's relationship to the caseworker and the agency. It is as though this parent's sense of failure can be tolerated only if he is able to say to himself, in effect, "This is not my fault; it is your fault because you do not trust me or value me as a person or as the child's parent."

The distinction between guilt and shame is important in efforts to help the parent restore some measure of self-esteem and use the foster care services constructively. Lynd differentiates guilt from shame, stating that guilt arises from a feeling of wrongdoing while shame arises from a feeling of inferiority (5). She continues: "Experiences of shame appear to embody the root meaning of the word —to uncover, to expose, to wound. They are experiences of exposure . . . of peculiarly sensitive, intimate, vulnerable aspects of the self. The exposure may be to others, but, whether others are or are not involved, it is always . . . exposure to one's own eyes." Lynd points out that, in an experience of shame, trust is seriously jeopardized or destroyed (6). Unprovoked belligerence often covers intolerable shame.

The issue of shame over parental failure as it appears in the foster care situation must be dealt with either directly or indirectly, or both, in order to establish a working alliance and achieve beginning trust. In some cases the problem of shame and consequent loss of self-esteem and ego identity cannot be approached on a verbal level; open recognition of the feelings is too threatening to the disintegrated ego. In such cases, the feelings of shame can be influenced only indirectly by the caseworker's attitudes and behavior. The caseworker's expectation of the parent's constructive participation in the child's placement, along with guidance and support in carrying it out, may help him, indirectly, to regain some measure of self-esteem. He is expected and supported to carry out functions that are, uniquely, his, to the full extent of his capacity.

Immediate casework contact with the parent anticipates and tends to reduce the intensity of his shame. The absence of efforts to engage the parent in some level of participation in the initial plan-

ning stage has the opposite effect: it tends to confirm his expectations that he will be treated as a bad parent. He is unaware that
this expectation mirrors his own self-image. His response to absence of action on the part of the agency points up a generality in
working with the parents of placed children. Casework passivity
and failure to take initiative in promoting the parents' participation in appropriate aspects of the child's life is likely to be interpreted by the parents as having a specific purpose: to shut him out
or to express tacit approval of his withdrawal. He does not see that
his own withdrawal, avoidance, or passivity may be responsible for
the lack of continuity in the working alliance. His lack of self-esteem, his shame, guilt, state of regression, or disorganization may
interfere with any wish he has to maintain the contact with the
child and the agency. Dynamically, then, it is not realistic to expect self-motivation in agency contacts as a prerequisite for service. It is desirable to initiate contacts with these parents, at all
points along the way, when they fail to make contact, and there is
reason to promote the continuity of the relationship on behalf of
the child, the parents, or both.[6]

THE VOLUNTARY CLIENT

The major distinction between the involuntary and the voluntary
client is that the latter seeks the service for his child on his own initiative and has some conscious motivation to use the service in
some way. In some instances he does this only upon the insistence
or threat from an outside agent, such as school, medical facility, or
protective agency. In others, he recognizes his need for help with
the child and takes action without outside intervention. In either
instance, however, he has some choices, limited though they may
be. Even the parent who applies to the foster care agency under
threat of court referral from a community institution such as
school, clinic, or others, has some alternatives open to him. For example, he can choose to accept or not to accept the referral, and,

[6] In exceptional cases it is necessary for the agency to initiate contacts with
the parents for legal or financial reasons, even though the needs of parent and
child would be better served if contacts were discontinued.

likewise, he can decide whether he will accept the services that are offered by the agency. In most instances this means that this parent, even though he may be marginal in his capacity to find a constructive solution to his problem, is healthier in this respect than the involuntary client who, because his ego disfunction is greater, makes it necessary for the community to impose a solution for the child's protection. This fact does not insure that the voluntary client is free of extremely serious problems in his parental functioning or that he is not resistive to or ambivalent about various aspects of his altered role, the agency's role, or the use of help to modify the conditions that necessitate placement. However, because he seeks service voluntarily he has an opportunity to explore his situation and his proposed solution, to respond to the agency's procedures and defined expectations, and to arrive, with the caseworker, at a joint decision. At the point of placement, he has accepted, at least consciously, the agency's service and its conditions for admission of the child. The agency, on its part, has the opportunity to observe the parent's initial pattern of responding to this experience and to evaluate and work with the parent's responses. Consequently, at the time of the child's transfer to the placement facility the initial stage in developing the working alliance has been experienced by both parent and agency.

Brief illustrations of the parenting situation of voluntary clients will point up some of the similarities and differences:

1) A divorced mother applied to an agency for placement of two preschool children. Although she worked as a secretary and was able to manage her job successfully, she felt overwhelmed and incapable of caring for the children. The five-year-old boy had developed problems of extreme self-destructiveness, emotional isolation, and nightmares. The day-care center refused to continue his care. The three-year-old boy reacted to the day-care arrangement with increasing anxiety and resistance to habit training for bowel and bladder control. The mother had secured personal psychotherapy in a clinic, but her problems were found to be too pervasive and deeply entrenched in her character for modification on a short-term basis. Her tenuous emotional adjustment made it impossible for her to care for the children personally, even if it had been pos-

sible to relieve her of the economic necessity to support her family. Personal therapy and the day-care placement of the children had, for several years, enabled her to maintain herself in a stable job situation and to cooperate in the day-care plans, but the increasing disturbance of the children reflected the insufficiency of mothering at critical developmental stages, and the mother's adjustment was deteriorating. She could not consider homemaker service because of her intense internal conflict about women in mothering roles.

2) A divorced father of two preschool children applied for their placement when his second wife, stepmother to the children, refused to continue their care and left the home. The father had found temporary foster homes for the children before applying to an agency.

The history showed that both his first and second wives had been delinquent, unstable characters and that he had always handled his problems by getting involved with drugs, running away, and changing jobs frequently. He had, at the same time, always retained responsibility for the children. He wanted to maintain his relationship with them and his responsibility for them, but recognized their need for long-term stable family life which he could not provide.

3) A mother and father were referred by a family service agency for the placement of their ten-year-old son. They had been pressed into requesting help at the family service agency by the school because of the child's chronic school problems, which dated back to kindergarten. He was withdrawn, could not be motivated to learn, was unable to concentrate, and had poor relationships with teachers, who found him unresponsive to any approach. His other problems included unrealistic fears, hoarding, nightmares, wandering away from home, stealing, inability to make friends, thumb sucking—all of which dated back to preschool years. The parents, in treatment at the family agency for a year, made no progress. They used the sessions to ventilate their hostility to the child and to blame each other for his condition. They felt that he had always been "odd" and that his problems increasingly interfered in the marriage. They were unable to move beyond this and were able to cooperate with each other only after the family agency caseworker

suggested placement as a possible plan. Their individual personal histories documented life-long problems, now apparent in their inability to modify their attitudes toward their son.

Other voluntary cases differ mainly in detail. For the most part, at the time of application, the parents recognize and acknowledge that they are unable to care for the child, and that either the child's problems, or their own, or both, necessitate foster care of some type. In some instances, unlike the involuntary client, the voluntary client is able to maintain a physically intact home and some level of economic stability, but deep-seated psychological problems interfere with minimally adequate parenting and with the effective use of individual or family treatment. Some are unable to tolerate foster family care, or to use help to accept such a plan, which they see as a direct confirmation of their own failure, but they can cooperate in a group care plan for the child. Most, however, can use help to accept foster family care when this is indicated. In the main, these parents are individuals whose inability to give the child sufficiently good parenting for minimally adequate development stems from severe personality disturbances which have their genesis in early childhood experiences.

Psychological Reactions to the Child's Placement

The child's placement solves some problems for the parent and introduces others. The parent gains respite from the daily impingement of the practical demands of child-rearing and the emotional stress in interpersonal relationships. Whether the placement is voluntary or involuntary, the parent has turned over responsibility to others to assure that the child is provided with adequate care, protection, and supervision. However, just as the child experiences the placement as a rejection by the parent and confirmation of something unacceptable in him, the parent experiences it as the confirmation of his parental failure. In addition, once the separation takes place he begins to experience the loss of the child's presence in both its positive and its negative aspects. The child's removal introduces changes in the psychological equilibrium of the parent and within the family. These changes necessitate the establishment of a new equilibrium in the individual family members and in any part of the nuclear family group which remains intact.

The parent's responses to the tasks of developing a changed relationship with the placed child and a new relationship with the agency are prominently influenced by parental ambivalence, shame, guilt, and loss. If the loss is that of an unconscious dependent, or even symbiotic, relationship with the child, the course of achieving a new emotional equilibrium is most difficult for the parent and is likely to be accompanied by regression. Whether the sense of loss, guilt, shame, or feelings of failure are paramount, the relationship with the child and the agency is often characterized by the commonly observed defense mechanisms of denial, displacement, and projection. In some cases these defenses may be expressed in rage against the agency or the court; projection of responsibility for the placement onto others, such as the school, agency, clinic, or court; irrational criticism of the surrogate parents; and unrealistic worries about the child and the adequacy of his care.

The parent's paramount psychological tasks, then, are to find a new dynamic equilibrium within himself and in his relationship with other family members and to develop the changed relationship with the placed child. In one way or another he works at these tasks intrapsychically. If he is absent, and not in direct contact with the agency or the child, or both, the process of adaptation and readjustment is unknown and unavailable for agency evaluation. Evidence from chronically itinerant parents, who have appeared intermittently to inquire about their children, suggests that some fantasy process is utilized to alleviate guilt and that the parent suffers from such low self-esteem that he accepts his parental failure as a part of his self-image. Often after his inquiry he again disappears. In some cases, the absent, nonitinerant parent who manages to work and stabilize himself in some form of family life fantasies a reunion with the absent child in some indefinite fu-

ture when his life will be better or circumstances will change. The
fantasies are his chief means of quieting his conscience and finding
a tolerable internal stabilization.

The parent who is not absent has three main channels available
to him to work on the achievement of a new equilibrium: (a) his
fantasies and thoughts, (b) his periodic direct contact with the
child, (c) and the agency caseworker. From a mental health point
of view, the face-to-face contact with the child and the participation of the caseworker have a high level of importance. Only the
contact with the child can afford an opportunity for realistic appraisal of the interrelationship, correct the fantasies and distortions
that develop during the separation, and open the way to the possibility of developing a better object relationship, to the extent that
the parent's capacity will allow. In some instances, the caseworker
may play a critical role in helping the parent utilize the experience
for growth, increased self-esteem, movement toward rehabilitation,
or stabilization of long-term placement or permanent separation.
Psychologically, emancipation of the child and parent from the
crippling, destructive elements in their relationship may be essential, when the crippling elements predominate and cannot be modified.

THERAPEUTIC USE OF FAMILY VISITS

The opportunity for the parents and the child to adapt to the altered parental role, in the early months of placement, is best
provided within the structure of the visiting arrangements. Within
these visits, the altered roles are experienced by both the parent
and the child in each other's presence. This experience, important
in itself, is also the fulcrum of much of the silent work in the adaptive process that goes on when they are not together, and is the
focus for important aspects of the casework helping process. The
visiting parent faces a whole new set of demands on his adaptive
efforts. His major tasks on the child's behalf, as defined by agency
expectations, are: 1) to help the child make sense of the reasons for
his inability to make a home for him, and 2) to free the child to
utilize the surrogate parenting and agency service available to

him. These expectations do not mean in any sense that the agency expects the parent to become the child's therapist; it means only that he, better than anyone else, can clarify the real reasons for the placement and encourage the child to accept and reciprocate love from the surrogate parents and help from the agency. By giving his approval to and supporting both relationships, the parent can greatly reduce the conflict of loyalties that often stands in the way of the child's use of surrogate parenting. The parent may be wholly unready to cope with these tasks or totally unable to do so without sustained help from the caseworker. Whatever the parent is able to do that benefits the child contributes in some degree to the parent's growth.

In helping the parent, the caseworker should keep in mind that this parent usually is a person who has not had sufficiently good parenting in his own childhood to enable him to achieve adequate parenthood himself; he is basically a deprived, excessively dependent person who wants to be given to in much the same way that his child is now given to by the surrogate parents, although this need may be concealed from himself and others beneath layers of complex, deceptive psychological defenses. When faced with the visiting situation, the parent's needs and conflicts come to the fore and heavily influence his behavior.

When the visiting arrangement is recognized as a dynamically important aspect of the total treatment strategy and aims, it is designed and carried out with attention to individual and family diagnosis and a balanced regard for each of the participants in the foster care system. Short of such differential planning, the parent and child are left to continue their previous pattern of interpersonal relationship, with its destructive and pathological elements exacerbated by the parent's defenses against painful, conflictual feelings. The most common maladaptive defenses observed in parent-child visits, are these:

Some parents follow an established pattern of avoidance by failing to observe the planned visiting arrangements or by visiting on impulse, without an appointment, when their need for contact with the child springs from some inner worry or loneliness.

Some visit consistently and handle their guilt, fear of loss of love, or competition with surrogate parents by over indulging the child with unrealistic promises, gifts, or permissiveness.

Some express their emotional dependence on the child with inappropriate confidences, physical seductiveness, and the like.

Some express their hostile feelings through subtle or overt depreciation of the child or abusive criticism of the surrogate parents.

Some express competition by setting up a triangular struggle among child, self, and foster parent, or self, foster parent, and agency.

Finally, some develop a secretive, dependent relationship with the surrogate parents—temporarily satisfying to both, but doomed to failure by the extent of the underlying needs and the ultimate excessive demands of the parent.

In any of these situations, these characteristic ways of relating to others are consistent with the internal dynamics and learned social techniques of the parent. They are a continuation and expression of some aspect of the problems that played a determining part in the parental failure.

Not only are these various forms of behavior, when allowed to proceed without intervention, destructive to the parent; they also endanger the child's care and treatment because they support and encourage pathological development and raise anxiety and hostility in the surrogate parents. The lack of planned intervention tacitly gives the agency's permission to the parent to continue maladaptive behavior that has already proven inadequate and destructive to him and his family.

The parent is not alone in continuing to act out his pathological patterns. The child, too, brings his learned techniques for relating to the parents into the visiting situation. He is able to arouse in the parent intense guilt, triangular competition, fear of loss of his love, worry, and such. His behavior is sometimes the spark that sets off the unrealistic promises, the jealousy and sabotage of foster parents or agency, and other destructive responses.

In short, both the parent and the child continue to interact, to express their internal needs, through the various interpersonal social techniques that they learned to employ in the original family situation.

In view of these observations the visiting arrangement should be designed to be both preventive and therapeutic. The general aims are: (a) to prevent incidents that complicate the conditions of the service and interfere with the child's use of his new environment, and (b) to offer help to both parent and child to modify the relationship in the directions that will better serve the welfare of each.

For families that cannot constructively use the foster home visit, the supervised office visit provides opportunities for working toward both these objectives. This visiting structure offers protection for the parent against the unmanageable feelings aroused when he is directly confronted by the parent surrogates and the consequences of his own acting-out behavior. It affords the caseworker an opportunity to observe the interpersonal interaction between parent and child and to use the observations as a basis for offering them specific kinds of help in understanding what is occurring and modifying their behavior.

In most instances, the parent can best accept the structure of the supervised visit when it is presented from the outset, matter-of-factly, as one of the agency's policies within the framework of the philosophy and aims of the total service.[7] The caseworker's explanation may include four elements: (a) The agency provides for regular visiting; (b) Visiting takes place in the agency's office; (c) The caseworker usually participates to help both the parents and the children with the problems and questions that are involved when the family is no longer living together; (d) Although visiting takes place in the office, provision is made for the parent to visit the prospective foster home or group facility prior to the child's placement.

[7] Some social workers have been troubled by the concept of the supervised visit because of the feeling that it violates privacy and freedom in the parent-child relationship. This attitude presupposes that there is a substantive positive, object-related quality in the relationship which should be preserved by privacy. However, the parent who is emotionally ill and handicapped to the extent that he is unable to manage visits beneficially for himself and the child has a right to professional service that is premised on the recognition of his condition and understanding of his real needs. Legal visitation rights are rarely called into question by parents who experience the supervised visit as a part of a plan designed out of concern for the needs of both parent and child.

This total approach tends to cut down potential feelings of rejection, depreciation, or neglect because it actively plans for the continued relationship, establishes a structure, and provides for agency participation, carrying into action the philosophy and attitudes that have been verbalized in the total interpretation of the agency's service.

The supervised visit lends itself to any or all of these preventive and therapeutic uses:

1) The presence of the caseworker with whom there is a defined, purposive relationship provides emotional support for parent and child.

2) Problems in communication can be identified and clarified.

3) Educative approaches can be utilized when indicated in matters ranging from simple techniques of play to appropriate role definition and performance.

4) Direct intervention can be employed when the behavior of either the parent or the child is psychologically destructive to the other.

5) Direct help before, after, or during the visits can be provided for the parent and the child, individually or in the family group, in relation to stresses in the interpersonal relationships.

6) Family visits reveal the family dynamics as they operate in the framework of the separated family, and reflect a continuation of some of the relationship patterns as they existed before the separation. These observations may yield entry to important aspects of treatment.

Unstructured, unsupervised visiting ordinarily is successful only in the absence of severe pathological conditions in child and parent. Parents' visits with children in foster homes work best when the placement is of relatively short duration and the child's return to his family can be anticipated. In such situations, the parent, is usually a relatively stable person whose relationship with the child is free from severe disturbance. Under these conditions, the parent's need for the participation of the caseworker primarily revolves around the structuring of visits, which requires the collaboration of the surrogate parents and the child. The caseworker's liaison function is connected with facilitating and interpretive functions.

The unselective use of parent-child visits in foster homes, common in much foster care practice, causes serious problems for the parent who acts out his disturbed feelings and creates severe conflict in the child and the foster parents. Viewed from the standpoint of the parent's welfare, any structure that allows or enables him to act out his self-defeating and destructive pattern of behavior in his relationship with his child is a disservice, not only to the child, but also to the parent. It should be kept in mind that even the most immature and disorganized parent wants what is best for his child even though he is unable to provide it. His disruptive actions are self-defeating and guilt-producing. However, without the agency's provision of structure and support, he may not have the ego strength to utilize the guilt constructively, that is, for self-discipline and self-control.

The casework time and energy that is used in attempting to stabilize such situations and, ultimately, in many instances, moving the child, would be better used preventively by arranging office visits from the outset.[8]

The Focus of Casework Help

The kind of help the parent-clients can use is differentially determined on the basis of a variety of factors. These factors include:

1) The parent's view of the purpose of his contacts with the agency.

2) The problem areas he presents for discussion which provide the opportunity for mutual identification of the areas of work to be undertaken at any given time.

[8] Many foster parents give up foster parenting as a result of the stress introduced by parental visits at the foster home. Sometimes the cause is not manifest, either because the foster parents do not feel free to acknowledge this stress as the real reason for their withdrawal (and give other, well rationalized reasons) or because the complex feelings are denied and come out only indirectly.

3) The degree of ego dysfunction in major life roles (parenting, marriage, work).

4) The nature of the defenses against underlying dependency which determine the degree to which he can use constructively the realistic dependence inherent in accepting help and the level at which help can be offered.

Theoretically, it can be assumed that the parent's fear of the helping relationship is at least equaled by the extent of his underlying need. The greater his fear, the more likely he is to restrict the use of the relationship to the most minimal arrangements for the child's care. For some parents, an offer of help for himself on his own behalf or exploration of feelings may cause him to avoid contact with the caseworker in any possible way. The parents themselves provide clues to the areas of help they want, or, can accept.

The caseworker's approach is a graduated one, beginning with the mutual concern about the child's needs. Support and guidance in the changed role in the relationship with the placed child are inherent in this aspect of help.

Next, tangible services in relation to environmental problems can be offered when the parent communicates facts that indicate the need for such help. This may involve practical planning in regard to financial help, employment, medical care, housing, and the like. The need for help in these basic areas of living takes priority over other problems. Although psychological problems and environmental problems may be feeding each other, they usually cannot be disentangled, and ego-functioning potential cannot be estimated until adequate efforts have been made to relieve or reduce environmental stress. If the parent demonstrates inability to respond to these efforts, the inner need to maintain a self-defeating or self-destructive environmental situation begins to crystallize. Attention to these matters, however, facilitates the development of trust in the caseworker, to the extent that the parent can allow himself to respond positively.

Third, an active response to crises or emergencies in which the parent needs help provides an opportunity which many deeply distrustful clients are able to use to test the caseworker's concern by seeing and experiencing a demonstration of the reality of that concern.

Finally, the parent who is not too frightened may be able to move quickly into using help on an emotional level, and in relation to any of his environmental or interpersonal problems. The approach then may include easing guilt and shame to mobilize improved ego functioning; identifying self-defeating patterns of behavior in interpersonal relationships and in role functioning; reinforcing desirable patterns of behavior; and promoting emotional insight in problem areas when it is needed and can be supported by the ego strength of the client.

It is of special importance with the client who has deep-seated dependent needs and regressive drives to encourage and support his capacity to act on his own behalf. As in early childhood development, the disturbed adult's growth in ego functioning is built on his mastery of each task that is within his functioning capacity. Sometimes he may have to stretch hard and he may be able to perform some tasks for himself only with the caseworker's active participation. Doing things for him should be limited to those situations in which it is clear that what needs to be done is essential and the client is truly unable to do it for himself. For example, a mother in need of medical care, unable to act independently to make the necessary arrangements, may need only an opportunity to ventilate her anxiety and verbal support from the caseworker. Or she may be unable to take this step without the support derived from the caseworker's presence. Or it may be necessary for the caseworker to make the arrangements and accompany the mother to her first appointment. Unless the parent is manifestly too disorganized to function on his own behalf, these graduated steps in determining the quantity and quality of help the parent needs safeguard the use of self-reliance to its optimal degree.

The work with parents of placed children is sometimes hindered by the fact that some social workers and psychiatric consultants, accustomed to the clinical treatment model, find the cooperative aspect of the parent-client role, as a participant in the foster care system, a bewildering complication. Conversely, child welfare caseworkers who are oriented only to the parent's cooperative role find the treatment aspect confusing. In fact, the separation of these two aspects of the client role is valid only for the purpose of clarifying related aspects of treatment. On the one hand, treatment of the parent for environmental and interpersonal problems in areas exclusive of the relationship with the placed child is artificial and unrealistic. On the other, an approach that arbitrarily limits the areas of help to focus exclusively on the parent's relationship with the placed child forecloses the opportunity for optimal use of help. Any progress the parent makes in functioning as a self-reliant individual contributes to his mental health, his constructive participation in the child's use of placement, and the possibility of a desirable outcome. The relationship of the parent with the placed child is an integral part of the parent's psychological life and equilibrium, and it cannot be separated and parceled out in the helping process without fragmentizing the very elements in the parent's life that should be emotionally integrated in the service of improved emotional health and more effective ego functioning. Parents who want and can use treatment for intrapsychic problems, however, as differentiated from environmental and interpersonal problems, can and should be referred to specialists in adult psychotherapy.

The major areas of work with the severely disturbed parent, including the therapeutic use of the supervised visit, are illustrated in two summarized examples of casework service to contrasting families, with different capacities for using help. The first case was selected, despite the extreme ego disfunction of the parents, because it typifies many of the major problems commonly met in working with parents, some of whom may be less disturbed and less distrustful, but who are different only in degree and who require similar approaches, modified in relation to the particulars of their individualized responses. No attempt has been made to discuss or illustrate work with the neurotic parent as differentiated from those suffering from character disorders or prepsychotic and psychotic reactions because few such adults are seen in foster care agencies, and because casework practice in relation to such clients is already well established and well defined.

THE WILENSKI CASE

Diane and Julie Wilenski, aged seven and five, were placed in temporary foster care by the juvenile court when police found them alone in the family's burned-out apartment. Several days later the mother, aged thirty-one, was found wandering on the street. She was subsequently committed to a state hospital with a diagnosis of schizophrenic reaction.

The father, aged thirty-five, had disappeared and could not be located. He and the mother had been living together up to the time of the mother's disappearance. Later it was learned that he had gone to the home of his parents in another state where he remained under their care, as he was suffering from a recurrent mental illness.

In the absence of both parents, the initial study focused on the children. Both children were found to be severely disturbed. Diane, the elder, was a self-destructive, hyperactive, impulse-ridden child. She was abnormally greedy; she slept poorly; her school work was consistently poor, although she had above average intelligence; she had no friends. Disturbances were present in behavior, in relationships, and in social and intellectual functioning. She was relatively free from symptoms only in her physical health. Strengths were seen in her mourning for the loss of her mother; her ability to learn in a one-to-one relationship; some reciprocal relationship observed in play with her sister; her ability to verbalize fantasies; and her positive response to limits. It was inferred from this evidence that she must have received some gratification in the mothering relationship. She seemed to retain hope for a satisfying relationship with a mother, but had not received enough affection for gratification of her needs. It was doubtful that foster parents could be found who could tolerate her behavior or provide the special educational and group experiences she required. A long-term placement in the agency's residential treatment center was planned.

Julie, the younger sister, although severely disturbed, used such nonaggressive defenses against stress as physical symptoms, intellectual constriction, and emotional isolation. Diagnostic psychological tests showed a high degree of creative potential, which she was unable to use. In relationships with staff members she showed superficial spontaneity. Because of her age and the nonaggressive nature of her symptoms, a long-term foster home placement was planned, with recognition that she would need a family which would be able to accept the potential acting-out behavior that would be likely to develop in the course of her care, and the individual psychotherapy which she might need later.

The degree and pervasiveness of disturbance in the two girls, and the mental illness of the parents, suggested that both children would require long-term care outside their nuclear family. Corroboration was found in exploration of the family history in later interviews with the mother and the paternal grandparents.

It was learned that the father had been hospitalized four years earlier with a diagnosis of schizophrenic reaction. That had been but one episode in a chronically unstable adulthood. The paternal grandmother informed the caseworker that, currently, the father could not remember anything, wandered away, and had laughing spells that alternated with despondency and suicidal threats. She said he was a quiet, easy-going man who loved children, but he often lost his jobs due to illness and had never been able to provide a stable home. He made no effort to visit his wife or children.

There was direct evidence from Diane that the mother's bizarre behavior was of long duration. She had kept Diane home from school as early as the first grade to help her "keep the little red men from coming into the house."

Initiating the Working Alliance with Mrs. Wilenski

A hospital report stated that the mother was mute, hostile, and uncooperative at the time of admission. Under medication and other therapies she improved steadily and became oriented to her surroundings, but showed some memory impairment.

When she had improved sufficiently, the caseworker was allowed to visit her. The visit took place after Julie's placement in a foster home and before Diane's placement in the residential treatment center. The worker faced a rather delicate problem regarding the effect of the latter plan on the mother, who hated her own hospital experience and identified Diane with herself.[9] The selection and timing of the information to be shared was of some importance in regard to the emotional impact it would have and its effect on her future feelings about the agency.

In the first visit, the caseworker found the mother friendly but guarded. Her affect about the children was sad and anxious. She seemed to comprehend the caseworker's explanation of her function and the agency's relationship to the court and the children. She wept when plans for the children were discussed, but expressed no opinion about them. She said she looked forward to rejoining her husband; she loved him and the children.

The mother was visited several more times in the course of her hospitalization. She was given information about the children's care and finally was told that Diane would be placed in a small group residence belonging to the agency; here she would be in a small school on the grounds and could get individual help with her school work and her trouble with other children.

It was noted that the mother seemed to have a strong symbiotic attachment to the children and was unable to differentiate them and their needs from her own needs and reactions.

After her discharge from the hospital, the mother obtained employment and housing through the hospital's rehabilitation program.

Focus of Working Alliance

The working alliance was approached through recognition of the mutual need of mother and children for a continuing relationship. This need was apparent from the children's expressed longing for the parents, especially the mother, and the mother's consistent emphasis on her concern for their welfare and her wish to be with them. The mother shied away from any supportive help as such; she

[9] Ordinarily, it is important that parents be given full information about the severity of the child's disturbance and progress reports keeping them informed of the child's condition. However, the selection and timing of such information must be carefully weighed in working with the mentally ill parent.

was in good physical health, and needed no assistance in obtaining medical care or in her employment or living situations. The helping process, consequently, was focused entirely on the parent-child relationship. The mother avoided contact with the caseworker except at the time of arranged visits with the children in the agency's office. She was frightened, ashamed, and suspicious, and covered her feelings with aggressive demands. But she cooperated fully in the visiting plans. The plan for office visits at monthly intervals, with the caseworker's participation, was presented to her as one among other routine policies of the agency. She readily accepted it.

The mother's emotional investment in the children was the cornerstone of her existence. She had both a legal right and an emotional need for regular visits. The children's need for visits with the mother was mixed. Although they mourned the separation, her extreme disturbance had been frightening to them, and visits could be expected to stir up conflict and anxiety. From a mental health point of view it was important that the children's ambivalent attachment to the parents be recognized and contacts continued in order to avoid, if possible, the fixation in development that is likely to occur in reaction to termination of such a relationship. Since both mother and children needed an ongoing relationship, the structuring, supervision, and casework help in relation to the visits constituted a critical aspect of planning that would make a difference between potential therapeutic use of visits and potential destructiveness.

These conditions, while somewhat dramatized in this case by the severity of disturbance in both the mother and the children, are different only in degree from visiting conditions in many long-term foster care cases.

The mother was offered a routine appointment immediately preceding each visit, to receive a report about the children and to discuss the visits or any other matters she wished. She refused the offer of appointments following the visits for the purpose of discussing any further questions she might have. The caseworker described her as literally fleeing from the building after every visit.

During the first two years of these contacts, she maintained an overtly resistive, suspicious attitude toward the caseworker, but directed her complaints about the children's placement against "the state," thus making the state the "bad mother" rather than the agency. In this way she was able to be a "good mother," and cooperate in the care of the children.

Use of the Structured Visiting Arrangement

Most of the communication that took place between the mother and the caseworker was within the structure of the family visits. The caseworker introduced a few simple, appropriate games and toys which could be used for everyone's participation or as a distraction for the children, should they be unable to relate verbally to the mother.

The pattern of the visits was in many ways typical of many other families. Mother and children needed the caseworker's participation to structure the visits, clarify distortions in communication, augment information about the children's daily life as was needed, and provide support or limits for both parent and child.

The caseworker noted that the visits tended to be noisy, as the children spent part of the time chasing each other or playing games, with much loud laughter. The mother related to this at their level, was always kind, but was unable to limit either the physical or verbal excesses which caused her and the children to become overly excited. The caseworker placed needed limits, sometimes by explaining that it was necessary to be more quiet because other people were working in nearby offices, or sometimes, indirectly, by her own quiet participation.

Diane, the elder child, at times wanted to sit and talk. Her mother always wanted to know details about her daily life in the institution, what she did during the day, how she got along in school, what she watched on television. During these conversations Julie played with the toys alone or with the caseworker or interrupted with her own concerns. Diane told her mother about things that happened that upset her, such as another child's transfer to a psychiatric hospital, children running away, or a housemother's illness. Often there was confusion and distortion in those reports, which were corrected by the caseworker, thus relieving the anxiety of Diane and her mother.

Diane talked a great deal about her wish to go to public school and how hard she was working to achieve this. Since both mother and child saw the school problem as the concrete evidence of the child's "craziness," much of their anxiety was focused on this subject. The caseworker's matter-of-fact clarification of the child's unreadiness and long-range perspective repeatedly served to restore a more realistic feeling about this issue and to keep it at a manageable level.

After some months, the children's wish to see their father confronted the mother with a conflict, since she wanted to please them but had avoided getting in touch with him. She reached out gingerly for the caseworker's support after a visit in which Diane pressed her to arrange a visit with the father. The mother used the caseworker's support to do what she felt was manageable for her. Eventually, she made a visit to the paternal grandparents' home and arranged for the father to come to the agency office to see the children. He did not appear on the appointed day. The caseworker was present to listen, allow the children to ventilate their disappointment, and clarify for both mother and children that it was the father's condition which interfered with his ability to keep his promise.

The most difficult part of the visits for the mother was Diane's verbalized fantasy of a future in which the family would all be back together. When this came up, the mother tried to change the subject. The caseworker's observation of this interaction gave her the opportunity to intervene at the time or to follow up as needed in subsequent sessions with the individual participants.

Gradually, as the mother experienced the caseworker's acceptance, support, firmness, and open sharing of information about the children, her suspiciousness decreased. The caseworker noted:

The mother has become much more trusting of me and the agency. She now seems to be quite accepting of the girls' placement, and is able to see that they are well cared for. She occasion-

ally goes off in a tirade about how the state has taken the children away from her; the state won't do anything to help anyone, and on and on. This usually happens when something worries her, such as a child's missing a visit due to illness or her worry about why Diane is not yet in public school. Some of her questions suggest that she is not clear about the nature of the residential treatment center and thinks of it as being similar to the state hospital, even though, when she asks questions, Diane tells her it is a nice place and how much she likes it. She does not appear to comprehend the kinds of problems Diane has; her overt attitude is that Diane is nervous and excitable, which she will outgrow.

On the whole, the mother has made progress. She is able to talk much more freely about her concerns about the children and even to ask for my help and advice in some matters regarding her job and living situation. She continues to bring more gifts for the children than she should, but this is now within reason in relation to her income.

Three months after this recording, a crisis occurred in the mother's relationship with the agency. It was necessary to cancel Diane's usual visit because of a severe regressive episode following the loss of a housemother. Her violent reaction contraindicated activity outside the institution. The mother reacted to the canceled visit with extreme agitation. Her underlying fear that the child was mentally ill just as she had been, previously thinly concealed, now emerged in her efforts to prove that both she and the child were all right. She obtained a lawyer and requested that he represent her in court to ask for the return of the children. The lawyer, after a conference in which he learned about the child's illness and the agency's interest in the welfare of both the mother and the child, agreed to refer her back to the caseworker. No effort was made to dissuade her from asking for court intervention. Instead, she was invited to talk with Diane's therapist as one means of getting further information about the child's condition. The long and consistent relationship was used to help her recognize the unrealistic nature of her fears. She knew from experience that the worker and the agency had been reliable, and was now able to respond to the reminders of specific instances of trust and mutual cooperation which she had experienced. She responded well to the various steps that were taken to restore her to a more realistic view, and subsequently consolidated a new level of trust and security in her relationship with the agency.

Had the mother carried through on her intention to go to court to ask for the children, the consequences, even though restoration of the children was unlikely, might have been damaging to her mental health, her trust in the relationship with the agency, and the security the children felt in their placements. It is in crises such as these with the severely disturbed parent that the strength of the working alliance becomes critical in safeguarding the total placement system.

The approach, throughout the course of the helping process, in contrast to an exploratory, uncovering one, is focused on ego support, identifying islands of strength, and protecting and promoting functioning in these areas. This mother, like many others, was able to maintain herself outside of a mental hospital, function adequately on a simple job, and cooperate in the care of the children largely because the casework service was designed to provide optimal support and balance in her relationship with the children and the agency.

Other parents need and are able to use help in other areas of living, beyond the levels of help seen in the foregoing case. Although many would not seek help in a family service agency or a clinic, they can use help in the foster care agency when the establishment of the working alliance on behalf of the child has served the purpose of reducing their fear and shame and when their motivation has been strengthened in the process of receiving the services for the child's placement. The areas of living in which these parents need and can use help may include marriage, work, parenting of children who remain in the home, homemaking, financial management, medical care, and such. The problems may be both interpersonal and environmental.

THE MILLER CASE

The Miller family illustrates the extensive help used by a mother in her work, health care, relationship with the placed children, a new marriage, and the effect of this help on the lives of the children.

Mrs. Miller, the divorced mother of three school-age children, sought agency help on the insistence of a school counselor. The children, girls aged twelve and ten and a boy aged five, were noted by their teachers to be irregular in school attendance, ill-kempt in appearance, fatigued, and chronically unable to keep up with their school assignments. The school counselor learned from Mrs. Miller that she was employed on two jobs and left the supervision of the two younger children to the eldest girl, who helped the youngsters get off to school in the morning and supervised them after school. Following the counselor's sessions with Mrs. Miller, the situation did not improve; it seemed to deteriorate further. Mrs. Miller appeared to be uncooperative; she denied the seriousness of the children's situation and refused to accept referral to a social agency. Finally, she became frightened by two incidents: suspected sexual acting out of the eldest child and an accidental fire in the apartment when the children were alone. She was in a state of panic when she applied to the foster care agency for placement of the children.

When first seen in the agency, Mrs. Miller talked volubly and compulsively about herself, the deprivations of her childhood, and her painful experiences with men. The interviewer noted that it was almost impossible to get her to focus on the children sufficiently to determine whether placement was needed, although she pressed urgently for their placement to avoid some feared catastrophe.

Mrs. Miller's compulsive talking about everything except the central issue of the children's placement served several purposes, one of which was to avoid the intense shame of exposure of her failure as a mother. In other life roles she was able to project onto others the responsibility for failure, but this defense did not serve in this situation. Once faced by the necessity to place the children and the reality represented by her presence in the agency, she could no longer deny or evade her failure.

Mrs. Miller, with better ego integration than Mrs. Wilenski, represents the parent who can benefit from both verbalization at the feeling level and active engagement in functioning as a constructive cooperator on the child's behalf.

In the second interview, the caseworker told Mrs. Miller that her other problems were important, but that she could deal with them better after the immediate problem about the children was resolved, "but it might be more comfortable, in a way, not to talk about the children, . . . most parents who come here feel as though they have failed pretty badly. . . ." This opened the door for the mother's verbalization of the feelings of shame which had been blocking her communication. Throughout the initial history-taking interviews, she and the caseworker, from time to time, recognized the ebb and flow of shame, guilt, and anxiety, but the shame over failure was uppermost and was only gradually diminished as Mrs. Miller experienced the caseworker's consistent acceptance and support and achieved a degree of restored self-esteem and ego identity.

Mrs. Miller's entire history had been marked by self-destructive, self-defeating behavior in her personal relationships with men, in her employment, and in the neglect of her health. The family history revealed periods of stabilization followed by periods of severe disorganization throughout the rearing of the children. In the interim between her two marriages she had maintained a common-law relationship with another partner. When these relationships remained stable, she had managed to provide adequate care and supervision for the children, but when each relationship began to deteriorate, the family went through long periods in which the mother and her current spouse accused each other of infidelity, fought, drank excessively, had serious economic problems, and neglected the children.

When she was alone, Mrs. Miller obtained work to support the family. She expected her oldest child to supervise the younger children. She changed jobs frequently. Her resistance to recognizing the children's condition did not seem to result from indifference but rather from an underlying feeling of desperation: she saw no alternative solutions and she was deeply humiliated by exposure of her failure as a mother.

In her relationships with the children, although she wanted and tried to give them the care she thought they needed, her problems interfered seriously with her parenting capacities. She was kind and tried to be understanding, but the relationships were dominated by her own needs. She tended to act out her sexual conflicts through the eldest girl, and was extremely infantilizing and unconsciously seductive with the little boy. The middle child was markedly left out. Each of the children showed corresponding developmental problems. The eldest girl identified with her mother's behavior in her relationships with men and was beginning to act out sexually. The second child was chronically depressed and withdrawn, feeling that she had little place or importance in the family relationships. The little boy was emotionally immature for his age and was beginning to show sexual identity problems. The two younger children were placed in foster homes, and the eldest in a therapeutically oriented school.

Despite Mrs. Miller's severe disturbance, she was able to establish a working alliance and a cooperative role in the course of the study and placement process. With guidance and support, she provided the necessary information about the children, clarified with them the reasons for their placement, supported their use of the facilities selected for them, and entered into the visiting arrangements, using the caseworker's help to understand what the children needed from her. Her relationship with the placed children and her functioning in other areas of her life were interrelated in her treatment. While she worked on her responses to the children's needs, she also moved into other problems. The major focus in her relationship with each child is of interest in following the relationship between her use of help in her major areas of disfunction and their influence, direct and indirect, on each other.

1) In the course of placement, the eldest child rebelled against the school's expectations and requirements and attempted to get her mother to side with her against the school. Mrs. Miller's ten-

dency to get caught in triangular situations, to identify with this child and to act out through her, emerged clearly in her role of visiting parent. The caseworker intervened by giving information about the child's need for the limits and expectations imposed by the school and by clarifying the importance of the mother's support for the school's position. The mother's ability to alter her behavior was due in part to the worker's guidance and support and in part to the structure of the visits, which placed limited, manageable demands on her for impulse control. She gained some intellectual awareness of the tendency to become aligned with her daughter because of the similarity of their feelings and because of the unrealistic and self-defeating nature of the child's responses, as well as her own. Thus, she gained, indirectly, some self-awareness and increased safety in bringing her other interpersonal problems to the casework sessions for discussion.

2) The second child, after placement, expressed her longstanding feelings of rejection by rejecting the mother. In the family visits she withdrew and the withdrawal was no longer lost in the general diffusion of family living. It was clearly visible in the structured limits (time, space) of the visiting situation. The major goal in this relationship was to help the mother give responsively to this child, in relation to her needs as they were observed and interpreted by the caseworker. The achievement of this goal involved the need for greater awareness of her feelings about this child and increased awareness of the total pattern of family interaction.

3) In her relationship with her son, the physical seductiveness was not discussed directly; instead, this and the infantilization were approached educatively as she was helped to learn to treat him as a boy needs to be treated in relation to his age level. In this context, the physical cuddling was brought under control and it was possible to discuss the boy's need for an increasing degree of autonomy and self-reliance. As Mrs. Miller followed a few simple suggestions for encouraging his self-reliant activity during the visits, she and the caseworker related this, in her interviews, to the goal of adult masculine adequacy and her relationships with men.

While these major goals in the parent-child relationships were oriented to the needs of each child, they played a dynamic part in the mother's use of help in other areas. Her self-esteem increased and her self-destructiveness was diminished. With strong support from the caseworker she undertook necessary medical care and stabilized her living situation. She frequently tended to regress to compulsive talking about her childhood. When limited and encouraged to stay with the reality problems of the present, she made small, steady gains until her environmental problems were relatively stabilized, although her tendency to move from job to job continued to threaten her financial security. In this connection, it became apparent that she expected exploitation and rejection from men and acted out in ways that provoked the rejection. She was encouraged to stay on one job and use the experience to examine her part in the now well-defined problem with employers. As she worked on this with some degree of success, she entered into a new relationship with a man whom she eventually married. Throughout the courtship and after the marriage she used the casework sessions to help her work out the vicissitudes in this relationship.

Intermittently, the eldest girl pushed to return home. The relationship with this child was the most problematic for the mother, since they were strongly identified with each other and the pattern of acting out with and through each other was deeply entrenched (7). However, through the strong and productive relationship, the caseworker effectively helped the mother contain the need to meet the child's request. The mother ultimately was able to discuss with the girl her need for the kind of help she was getting in the school. The mother was aware of her inability to make a stable home for the children, as she could see from trial weekend visits that she could not manage her relationship with her husband and also a full-time maternal relationship with any of the children.

In a briefly highlighted fashion, the kind of help that is needed and can be used by certain of the parent-clients in the foster care agency has been pointed out. Without help, such a parent continues in a self-defeating pattern of living and moves the children in and out of foster care, with a resultant deterioration in the children's capacity to use their placement experience for growth.

CONCLUSION

In summary, the aims of the casework service to the parent are fourfold: (a) to gain his cooperation in creating an optimal climate for the child's use of foster care services; (b) to help him achieve a more satisfactory personal life; (c) to protect the children from removal from foster care under adverse, damaging circumstances; and (d) to assure the restoration of the family whenever this is advisable (8).

Restoration of the Nuclear Family

The conditions under which parents and children are reunited as a family require the same careful appraisal as the conditions under which they are separated. However, the conditions that determine the capacity of parent and child to reunite successfully often are less visible than those that bring about the separation. The attitudes of those who provide the service are often more complex at this stage in the service process, and may influence agency staff members in their approach to the issue of reuniting parent and child. The subjective attitudes of staff members that most commonly interfere with objective decision-making at this point arise from either over-eagerness to restore the child to the family (in order to reduce the long-term placement caseload, for financial or philosophical reasons, or to solve problems that arise in the placement) or from reluctance to consider reuniting the family (due to emotional investment in or over-identification with the child or the surrogate parents, and anxiety about the parent's capacities). Manifestly, either of these two attitudes interferes seriously with the diagnostic and helping process.

Self-awareness and correction of the subjective involvements are crucial to the caseworker's constructive participation in this stage of decision-making. When the caseworker achieves an open-minded, objective diagnostic approach to the issue, half the battle is won, but it is implicit in the dynamic nature of the foster care system that this attitude usually can be achieved most uniformly in a staff when the agency's philosophy promotes and supports it.

As discussed in Chapter II, the tentative assessment of potential outcome has its inception in the intake study process and goes hand in hand with the initial individual and family diagnosis and the type of plan made for the child. Just as the prediction of duration of foster care is tied to diagnosis of the parents' past and present capacities, the diagnosis of readiness to resume care of the children likewise is based on present functioning and its relationship to past functioning.

In voluntary and involuntary cases, the issue of reuniting the family may be initiated by either the parent or the agency. In some instances, the question has been an integral part of the collaborative process throughout the working alliance. In others, it is initiated at some point along the way, when either the agency or the parent is attempting to solve some problem, appropriately or inappropriately.

Regardless of the source or the motivation for the initiative, the primary question that needs to be explored has to do with parental capacity. Understanding motivation may help to illuminate the assessment of capacity, but motivation is not the main issue. This point is emphasized particularly because when the parent's motivation is thought to be unsound the question of capacity is sometimes disregarded, and conversely, when the parent is thought to be well motivated his capacity is insufficiently emphasized. The central question is: Will it work? The condition and capacities of the parents, the condition of the children, and the environmental opportunities are the three major factors that determine whether a satisfactory family stabilization can be achieved. The environmental opportunities may be modifiable by the use of agency and community resources if other factors are sufficiently favorable.

The Wilenski case, discussed in Chapter III, illustrates the situation of a mother who sought the restoration of the children under wholly unrealistic conditions. The mother was motivated by guilt and panic, but, more importantly, her mental illness combined with her life situation clearly indicated a lack of capacity to make a home for her children. The guilt and panic, as motivations, simply served to cloud her judgment regarding her capacity.

Had the mother achieved a better level of mental and emotional stability, the condition of the children would still be an important factor in her capacity to care for them successfully. Diane's extreme disturbance placed a heavier demand on the persons undertaking her care than could be absorbed by even the most mature and stable parent. Her care required a team of child care workers to share and distribute the burden of her extremely disturbed behavior. Parents may progress to a stage where they would be able to give adequate care to a child who does not introduce excessive emotional stress. The child's condition, as well as the parents' current capacity, determines the potential success of a reunification of the family.

In appraising the readiness of the parents to provide adequate care for the child who has been placed, the questions pertinent to the decision-making process are: What changes have taken place in the parents, the children, and the situation since the separation of the family? What is the evidence? What can be anticipated on the basis of this evidence? Such an evaluation can be structured around the following:

1) The current ego status of the parents, their adaptiveness and capacity to absorb and cope with stress, as differentiated from the conditions at the time of placement;

2) The child's condition;

3) The interpersonal relationships among the family members;

4) The current family organization and stabilization;

5) The environmental situation.

Another case illustrates these issues.

THE PORTER CASE

Jenny Porter, a twelve-year-old girl, became separated from her parents when they fled from a hotel because they were unable to pay their bill. In the chaos, Jenny had gone for help when the hotel owner chased her father. When she returned, the family was gone. She went to a restaurant, whose owners were known to her family, in the hope that they would meet her there. When they did not appear, the restaurant owner called the police to arrange for her care. She was placed by the juvenile court in a temporary care facility.

The following summarized history was obtained from Jenny over a period of several weeks:

Jenny's family, consisting of her parents, herself, and a younger sister and a younger brother, had been itinerant for several months, traveling across the country in the family car. Her father had left his post in an army camp in order to avoid arrest. They had arrived in the city about six months before the hotel episode. Her father had been in the service all of Jenny's life. Her mother was European, and the family lived abroad where her father was stationed until she was about five years old. Since that time they had lived on two different army posts in the U. S. She described her father as being about fifty-years-old, with grey hair and "handsome!" She knew nothing about his family. She described her mother as much younger than her father, around thirty-five, and pretty, with black hair and dark eyes. The mother spoke with an accent, as she knew little English before coming to this country. She had never worked; she stayed at home and looked after the family. She liked to sew and made most of Jenny's clothes. Initially Jenny told the probation officer that her parents drank a lot, fought, and cussed, but the family always had enough to eat. Later, however, she gave a more favorable picture to the foster care caseworker. Her parents fought only a few times; they were good to her; her father liked to take the children fishing and swimming and gave them anything they wanted unless he didn't have money.

Jenny had no recollection of her life abroad, except that she spoke no English when she came here. She had difficulty in the first grade because she had to learn English. She repeated the first grade after they moved. At home she had no household chores, but

her father paid her to stay with the younger children when the
parents went out evenings. She gave the impression that her father
was the dominant parent.

School reports obtained from Jenny's former place of residence
stated that she worked well in her classes, attended school regularly, and seemed to be well cared for. She was shy, but well liked
by teachers and classmates. No problems were noted.

The initial diagnostic study and subsequent observations of
Jenny confirmed the early impressions of a relatively healthy child
of average intelligence. She was in good physical health, related
well to adults, made good peer relationships, and seemed fond of
younger children. She was obedient and made great efforts to
please. She looked after her personal appearance and her room.
Her interests were in friends, school, clothes, and social activities.
She expressed no criticism or hostility toward her parents for desert-
ing her. She appeared to repress all negative feelings and to handle
them by extreme compliance. In the problem area, it was observed
that she was unable to recall the events directly preceding
and during the crisis of the family breakdown; she had a problem in learning mathematics; and she evidenced a tendency
to overstretch in studying and mastering her school work. However, she also enjoyed school and gained real satisfaction from
learning.

It was learned from the army that Jenny's father was wanted for
forging checks and for absence without leave from his army post.

From the history and the observations of Jenny's development,
the caseworker inferred that the family life had been relatively stable and had satisfied the child's major developmental needs. Jenny
was free from severe problems and related and functioned well.
The child's tales about parental drinking and fighting seemed to fit
into the circumstantial situation of their run-away, separation from
Jenny, and problems with the law, but this entire picture was inconsistent with the extensive evidence that the child had grown up
in a stable environment, in which she had experienced much pleasure in family life.

The caseworker made tentative inferences that the family breakdown had occurred under some special stress, and that the continued absence of the parents may have resulted from fear of going to the police to find Jenny, since the father was running away from arrest. On this basis, she anticipated that the family might be reunited, and this possibility was considered in the foster care planning. In the prediction of outcome, the absence of evidence of long-standing, severe, deeply entrenched family problems suggests the possibility of a favorable prognosis, even though the current situation of the family is characterized by many signs of severe breakdown.

Two years after Jenny's placement, her mother called the foster care agency. On the previous day she had learned of Jenny's whereabouts from the agents, who had finally located the family and arrested the father. A brief summary of information obtained from the mother in a series of interviews follows:

The family had been running away for more than two years. The father had been in the army for over nineteen years and had only three months left to serve in order to obtain his pension when he took the family and left in a panic over his financial difficulties. The mother described their life as going along smoothly until the trouble two years ago. They had financial problems when they moved to this army post. They had to live outside the post due to a long waiting list for military housing. They were unable to find a furnished apartment and had to rent a house and buy furniture. Moreover, the father had to purchase a car for transportation to the post. The father handled all the finances and rarely spent any money on himself, but liked to buy things for her and the children. He did not tell her how serious the financial problem was, although she knew something was wrong. He was expecting money from some property he owned and thought he would then be able to pay the bills, retire from the service, and get a well-paying job as a mechanic. Only when he took the family on a camping trip and decided not to return to the post did the mother learn that he was running away to avoid trouble over a forged check. In looking back, she thought she should have insisted on returning to their home at the time, but she felt helpless; she had no relatives in this country, no work experience, and didn't know what else to do. Now that she has been working since the father's recent illness, she finds that she is able to manage a job and the children and she feels more confident. She also felt that she should have participated in the financial affairs because she thinks they could have managed without getting into the problems that placed Mr. Porter under such heavy pressure.

The separation from Jenny occurred when they were trying to leave a hotel because they had no money to pay the bill. The hotel manager chased them, went after the father with a club, and Jenny ran for help. In the excitement and panic, the parents managed to get the family into the car and got away. When they saw that Jenny was missing, they drove around looking for her, then, at the mother's insistence, the father agreed to telephone the police. He returned, saying the juvenile police told him she was in custody and would be put in a home. The mother believed him, but she saw later that he had told her this because she was upset and crying. When months passed, he again assured her that he had called and that Jenny was all right, but he had done this because she was having nightmares and crying in her sleep.

After the separation, the father got jobs cooking in hotels and the mother got some books and tried to teach the children what they were missing in school. At times, when they had no money, they slept in the car, parking in different places. A year ago, the father became seriously ill and was hospitalized for three months. Part of this time the mother lived in a mission with the children, then decided she would get a job and move out as she hated the kind of people (alcoholics) who were around them. She immediately found work as a waitress in a first-class hotel dining room and moved into an apartment.

After his recovery, the father obtained a job at the same hotel as a chef. They worked alternate shifts, in this way supervising the children. When alone, the mother arranged for supervision of the children by a reliable neighbor in the building. The children were entered in school and the mother thought they were doing well, al-

though both were one grade behind as a result of their recent moves.

In relation to the father's arrest, the mother was resigned, saying they all knew it was only a matter of time. Mr. Porter probably was traced through his Social Security number.

Within two weeks after his arrest, the father again became acutely ill and was hospitalized for surgery, from which he made an adequate recovery. While he was in the hospital, the mother talked with the Army lawyer who looked into the father's situation and told her that the entire matter could be straightened out, that the father would have to repay the money for the forged check, pay a small fine, complete his three months' service in the army, and then would receive his pension. He had an excellent record with many commendations up to the time of the crisis.

Mrs. Porter was one of two sisters. She had been reared in a small town. She described a close relationship with her mother. She had a three-year apprenticeship as a seamstress after attending school until she was fourteen. Her father was strict; he reared the children to obey and respect adults, and she has done likewise. Her father died a year ago.

Her parents loved Jenny and spoiled her. In Europe, they had a happy life, had many friends, and enjoyed outdoor activities such as fishing, camping, and picnicing. Jenny had been a healthy, "good" baby. She had gone to nursery school at the age of three and adjusted well. Mrs. Porter thought that none of the children had ever presented any special problems. The younger children adored Jenny, who was a very good older sister to them.

From the outset, Mrs. Porter was eager to see Jenny and assumed that they would be reunited immediately. However, she was responsive to approaching this in a step-by-step fashion. A visit between her and Jenny and another with her and the children were planned.

Mr. Porter, in an interview in the hospital, gave substantially the same information as the mother and Jenny had given, but was able to supplement a great deal regarding the causes of the crisis in his career and family life.

Although puzzled and unable to explain his actions, Mr. Porter was aware of the circumstances that caused the mounting, intolerable pressure. He did not think it was the financial problem in itself, but rather the conditions of his work. For years he had been responsible for special services, in which he organized and supervised sports and recreational facilities. He had always been "his own boss" to a certain extent, and his work was highly regarded by his commanding officers. Suddenly, a supervisor was needed to train "young kids" in maintenance engineering. Since his record showed that he had this skill, he was transferred to this job. The boys were irresponsible, and often did their work poorly. Mr. Porter was "chewed out" by an officer when anything went wrong. In addition, he received word that he was being considered for a transfer to Germany during his last three months of duty. He couldn't face uprooting his family and going through all of the hardships of a transfer again. He thought it was unfair after his many years of duty overseas; the young fellows he supervised had never been overseas and some of them should have been sent instead. He still could not understand why he had acted as he did in response to these stresses. In retrospect he thought perhaps he should have seen a psychiatrist.

Mr. Porter's medical problems had necessitated repeated surgery, and he had been dangerously ill. Now, in the Veterans Hospital, he felt confident about his recovery. He had been in a great deal of pain at various times in the past several years, but did not give the details to the army physician and therefore did not have a thorough examination until he was taken to the hospital here for emergency care. He would continue to need regular medical care in the future.

Mr. Porter described his relationship with Jenny as a very close one. Because she was the eldest he had always felt closest to her, although he was also devoted to his two younger children. He was eager to see her, and had already received two letters from her. He had no question about reuniting his family, but felt that he should be out of the hospital before making plans. He had learned from his lawyer that he would probably have a "minor" court martial and would be allowed to complete his army service in the post near this area and obtain his pension. He did not want to move the family again.

The visits between Jenny and her family members supported the impressions of a cohesive family with substantial capacity on the part of the parents for meeting the needs of the children. In the individual visits Jenny communicated openly with her mother, but was self-contained and somewhat aloof in the family group visit. Her mother and siblings were eager for her interest and response. In none of her relationships did she directly express any feeling about the long separation and the family's failure to find her.

Analysis of the Porter family in the areas identified earlier illustrates their application to the available data.

Current Ego Status of the Parents

Mrs. Porter had responded to this experience with growth and increased capacity to cope with the family's problems. In the face of her husband's illness she had broken out of her passive compliant role, had obtained a job, found housing, established the children in school, and arranged for adequate supervision during her working hours. She was able to support the family on her income. She visited her husband regularly in the hospital and maintained an internal cohesion and continuity in the family, despite Jenny's absence and the father's hospitalization. She maintained her standards and values in the face of extreme external disorganization. Her increased adaptiveness included a gain in personal confidence and the capacity to look back on the crisis, evaluate some aspects of her part in it, and modify her behavior.

Mrs. Porter had not been able to cope with her own and Mr. Porter's fear of his arrest and whatever other deterrents entered into their failure to locate Jenny until after Mr. Porter's arrest. The immediacy of her action in seeking out the child following his arrest suggests that her passivity was directly connected with her relationship with Mr. Porter.

Mr. Porter's hospitalization at the time the parents became known to the agency made evaluation of his current ego status almost wholly speculative. Nevertheless, there were indications that, once the running-away was halted, he was again able to evaluate his situation and plan for the future fairly realistically. The absence of severe depression combined with the insight regarding the irrationality of his behavior suggests that he may be able to achieve his former functioning level and maintain it if his life circumstances do not again produce the specific kinds of stresses that he is unable to tolerate. By his own account, the responsibility for training young men, still adolescent in their development, created an untenable psychological situation. He connected this with his bitterness toward the commanding officers on two counts: their criticism of his work and their proposal to transfer him overseas. His vulnerability to the "irresponsible kids," may have been connected with some conflict over his own repressed adolescent impulses. This appeared to be the trigger that set off his anti-social solution to his other problems.

There was a likelihood that he would not again be placed in a similar psychologically untenable position. The army agreed to send him to a post near his family to complete his service. He had now expressed openly his inability to cope with the type of work to which he had been assigned. On the basis of his good record his wishes were respected. Upon leaving the army, his dependence on the structured life provided there might be compensated for in two ways: (a) He had tested his capacity to work in a private job during the past two years; (b) His wife had emerged from her passive, compliant role and the circumstances of his repeated hospitalizations had forced them into a more balanced sharing of responsibility for managing the finances and other aspects of family life. This changed equilibrium had worked out well for both of them. In brief, the acutely turbulent aspects of his adjustment to the transfer from army to civilian life seemed to have been experienced and to a degree mastered in the running-away experience.

Mr. Porter's precarious health might be expected to cause further complications, but Mrs. Porter had already demonstrated her capacity to cope with this in the dual roles of breadwinner and mother.

In summary, the adaptive capacities of both parents appeared to be sufficient to manage the reabsorption of the placed child into the family if the child's adjustment, the interpersonal meaning of the child in the life of the parents, and the environmental situation were such that they did not introduce excessive stress.

The Child's Condition

Jenny, as we have already observed, had no outstanding problems in any area. If her presence in the reunited family introduces serious stresses, they might arise from the specific nature of the interpersonal relationships and the dynamics of the family system.

The Interpersonal Relationships
and Family Dynamics

Both parents expressed love for their child directly and indirectly in many object-related ways. What, then, other than the obvious circumstantial reasons, made the parents unable to seek her out during the long separation? There is insufficient information to understand the underlying causes, and the coalescence of psychological and environmental conditions that brought this about. However, some available information provides a basis for speculation. The father's marked closeness to Jenny was noted by Jenny and both parents. One can do no more than raise a question about this. Was this father-daughter relationship threatening to the father, the daughter, or the passive compliant mother, who was unable to recognize or communicate her feelings? Jenny's pubescence and approaching adolescence cannot be ignored, as the adolescence of any child in any family is likely to introduce important changes in the family dynamics. How does this affect the evaluation of the potential success of replacement? It has only a secondary place in the decision-making. The child's observable adjustment and the parents' observable capacities are the primary issues. On the secondary level, the awareness of potential interpersonal stress and specific vulnerabilities to that stress enables the agency to work toward a replacement plan that includes the provision or referral for subsequent service if it is needed.

Little has been said about the two younger children and their place in the family. Observations were that they appeared healthy and were functioning well in school and at home. In the visits and interviews they seemed to receive their share of participation, but all of the family revolved around Jenny, eager for her attention and approval, which she gave. Mrs. Porter gave tacit and overt encouragement to this balance in the relationships.

Current Family Organization

The family organization and degree of stability have already been described in the context of parental ego functioning. The family life had been re-established and stabilized, with the children in school and receiving good care and the daily routines and interpersonal responses to the individual needs of all family members were adequate and apparently satisfying. This equilibrium was not new; it had been well entrenched for about one year.

The Environmental Situation

The environmental situation in relation to income, housing, school, medical care, and supervision of the children was adequate. The housing arrangement, however, provided only minimal space and would be insufficient if both Mr. Porter and Jenny returned home. This would necessitate resettling in new housing, with possible concomitant changes in school, job, and so on.

This environmental problem raised issues of timing. In this instance, the family, with help from the caseworker, postponed the child's return to the family for several months to allow her to complete her school semester and to allow the parents to determine whether a change of housing was needed. Had there been no environmental problem, the timing would have depended on the family's capacity to work out the transfer on a transitional basis, to provide an opportunity to integrate some aspects of the change. Some children and their parents are able to make active use of the help of the caseworker during a transitional period. Others are not. But often the family members are responsive to the agency's guidance in steps of the transition, if the reasons are valid and clearly identified.

PREVENTION OF FUTURE BREAKDOWN

Manifestly, the preponderance of evidence in this analysis was on the side of a favorable prognosis. Another secondary but important issue in working with the parents is the identification of family patterns that played a part in bringing on the previous crisis. It will be recalled that these parents did not communicate and share their troubles, and neither one sought outside help to solve a critical situation. In retrospect, it can be speculated that the entire sequence of events and their destructive consequences might have been prevented had there been better communication between the parents or had the father been able to seek outside help. Modification of this pattern is one of the caseworker's goals in the work with the parents.

The restored family is a vulnerable family. Educating the parents to use outside help is one of the significant goals in the process of helping the natural parents. The Porters had built-in independent problem-solving techniques that had served them well in marriage and child-rearing for years until a specific set of conditions brought a serious breakdown in family functioning. Other parents, with less capacity for independent problem-solving, likewise need to learn how to use and when to seek outside help. The educative process in this regard is both implicit and explicit. The learning process goes on as an intrinsic part of the replacement process. The caseworker's verbalization of the validity of seeking help as a mature approach to prevention of crises reinforces what the parent may learn only partially from experience.

REFERENCES

1. *Webster's Third New International Dictionary*, G. and C. Merriam Company, Springfield, Massachusetts, 1967.
2. Draza Kline, "Service to the Parents of Placed Children: Some Changing Problems and Goals," *Changing Needs and Practices in Child Welfare*, Child Welfare League of America, Inc., New York, 1960.

3. Carel B. Germain, "Social Study: Past and Future," *Social Casework,* Vol. XLIX, No. 7, 1968. This is an illuminating discussion of the need and current trend to broaden conceptions of casework.
4. Frances Scherz, "Intake: Concept and Process," *The Intake Process: Six Papers on Intake Procedures and Short Term Treatment,* Family Service Association of America, New York.
5. Helen Merrell Lynd, *On Shame and the Search for Identity,* Science Editions (Inc.), New York, 1961, p. 22.
6. *Ibid.,* p. 27.
7. For discussion of these acting-out mechanisms, see Ner Littner, M.D., "The Caseworker's Self Observation and The Child's Interpersonal Defenses," Smith College Studies in Social Work, Vol. XXXIX, No. 2.
8. Kline, "Service to the Parents of Placed Children. . . ."

CHAPTER V

THE FOSTER FAMILY

Common Components in Foster Family Care

Who are foster parents? What is their job? What is the nature of their relationship with the foster child? The child's natural parents? The agency? What are the components of the working relationship between agency and foster parents as it derives from agency purposes and goals?

The answers to these questions, self-evident as they may appear at first glance, do not yield readily to unified formulation. This fact is abundantly documented by the failure of foster care specialists to reach agreement on the answers through several decades of debate. Some of the disagreements arise from the fact that experts within social work and from other disciplines view the questions from quite different angles, depending on their philosophical orientations to foster family care services and their explicit segments of experience. The experiences vary in relation to different types of clientele, different geographical areas, and differences in the functions of the agencies.

Foster parents, likewise, do not fall into homogeneous classification. They reflect the subcultures of the geographic areas and communities in which they live; they differ in their psychological, educational, social, and economic characteristics and their motivations and foster parenting capacities; in the type of care and kind of child they wish and are able to handle; in the kind of agency they seek; and in the help they want, need, and are able to use in carrying out their roles as surrogate parents.

The foster child clientele, too, shows a range of social, cultural, and psychological characteristics and service needs. It includes children of all races and of different subcultures. It includes emotionally deprived and psychologically damaged children, those handicapped innately or by educational and cultural deprivation. It includes children from broken homes, in which minimally stable family life has never been present; children whose parents are incapable of planning for them and for whom adoption is not feasible; children who have been abandoned, whose parents may or may not return to play some role in their future lives; children whose parents cling to an ongoing relationship, living on the unrealistic fantasy that they will some day re-establish a home; children whose parents have capacity and motivation to re-establish a home and who, some day, may have the opportunity to do so. It includes children who are removed from the care and custody of their parents by court action before their referral to the foster care agency, some of whom are transferred for service to a community far removed from the location of the family residence. And it includes children served in the immediate community of the family residence, whose parents are accessible to child and agency. In the course of their experience, few, if any, practitioners see a cross section of this clientele and the differing needs.

The wide variations within agencies, among foster parents, and in the clientele group suggest that the establishment of a uniform concept of the components of a foster family care service can be made only in the broadest possible terms, within which many individual variations reflect the philosophy, functions, and resources of each agency and the clientele that it serves. This problem of diversity will be approached here through discussion of three factors which are common to foster family care and which are systematically related to each other, despite variations in agency philosophy, clientele, community, or type of care. These three factors determine the unique nature of the role of foster parents and their relationship to the agency.

AGENCY RESPONSIBILITY AND
SUPERVISORY FUNCTION

The nature of the agency's responsibility for a placed child's welfare is a primary factor in determining the role and functions of foster parents and some of the components in their relationship with the agency. The agency's defined function, professional commitments, and legal obligations combine to make the agency responsible and accountable for the child's welfare for as long as he remains in placement under agency care. The agency cannot delegate its primary responsibility; it can and does utilize the foster parents as an instrument for discharging certain aspects of that responsibility. Hence, regardless of interest, investment, and parenting abilities, as long as he is not the legal parent the foster parent remains responsible to the administrative agency that represents the legal parent or the state. Consequently, the agency must exercise a supervisory function as one component in its arrangements with foster parents (1, 2).

Within this frame of reference the degree of autonomy of foster parents may vary considerably from agency to agency and case to case, depending on the type of care the foster parents have undertaken, the agency's assessment of their parental abilities, the role of the natural parents, and certain agency policies. Likewise, the modalities and techniques used by the agency for implementing the supervisory function may vary. These differences ramify into the entire stucture of services and the decision-making processes.

SHARED RESPONSIBILITY FOR THE CHILD

The structure and process of the supervisory function are influenced by the shared responsibility for the child. This responsibility is distributed among agency, foster parents, and those natural parents who retain residual legal rights and continue to participate in a relationship with the child. The powers and duties vested in the agency, either by voluntary agreement with the parents or by judicial action, include the selection and evaluation of the facility in which the child lives; assurance of continuity of care; provision for retaining the child's connections with his past life and for his ongoing relationship with his nuclear family; the initiation, authorization, and evaluation of such auxiliary services as special medical, psychiatric, or educational services; and, should it be indicated, determination of the need for change in the child's placement. Among the legal rights retained by the natural parents or legal guardian (court) are those related to consents for major surgery, traveling outside the state, military service, or marriage while the child is a minor (3).

It is manifest, then, that although they undertake the child's direct care and are vested with decision-making authority regarding the child's daily living, the foster parents usually cannot be empowered to make independent major decisions that have far-reaching effects on the child's life. However, the foster parents' emotional investment in the child and the child's reciprocal relationship with the invested adults (the key to the benefit the child derives from foster family life) require a satisfying degree of participation by the foster parents in the decision-making process. Neither the child nor the foster parents can accept, emotionally, decisions or plans that are made without significant participation by the foster parents if an important parenting relationship has been developed (4). The art of utilizing the shared responsibility for the child's benefit is at the heart of effective foster care service. A major prerequisite is a satisfying working relationship between the foster parents and the agency's representives (caseworkers and others) within which open communication, sharing, and participation are part of a continuous process.

USE OF THE FOSTER FAMILY MILIEU
ON BEHALF OF THE CHILD

The third significant factor common to all foster family care, and a major determinant in the unique role of foster parents, is the use of the family milieu on behalf of the child. Surrogate parenting, in the milieu of the family, is distinguished from other types of occupational services to children by virtue of the fact that it involves the entire family system and its dynamic equilibrium. Regardless of the type of care undertaken by the foster parents, whether temporary, long-term or permanent, salaried or otherwise, the entire family and the family life are brought into the relationship with the child and into the range of dynamic transaction with the agency, influencing and influenced by the foster child, his family, and the agency's services. Even in the temporary care of infants, the baby becomes a part of the dynamic interaction of the nuclear family life, affecting in some way the environment of each individual in the family and the interpersonal relationships in each interacting unit in the family.

The presence of the foster child also ramifies into the extended family relationships (especially grandparents), and the family's social and community relationships. The foster parents' relationships to the child and the agency, which differ in these respects from those of other occupational typologies, impose on the agency a helping responsibility not only in the interest of the placed child but also on behalf of the foster family, whose welfare, affected by the presence of the foster child, directly affects the welfare of the foster child.

Role Definition and Relationship
with the Agency

PRIMARY AND SECONDARY ROLES

The role of foster parents has been a subject of debate for decades and the persistence of the debate suggests the inherent complexity of the subject. Professional publications note confusion and ambiguity among foster parents, foster children, natural parents, and caseworkers concerning the powers, duties, and responsibilities of each of the individuals in the foster care system, the foster parents' relationship with the agency, and the nature of the helping process. Kadushin called attention to the problem by reporting "There is no clear-cut definition of the foster parents' relationship with the agency so that they are sometimes regarded as clients, sometimes as colleagues, sometimes as paid employees" (5).

However, there is a danger of overstating the problem. The complexity of the role of the foster parent, and reciprocally the roles of other individuals in the foster care system, is not unlike that of individuals in other service structures in which a system of interpersonal relationships is the medium for producing the service. In any such system the collaborating individuals function in both primary and secondary roles which may overlap with each other, shift temporarily, or proceed simultaneously. Accordingly, a foster parent may be, simultaneously, a foster parent, an agency employee, and, at some points, temporarily, a client. There is substantial evidence that role confusion is neither inevitable nor unalterable, but rather that role clarity and role confusion in the foster care system are evidences of a dynamic interplay of inner and outer processes that call for analysis and understanding.

Role clarity has its inception in the agency. When the agency is unclear, inconsistent, or vague in its philosophy, program of services, policies, and role definitions, it is literally impossible for the caseworker to perceive and define the reciprocal roles in the foster care system. Under these conditions, any existing inner needs in the foster parents or in the caseworker which may be an added source of role confusion cannot be identified because the reality of agency confusion hides the contributing causes. Conversely, when the agency provides clear and consistent programs and policies, there is relatively little role confusion. When it occurs its source can be identified and appropriate measures for meeting the problems can be taken. Agencies may differ from each other in their philosophy and approach to foster care services, but internal coherence is an essential prerequisite to a coherent foster family care service in which the reciprocal roles of foster parent, caseworker, and natural parent are worked out at an effective level.

In the view of the authors, the foster parents' primary role is that of surrogate parents to a child, within their own family setting, under the supervision of an agency that is responsible and accountable for the child's care. Secondarily, the foster parent may be an agency employee, and, at times he may shift temporarily to the client role. He may occupy both or neither of these secondary roles, but if he does, it is for the purpose of enabling him to discharge his primary role as foster parent.

FOSTER PARENT AS AGENCY EMPLOYEE

In a study conducted by one of the authors (6) in which all of the foster mothers in an experimental program were employed as agency staff members, interviews with the foster mothers showed that without exception they thought of themselves, their motivations, and goals primarily in terms of their foster parenting role. They viewed their employee status, the salary, individual supervision, and group training program as the means by which they could achieve their goals as long-term foster parents to the children placed in their homes. There were two prominent factors in their perception of the primary role. First, the agency conceived and defined the roles in this way and communicated its expectations to applicants in the process of recruitment, screening, and study. Second, the agency accepted only those applicants whose primary motivation was the foster parenting one. The employee role was an enabling rather than a primary role, by agency definition, and, reciprocally, by the foster parents' perception.

MISCONCEPTIONS OF FOSTER PARENT
AS CLIENT

The misconceptions of foster parents as clients arise in part from the observed therapeutic needs and some of the mixed motivations of foster parents. Many foster parents need and use therapeutically oriented help from the caseworker in the course of meeting the problems of family life and of foster parenting. The skilled caseworker provides enabling help which is therapeutic in effect, as a matter of course, when it is needed. However, for the qualified foster parent, neither his nor the agency's central purpose and expectations are consistent with the client role as a primary one. In exceptional situations, the foster parent and the caseworker may arrange a temporary shift to a defined treatment focus in relation to a specific problem that interferes seriously with the foster-parenting function. This, however, should be a temporary, enabling procedure, mutually defined. When it is not so defined and understood, both the foster parent and the caseworker are in a muddle of confusion. (The therapeutic component in the helping process will be discussed separately in this chapter.)

FACTORS IN ROLE CLARITY

In three widely diverse agencies known to or studied by the authors, salient factors in role clarity, and positive, effective working relationships, included these:

1) Each agency attempted to base the placement decision on an adequate family diagnosis and made a projected plan in relation to the expected duration of care.

2) Each was clear about the services it offered to the children, the natural families, and the foster parents.

3) Consequently, each usually was able to define the agency's expectations and respective roles of the foster parents, parents, and agency staff.

4) The foster parents were selected primarily for their interest in and apparent capacity to fill the requirements for foster parenthood.

5) Casework staff members, in the main, were provided with the time and resources to give the frequency and continuity of service needed by the foster parents and to carry out the functions inherent in the caseworker's role.

6) All three agencies viewed the foster-parenting role as primary, although they freely provided therapeutically oriented help as needed. One agency uniformly paid fees for service; another paid fees only in unusual situations; and one, already discussed, employed the foster parents as staff members (7).

Role confusion in the foster parents was limited to a small percentage, in which the source of role conflict could be clearly related to internal problems of the foster parents or the caseworker, or lack of experience of one or both.

To understand foster parents' role conflict in relation to the agency, one must look first at the reciprocal motives and expectations of each. The agency seeks foster parents in order to achieve two major objectives for the child who can use family care, as distinguished from group care. The first objective is to provide individualized, close, substitute parental relationships for the child as the matrix for ego growth and superego development and as a model for family living. The second is to provide a family environment in which the child can learn social skills and techniques for living as a member of a community. To meet the agency's expectations, foster parents need an opportunity not only to integrate this experience emotionally, but also to learn new skills that embrace a synthesis between the normal family environment and the special conditions of surrogate parenting in a system of relationships that include shared responsibility with agency and natural parents. This is, in part, a learning process for foster parents, caseworker, natural parents, and child. Each has a stake in the success of the learning process.

The motives and expectations of the foster parents are somewhat more complex than those of the agency. The stated motives of foster parents usually include religious or social motivations in connection with the wish to enlarge the family. The underlying motivations are usually multiple and are not manifest. In any event, in becoming foster parents they make two deliberate choices.

First, they choose foster care rather than adoption or enlargement of the natural family as the means of expressing their wish for more children.

Second, they choose to carry out this wish under the auspices of an agency in preference to private or independent foster care.

Since independent foster care is available in most communities, it may be assumed that most applicants, initially, are attracted to agency foster care because they see in it some advantage which promises to outweigh the disadvantages. Beyond the initial application, one of the major purposes of the screening and study processes is to inform the applicants fully about the respective roles and functions of foster parents, natural parents, and agency, the agency's specific expectations and the policies and procedures that govern its services. One of the purposes of sharing this information is to engage the applicants in a realistic assessment of their wish and capacity to enter into this type of relationship. If the study process has been carried out adequately, when the applicants decide to proceed, we may assume that they are making an informed choice.

The choice meets the foster parents' needs in some ways that are conscious and some that are unconscious. Regardless of the specific motivations, they have in common a need to share, in some way, the duties and responsibilities of parenting with an institution that represents a reliable authority. They may hope that the agency's expertness in child care will shed light on problems with their own children, or they may need emotional support in their child-rearing efforts that extend beyond the biological family, or some other special support or response. This choice, as in all human action, reflects a confluence of different motives and impulses, both conscious and unconscious, some of which are in harmony with each other and some of which are in conflict. Consequently, many foster parents participate in this experience, with some hopes and expectations of which they are not fully aware. The outcome is that in the process of providing the service one may find that some of the areas in which foster parents wish to have autonomy coincide with the agency's role definition and some do not. Some of their reactions to situations arising in the course of their experience are realistic and some are not. No degree of clarity of role definition communicated verbally and by the caseworker's actions can obviate this. Only the caseworker's understanding of the foster parents as individuals provides the key to approaching the resolution of problems that arise.

Such conflict does not mean, necessarily, that the foster parents have not been fully informed, or that they are unsuited to the foster-parenting tasks, or are improperly motivated. It means simply that, as human beings engaged in a complex set of collaborative relationships, their internal needs may not coincide with the demands of the external situation and casework help toward accommodation, adjustment, and modification is an inherent part of the foster parent-agency relationship.

The caseworker, too, may react to the service or to particular individuals in the service system with role confusion. Either the caseworker or the foster parents may displace to the issue of role confusion, feelings, attitudes, and expectations that belong elsewhere. To illustrate: (a) The caseworker who has left-over childhood anxiety about school teachers may fail to visit the new school on behalf of a foster child who has special educational needs, rationalizing that this is one of the duties of the new foster mother, without specific clarification with the foster mother regarding either the agency's policy or the foster mother's wishes. (b) A foster parent who is greatly threatened by the child's relationship with his natural parents may make independent plans for a child's vacation without regard for the parental visiting plan or consultation with the caseworker, displacing the conflict to the area of role confusion. (c) The caseworker and the foster parents may be mutually competitive for the child's favor and may displace the competition to the area of role confusion.

In brief, the problem of role confusion is not inherent in the foster parent role as such; it derives either from confusion within the agency, from internal problems of the caseworker or of the foster parent which interfere with role functioning, or some combination of these. It is an inherent part of the supervisor's function to help the caseworker with feelings that interfere with coherent role interpretation and implementation and it is a part of the caseworker's function to utilize his professional skills to help the foster parent resolve the problems that cause resistance to appropriate role implementation. When the caseworker and the foster parent are clear about their reciprocal roles, any confusion of the child and the parent can be dealt with in accordance with its true meaning.

Major Psychological Tasks of Foster Parenting

Surrogate parenting involves learning, adaptation, and change for the foster parents and the other family members. The foster parents' psychological tasks embrace a relationship with the child, his natural or surrogate family, and the caseworker. Concomitantly, the changes that take place in equilibrium in the foster family relationships in response to the arrival of a newcomer require special efforts on the part of the parents to re-establish an equilibrium in which some shift in relationships takes place.

The type of foster care undertaken by the family influences the nature of the psychological tasks of the foster parents and the family's responses. The demands made by the temporary care of infants are different from those made by the temporary care of older children, and those made by children in extended care differ from temporary care tasks. For example, the newborn infant in temporary care has had no psychologically important previous mothering experience. The developmental stage to which the mother and other family members must respond is limited to the early stage of infancy and the type of care required by infants. The experience of repeatedly receiving the infants and separating from them become the major factors that influence family equilibrium.

Discussion of the major psychological tasks of foster parenting will focus on those that characterize extended foster parenting, which encompasses the responses to the child's successive maturational states, rather than temporary care, since the latter can be explicated from the more comprehensive approach.

Although only the tasks of mothering will be discussed in detail, it is implicit that some aspects overlap with the fathering role. Also, it will be noted that the degree of separation anxiety in the foster parents strongly influences the foster mother's freedom to use her mothering capacities fully, and that the agency's activity is inseparable from the issue of decreasing or increasing this anxiety, which is a normal accompaniment to foster parenting.

THE MOTHERING RELATIONSHIP
WITH THE CHILD

The psychological tasks that confront the foster mother are in some ways similar to those experienced in natural parenthood, but they are different from them in significant ways. They are influenced by the child's previous experience with one or more other mothers; by the child's age and stage of development when he enters the foster family; by the agency's outlook or expectation regarding the length of his stay in the foster family; by his ongoing relationship with his natural family; and by the needs, hopes, and expectations of the foster family in undertaking foster care.

Despite these important differences, the chief psychological tasks in all mothering correspond with the developmental stages of the child (8). Most foster parents, experienced in rearing their own children, have already learned something about their core capacities as parents and the stages of child development with which they are comfortable and those that they find exceptionally troublesome. Even though the mother may respond better to some developmental stages than to others, she struggles to empathize with the child through each successive stage of growth and to help him throughout his growing-up years.

Clinical studies and observations of child development have shown that the mother's deep identification and unity with the child are essential to his growth. Experts agree that this tie is inherent in motherliness (9). The child's innate need to become increasingly independent and ultimately to break the tie presents the mother with the central psychological task in her mothering role. Deutsch stated the conflict this way: "Woman's two greatest tasks as a mother are to shape her unity with the child in a harmonious manner and later to dissolve it harmoniously" (10). For foster children, regardless of age, ego development depends on the achievement of this unity with the child-caring adult, just as it does for other children. But the tasks of the foster mother are complicated by the psychological issues involved in the past separation experiences and what is anticipated for the future.

In the first year of the baby's life, the healthy mother intuitively establishes the physical unity essential to the infant's earliest developmental stage. She provides for his physical needs and bodily care, and gradually modifies her closeness to the child in response to his maturational changes. In about the second year of the child's life the mother's task is to train him in instinct control, without being either too permissive or too restrictive. Few mothers achieve this fine balance, but they strive to understand what is best for the child in making the transition away from the physical unity to the psychological empathy which characterizes the demands of the subsequent developmental stages. At this stage, however, the child is rebellious, destructive, and messy. This is a difficult stage because much of what is pleasurable for the child is disgusting to the adult. It is a rare mother who does not experience at least some degree of annoyance and frustration during this period, under the best of circumstances. But this period, though difficult for the parents, is of crucial importance in the child's future growth. This period of development includes learning impulse control, the early stages of individual autonomy, and fitting into some of the demands of family life (society, in the later stages). The foster child at any age may need help to develop the trust essential to the strengthening of impulse control and to the successive steps in autonomy and self-reliance, since the placement experience has a tendency to induce regression.

The mother moves on with the child through the developmental years, helping him move beyond the exclusive relationship with her to mastering and enjoying his separate individual relationships with the father, other children in the family, and playmates. She helps him face the separation attendant upon his entrance into school. If his earlier development has proceeded well, he accomplishes this task with relative ease when the mother's healthy, realistic anticipation of it as a desirable experience for the child predominates over the innate wish to hold onto the closer tie. For the child, the innate striving for growth is reflected in stronger efforts toward independence at each stage of development. Sometimes the entrance into school is marked by persistent anxiety, seen in prolonged overt resistance or symptom development. For the foster child this anxiety may result from experiences that interfered with his prior development in a different mothering relationship, and the foster parents are faced with the task of correcting the earlier experience.

At adolescence, the normal rebellion and the struggle for emancipation and for the reintegration of ego identity may be acutely exacerbated for the foster child, who has an added burden of solving his problems of identity and emancipation as they are influenced by the earlier separation conflicts. The rebellion of a foster child may present acute stress in the family relationships, as the bonds may seem more tenuous than those of the biological family members.

The foster mother, like the biological mother, when entering into a relationship that can grow into a close mutual bond, knows that the purpose is to help the child move through the stages of childhood toward ever-increasing independence and ultimate emancipation, even though deep within her she does not want to lose the close relationship of childhood. For the foster mother the knowledge that the full separation may occur before the foster child grows up is an important psychological issue.

THE FATHERING RELATIONSHIP (11)

The inherent psychological tasks of the foster father are less intense than those of the mother; nevertheless, the foster father is called upon to share the direct and indirect demands brought by the introduction of the foster child in the family. His key role in providing emotional support, empathy, and direct help to the mother in the child-rearing functions is not unlike his role as natural father. The quality of his direct relationship with the foster child, too, is of great importance. His representation of the expectations, standards, and reality of the outside world often is a new and vital experience for the foster child, who in many cases has had little opportunity for a relationship with an adult male who is, psychologically, the head of the household, the provider, and the representative of the adult world outside the home. In the home, the foster father may be called upon to play a critical role in helping the child relate to the mother or in helping him overcome his fear of himself as the father, if the child, from previous experience, has learned to trust one parent more than the other.

Like the foster mother, but usually in more attenuated form, he must cope, psychologically, with the specific developmental stages of the foster child and reawakening of the vestiges of those stages which remain in his own make-up, as they do with all adults.

The demands for expanded ego functioning on the part of both parents reach into all areas of family life. All members of the family must give up something of the parents' attention. What they lose and what they gain become a part of the intricate dynamics of family and individual growth.

THE MOBILIZATION OF
SEPARATION ANXIETY

The issue of separation anxiety is inseparable from a discussion of the psychological tasks of the foster parents. Foremost, the agency's practices and procedures exert a substantial influence on ameliorating or exacerbating the anxiety about separation that is inherent in foster care. Vague generalizations, evasions, or indirection in regard to duration of placement heighten the conflict for the foster parents and concomitantly for the child. Both need knowledgeable assurance from the agency regarding the outlook for their future time together. However, the question regarding the length of stay often contains unknowns, and the question might well be raised, "What kind of valid assurance can be given?" Any kind of assurance rests on clarity and consistency in agency policy and an ongoing diagnostic assessment regarding the probable outlook of the duration of care. Any vagueness that contributes to the foster parents' anxiety is not only transmitted to the child, but also interferes in the use of the foster mother's capacity to develop and maintain the appropriate degree of psychological unity with the child.

It should be noted in this connection that cautioning the foster parents to limit their emotional investment in order to protect the child on the grounds that he may some day return to his natural parents (or be transferred to an adoptive home) at best serves only to allay some anxiety in the caseworker; at worst, it serves to keep foster parents and child in a state of ambivalence and anticipatory anxiety that defeats the very purposes of foster family care. Conversely, concrete, specific information about the natural parents, their whereabouts, condition, and prospects, and the actual participation they maintain in their relationship with the placed child carry a realistic message with which the child and foster parents can come to grips and which provides a legitimate and necessary focus for casework management and discussion.

The case of Tom and Barbara Dean (cited in Chapter III) is a case in point. It will be recalled that Mrs. Dean, a chronically unstable, mentally ill mother, requested placement of the two children for a year. This request was manifestly unrealistic. With help, she was able to correct what she told the children. Subsequently, the children and the foster parents were given measured assurance that they would be together for a long, indefinite period of time. It was understood and agreed by all concerned that if and when any change was expected, everyone would talk this over well in advance; meanwhile, everyone could settle down, knowing that there would be no serious discussion of change until the mother's total life situation was greatly changed, regardless of her impulsive expressions of her wishes which could be expected to recur from time to time. Subsequently, over a period of five years, Mrs. Dean intermittently told the children and the foster parents that she hoped to take the children home within a year. Knowledge of the mother's unstable situation and her precarious adjustment enabled the caseworker to handle the impulsive promises realistically with the mother, children, and foster parents, allaying the anxiety that was aroused. Gradually, each of them gained understanding of the mother's problem and no longer took her statements at face value. The caseworker's activity was the critical element in establishing and maintaining this equilibrium.

Intense separation anxiety can be mobilized in the foster parents not only by parental activity or misdirected casework activity, but also by any separation from an important person. For example, the loss of a caseworker can set off a chain reaction in the foster care system. The foster parents, in addition to feeling the loss, may feel threatened by the potential effects of the change in regard to continuity of the child's care, approval of the new caseworker, and effective management of problems that have been difficult, such as Mrs. Dean's impulsiveness. The natural parent, likewise reacting to the loss of the caseworker, but with less capacity to cope with loss, sometimes acts out the separation reaction by reaching out for

closer contact with or restoration of the children, when the parent
is actually in need of comforting and in no condition to provide a
home. The inexperienced caseworker entering such a case may also
be anxious and unsure in his work with the impulsive parent.
Thus, the caseworker may unwittingly transmit the anxiety back to
the foster parents and the child, keeping the family in a state of
disequilibrium. The essential safeguard against the contagion of
separation anxiety when there is a change of caseworkers is continuity in casework supervision, geared to insuring the new caseworker an adequate understanding of each of the individuals in
the foster care system. The case record, too, can be a vital instrument for insuring consistency and continuity of case management if
it is utilized for this purpose by the agency and individual staff
members.

REACTIONS TO SPECIFIC PROBLEMS
IN THE FOSTER CHILD

Foster parents' reactions to specific problems in the foster child,
as differentiated from the general problems common to the foster
parent role, introduce another factor in the adaptive tasks. The
term "matching" has often been used in reference to the selection
of foster parents whose make-up, temperament, and interests seem
appropriate to meet the needs of a particular child (12). The
agency tries to avoid bringing together a child and foster parents
who have identifiable vulnerability to each other's problems. Such
vulnerability may occur in any area. For example, some foster parents overreact to lying or stealing. Others are acutely anxious
about sexual problems. Some are unable to accept learning problems, etc.

Despite the best efforts of an agency, some mismatching is inevitable. Even the most comprehensive in-depth studies do not always
reveal the presence of a potentially troublesome conflict in the foster parents or latent problems in the foster child. In long-term
foster care a specific problem may emerge long after the child has
become well integrated into the foster family, in reaction to a particular developmental stage or as an expression of an earlier, quies-

cent conflict which is reactivated by some maturational or environmental change. In many instances, however, the intense reactions of foster parents can be modified through the helping process.

An example will illustrate the vulnerability of foster parents to a specific problem and the responsive casework intervention.

A twelve-year-old boy who had lived with a foster family for six years had experienced many serious medical and emotional problems. He had reacted to his mother's death and to his father's desertion with depression, defiance, and destructiveness. He developed poliomyelitis and sustained severe residual damage in the muscles of one leg, which required repeated surgery as he grew older. His school performance suffered and his peer relationships in school and at home were increasingly tense, marked by periods of withdrawal, jealousy, and anger. The foster parents, with help from the caseworker, were able to provide an environment that was well adapted to his needs. They were sensitive and wise in helping him with his reactions to the physical and emotional stress. They welcomed and supported direct casework help for the child in connection with these traumatic events.

When, at the age of twelve he was reported to have molested a five-year-old girl, they reacted with a total inability to tolerate or discuss the problem. Despite their long and genuine investment in the child, they felt that he must leave the family and the community. A physician in the local community, greatly agitated by the incident and without knowing the details, threatened to take legal action against the boy if the family did not "get rid of him." The foster parents' specific vulnerability was located in two areas: the sexual acting-out and the community tension and disapproval. They could not tolerate becoming the object of community criticism in regard to a problem which they, too, abhorred. When such a crisis arises, the caseworker's intervention must be both swift and sufficiently comprehensive to reduce acute reactions in all the interacting participants. In this instance, intervention was needed on three fronts: with the foster parents, with the physician who spearheaded the community agitation, and with the child.

Investigation of the incident revealed that in the so-called molestation the two children had looked at each other's genitals.

The disparity in their ages was the trigger for the intense reaction of the adults.

With agreement of the foster parents, the caseworker reopened direct work with the child and assumed responsibility for working with the physician who had insisted on the boy's removal from the community. Thus, the pressure on the foster family was diverted to the agency. The physician agreed to allow the agency time to secure a current psychiatric evaluation, and the foster parents concurred. This measure secured time, which is an essential factor in the cooling of crisis reactions, and in the establishment of an atmosphere in which the problems can be discussed.

The foster parents, relieved of environmental pressure, were able to discuss some aspects of their anxiety. How could they explain this to their own children? Was this a potentially dangerous symptom? The child had been a part of their family for six years; why did this happen? Who was at fault? As they discussed the immediate concerns, they gradually became somewhat desensitized and moved further into examining the anxieties they had experienced in connection with the sexual development of their own children. They did not discuss their own sexual conflicts, nor did the caseworker attempt to explore beyond their expressed concerns and anxieties. These parents, like many others, were able to establish a new equilibrium by learning from an experience that was painful and by using the educative, supportive help of the caseworker to tolerate the crisis and resolve it in favor of growth rather than retreat.

Although intense vulnerability to sexual acting-out arises from repressed, internal conflicts, repressive attitudes (until recently) have been a traditional part of middle-class culture, and internal conflicts are tacitly reinforced by community attitudes. Consequently, when a child's behavior touches off an acute reaction to this or other types of problems that have strong community import, the caseworker's activity and attitudes may be a critical factor in modifying and diluting the parents' feelings. The educative approach within an empathic relationship is especially valuable because it operates at two levels of communication: (a) The foster parents gain intellectual understanding of a subject that has been clouded with taboos or social disapproval and can see the child's behavior in the context of normal curiosity and experimentation, or as deviating in ways that can be understood. (b) Indirectly, and to some extent below the level of awareness, they may gain some acceptance of their own childhood impulses and temptations and consequently feel more at ease within themselves and less vulnerable to these specific problems of the children.

Foster parents' reactions that are amenable to casework help may vary in degree, from mild reactions to those of crisis proportions which require the use of emergency intervention measures. In some instances, the internal conflict is such that the parent cannot gain any significant tolerance for the specific problem to which he is vulnerable. In these instances, the casework approaches fail.

RELATIONSHIP TO THE CHILD'S NATURAL FAMILY

The major task of the foster parents in relation to the child's natural family is not only located in the direct interpersonal relationship with them, but also in understanding and managing their own feelings about the natural parents and their reactions to the child's feelings about his parents and siblings. The child's feelings about his parents are likely to be an ambivalent mixture of longing, rage, shame, and guilt, but they often are hidden. If the foster parent is to achieve empathy with the foster child, one of his tasks is to be in rapport with these feelings and to open the doors of communication, freeing the child to talk about his family when he feels so inclined. This task is not an easy one because the child must first learn that his foster parents accept the multiple relationships and do not take sides with either his positive or his negative feelings. Such understanding rarely comes spontaneously from intuition. The psychological conflict in the child usually requires intellectual understanding on the part of foster parents in addition to emotional capacity for acceptance. It is one of the educative functions of the caseworker to explain the nature of the child's mixed feelings about his parents. The usefulness of intellectual awareness is dependent, in part, on emotional capacity for rapport with this specific experience. Like other psychological tasks of foster parenting, it is an integrative task that involves emotional growth and learning. Capacity to understand and accept the child's needs in this respect may then be realized through the combined educative process with the caseworker and the experiential process with the child. This is not to say that this task is readily mastered or mastered with finality. Negative feelings about the natural parents re-emerge from time to time when foster parents feel free enough with the caseworker to communicate openly. Opportunity for ventilation, acceptance of these feelings, and refocusing on the child's long-range developmental needs is important in the on-going helping process.

The next aspect of the foster parents' involvement with the child's family takes place in the child's reactions to direct contacts with his family members. The foster parents easily may misapprehend the child's reactions, since in many cases they tend to take some defensive form. Some children react to visits with symptomatic behavior: they withdraw, stay in their rooms, refuse to eat dinner with the family, sulk silently before the television set while the other children play games in the yard, and the like. They may announce that they hate their parents and never want to see them again, or conversely, that they are going home tomorrow to live with their parents. They may state solemnly and defiantly, "You can't tell me what to do; you're not my mother." How can a foster parent respond to this? One of his learning tasks is to use his feelings, his experience, and his judgment in a disciplined way. He needs to learn to see these episodes for what they really are: a part of the inherent, painful struggle of the child to cope with his ambivalent feelings about his parents, a struggle that helps free him to accept and reciprocate the love of his foster parents.

The third aspect of involvement with the child's natural parents is the direct, interpersonal contact involved in the visiting arrangements. The dimensions of the psychological task which direct contact presents to the foster parents are largely determined by the agency's management of the family visits. Traditionally, all parents have been expected to visit their children in their foster homes. This practice reflected in part a legalistic attitude regarding parents' rights and responsibilities and in part a tendency to ignore psychological realities. Agencies and courts have expected foster parents to provide for visiting arrangements, regardless of the severity of the disturbed and disrupting behavior of the parents, or the child's reactions to visits, or the foster parents' preferences and capacities to deal with the problems. Often foster parents, unable to manage the impact of the disturbed parent-child relationships, have requested removal of the child, or the agency and the natural parent agree to transfer the child to another foster home in the hope that other foster parents will do better. In some agencies this practice gradually has given way to supervised visits in agency offices in situations that appear to present complex problems that upset the child or threaten the stability of the foster home. In many agencies, however, parent–child visiting in the foster home remains a common practice without regard to the suitability of the arrangement. It is doubtful that it can be carried through successfully in more than a small minority of cases; often it is disastrous.

Ordinarily, the psychological tasks created by parent-child visits in the foster home are within manageable limits for the foster parent when: (a) The conditions requiring placement and the defined goals are acceptable to the parent and to the foster parent; (b) The purposes of visiting are clearly defined and understood; (c) A mutually acceptable visiting structure is established and maintained. The establishment and maintenance of these conditions require the active participation of the caseworker at the outset and throughout the duration of the arrangement.

It is self-evident that the agency's management of visiting arrangements determines the magnitude of the psychological tasks demanded from the foster parents and the kind of help needed from the caseworker.

RELATIONSHIP WITH THE AGENCY
AND CASEWORKER

Just as the foster child and the parents have specific emotional responses to the agency and its representatives, as a symbolic parental authority, so do foster parents. Basic in this are the universal struggle between dependence and independence and the conflict inherent in competitive strivings and their sublimation in learning. The reasonably mature adult strives to function self-reliantly within an interdependent society and at the same time to use help realistically, to share responsibility appropriately, and to shift from major to minor roles, and vice versa, as needed in collaborative work. The structure of many life situations, in the family, the community, and the job, requires some collaborative efforts and interlocking roles. The degree of success varies greatly within and among individuals. Some are almost totally unable to achieve a psychological equilibrium in collaborative relationships. Such a situation represents an insurmountable problem for caseworkers engaged in foster care services and for parents who undertake foster parenthood. Fortunately, most individuals who are qualified for these tasks in other areas are sufficiently mature to learn to make the necessary accommodations and find gratification in collaboration. However, some degree of vulnerability to threats of competition or to personal autonomy and self-dependence is present in most individuals. The threat may be mobilized by the very nature of the collaborative structure or by some evidences of competitiveness in one or both collaborators.

The foster mother who depreciates the young, inexperienced caseworker may be defending her own fortress of adequacy, threatened by the very fact of the caseworker's youth and the authority vested in him by the agency. Likewise, the foster mother who shuts out the participation of the caseworker is likely to be protecting her own sense of adequacy and self-reliance. These are over-determined defenses, but they are not necessarily incompatible with adequate foster parenting. In most instances, resistance decreases as the foster parent develops a relationship with the caseworker which is appropriately supportive and noncompetitive. In exceptional instances, the resistance must be brought into the open for mutual understanding in order to achieve an effective working relationship.

The ideal goal, of course, for any collaborator (foster parent, caseworker, or others), is to experience a growth process that eventuates in the gratification that can be derived from mutual efforts toward mutual goals. This is not a static equilibrium but rather a changing one in response to changing elements in the interpersonal relationships with caseworker and child and influenced by other concurrent experiences. Growth in this area, as in others, is not necessarily on a consistent upward curve. Reverses occur in reaction to specific types of stress, such as change of caseworker, loss of a close relative or friend, or some specific threatening behavior by the foster child, own children, spouse, or others.

Negative feelings, subtly or indirectly communicated to the caseworker, may originate in the problems of the child, the natural parents, or the demands of the agency, and they may be displaced into the working relationship between foster parent and caseworker. One of the emotional demands on the foster parent is to learn to work out the relationships with the agency and the caseworker and to find an equilibrium consistent with his own personality and character structure. This task, like the others discussed earlier, can be impeded or facilitated by the caseworker's attitudes and activity and the agency's policies and procedures.

Evaluating Foster Parent Qualifications: the Concept of Emotional Maturity

In evaluating applicants for foster parenthood, the agency is looking for positive parenting capacities in relation to this specific undertaking, as differentiated from qualifications for other types of job activities. The major emphasis is on identifying the qualities and conditions necessary to meet the essential needs of agency-placed children and the problems that would seriously interfere with the use of the positive capacities.

Foster parents, like other people, differ from each other psychologically, educationally, and socioeconomically. They differ in their motivations, parenting capacities, adaptive flexibility, capacity to accept the foster child's status and original family relationships, their responses to and expectations from the foster child and the agency, and so on. Since there is great variation in the personalities and situations of qualified prospective foster parents, it is necessary to establish some flexible guidelines within which to evaluate and gauge the potential success of foster parent applicants.

In seeking foster parents, the agency is hoping to provide a workable, growth-producing environment for a child within the constellation of the family. There is no single road to this end. The ideal situation for any child is a family in which he can realize his optimal potentials. In the community at large this goal is sometimes achieved for children in family life, but more often there are many variations and levels of family life short of optimal conditions which provide a sufficiently good environment to promote physical and emotional maturational processes.

One then approaches the question: Is there or can there be any single set of criteria for foster parent qualifications? Specific physical standards and certain social requirements can be, and have been, designated by state licensing agencies. These are concrete, obvious, necessary, and readily identified. They typically cover such matters as adequate housing, sanitation, accessibility to educational and medical facilities, moral character, certain health standards, and the like. Beyond these readily definable qualities, how can one approach the issue of intangible qualifications and avoid the pitfalls of either unrealistically high expectations or the acceptance of applicants who do not have minimal qualifications for successful foster parenthood? Certainly, a set of criteria cannot be substituted for the expert diagnostic judgment developed by a well-trained, experienced practitioner; nor can such judgments be contained within the limits of static criteria. In the final analysis the evaluation of the capacity of applicants for the tasks of foster parenting rests on the knowledgeable weighing of interrelated factors in individual and family dynamics. But the interviewer does need some systematic concepts of individual and family dynamics as a frame of reference within which these operational judgments are made.

Emotional maturity is often cited as the broadest general requirement for sufficiently good parenting for any child. Although maturity is a relative state of character organization, it offers an approach for consideration of the applicants' potentialities. Within the concept of emotional maturity, three areas have been found useful in evaluating capacity for foster parenting. These are: (a) the capacity for giving and receiving; (b) adaptibility, reality testing, and learning; and (c) ego identity and ego integrity.

GIVING AND RECEIVING

The issue of giving and receiving in relation to maturity is an important one in foster parenthood. Since the foster child is not a biological member of the family and cannot have the same meaning to the parents as their biological children, the reaching out for foster parenthood has motives different in some respects from those of biological parenthood. It has long been recognized that applicants seek foster parenthood at a time when they feel some need which is not satisfied by their current family inter-relationships. Charlotte Towle suggested that the internal motivation "often arises out of some unmet need to give and to receive" (13). This unmet need may reflect, in part, a strong self-concept as parents, free energy to reach beyond the boundaries of the biological family in a giving relationship to children in a biological line different from their own, and belief in a value system that includes sharing and giving to the full extent of one's capacity. This level of maturity can be observed in many foster parents, even though other felt deficits, problems, or internal conflicts in their lives contribute to their motivation. At the opposite end of the maturity scale, the motivation may be primarily an expression of narcissistically oriented needs, which leave the applicants with a sense of emptiness in which the need to receive heavily outweighs the giving capacities characteristic of maturity.

Franz Alexander's concept of the mature person describes an essential balance between giving and receiving which is pertinent to foster parenting: "The mature person is no longer primarily a receiver. He receives but he also gives. His giving is not *primarily subordinated* (emphasis ours) to his expectation of return. It is giving for its own sake." Lest this definition of maturity be taken as an absolute, Alexander warned,

The platonic ideal of maturity in a pure and complete form is never found in nature and is only approached by human beings to a greater or lesser degree. Every adult carries in himself certain emotional remnants of childhood. . . . It must be realized that there is a proportion between receiving and giving which has limits for each individual and which cannot be transgressed without ill results (14).

For the placed child, the capacity of the foster parents to subordinate their "expectation of return" to "giving for its own sake" is of the utmost importance. It is this capacity that sustains the foster parents through long periods in which the child may be unable to respond overtly to their care. If one faces the fact that the care of most foster children cannot possibly be primarily gratifying, one then can face realistically the requirement that the foster parents must have achieved a level of maturity and a life situation in which they have energy free for giving without a dominating need to receive direct gratification from the child's response. One then must also give attention to Alexander's warning that the individual's limits for giving without sufficient receiving to balance the scales for his own individual equilibrium "cannot be transgressed without ill results." This means that the agency must assess both the applicants' capacities to give and the potential sources from which he receives gratification. It is in recognition of the potency of the latter factor that some agencies purposefully provide gratifications through the relationship with the caseworker or through a planned agency program designed for foster parents, and by so doing tip the scales in the direction of enabling the foster parents to stay with the job through periods of excessive drain on their energies (15).

Indications of the parents' level of maturity in giving and receiving can be drawn from many sources of the foster home study. In general, in talking about themselves, their children, marriage, work, and various facets in the "giving-receiving" equilibrium, the emotional awareness of the individuality and needs of other family members, as differentiated from their own wishes and needs, is one of the early clues to the predominant pattern (16).

Exploration of the parental experience with their own children at critical developmental stages yields many evidences or indicators of the emotional balance in the giving-receiving equilibrium of the parents. The mother's capacity to help the child in his steps toward independence, for example, is reflected in her handling of his first school experience, which brings a new level of separation for both mother and child.

The father's level of maturity in the parenting role is reflected in his participation in promotion of the developmental tasks of the children, emotional support of his wife, and his capacity to gain gratification from work. The latter is considered by Benedek and others as a key factor in the father's parental maturity. The presence of the capacity to work, however, does not insure parenting capacity, since there are motivations and gratifications in work other than those of achieving aims for the benefit of the family. But, given the opportunity to work, if the father is insufficiently motivated by the wish to take care of his family and unable to gain gratification from this, during the normal work years, something has gone wrong in the parenting aspect of the maturational process. The father is then unlikely to be able to enjoy his family or to give the support to his wife and the guidance and affection to the children which they need.

Applicants whose verbalizations or behavior in relation to the children are predominantly self-oriented are unlikely to have sufficient free energy to give the interest, affection, and care necessary to cope with the needs of a foster child, since such self-absorption reflects some emotional conflict or maturational problem that interferes with adaptive living. At the opposite pole, those who, in words or actions, exclude their own needs from consideration are unlikely to possess the resilience and recoverability necessary to cope with crises or prolonged stress. Extremes of giving too much or giving too little are apt to be equally defeating in the long run. Such extremes usually are not difficult to identify; like all extremes, they tend to stand out rather starkly.

Giving too much can be viewed from the standpoint of both giver and receiver. For the parent to give too much from the point of view of his own ego (except in situations that realistically demand temporary overstretching, such as in an acute family illness), reflects some lack of self-knowledge regarding his own ego span and the danger that he will be prematurely worn out. When he gives too much from the point of view of the recipient's welfare, it

suggests that the giving is in some degree emotionally over-determined as occurs in intransigent over-protection and infantilization.
The diagnostic question has to do with the degree and extent of
these problems and their modifiability. Does the parent respond
adaptively to reinforcement of reality-testing which is introduced
by helpers, such as spouse, teachers, caseworker, or others? The
parent who can use help at this level to modify or control the
over-protective impulse manifestly does not have a serious problem
in either his capacity for object relationship or his adaptability.

The issue of giving and receiving in relation to the agency is an
important dynamic in agency-supervised foster care. The applicant's wish or need for something from the agency as an adjunct to
the placement of the foster child has already been discussed. This,
too, can be viewed in terms of maturity. The sought-after relationship with the agency may reflect a predominant wish to give and a
secondary wish to receive. These wishes are illustrated by the applicant who welcomes the sharing, helping relationship, commonly
expressed by foster parents who say, "We want to do it; we feel
that with your help we can do it." The applicant who comes to the
agency with a predominating need to be given to is likely to reveal
his need in unrealistic dependency, excessive demands, or in other
ways that reflect heavily weighted self-preoccupation.

ADAPTABILITY, REALITY TESTING,
AND LEARNING

In evaluating emotional maturity for foster parenthood, a base
line must be established regarding the applicant's perception of
reality, his adaptability, and his use of experience for learning.
One considers the ability of the applicants to appraise themselves
and their situation realistically as well as their environment. One
asks: Is the applicant's behavior adaptive or is it unrealistic? Is it
predominantly responsive to reality as it is today, or is it primarily
controlled by inner compulsions? Are the stresses of living met by
growth in problem-solving techniques or by entrenched regressive
patterns?

Tensions are normal to family life; stress and crises occur in all families in response to environmental conditions, interpersonal relationships, health problems, and the like. With sufficient adaptive capacity, the adults in a family solve most problems in a manner that does not seriously interfere with the growth-producing environment and solve some problems in ways that contribute, directly or indirectly, to the positive growth of the children. At the other end of the scale, a consistent pattern of running away from problems by withdrawal, interruption of communication, or giving up activity designed to solve the problems creates barriers to growth which may be insurmountable. The gross indicator of adaptability is found in evidences of learning and growth in response to stressful experience.

In making an assessment of these ego functions, there are two aspects of study that go on simultaneously and act as a check against each other. These are: (a) the study content; (b) the applicants' responses to the study process.

The life history, even when it is brief, usually reveals some stresses or crises that the applicants have experienced, and the characteristic patterns of response can be explored. The adaptive person sees most problems fairly realistically and evaluates them in reasonable proportion to their true importance. Retrospectively, the growth process contributes to the ability to look back upon an experience and see it in more realistic perspective than was available at the time of the experience. The ability to do this derives in part from the process of learning from experience. One of the common examples is the young adult who makes a bad marriage. A second bad marriage suggests some inner compulsion to repeat nonadaptive, unrealistic behavior. A second marriage that is a good marriage, reflecting essential qualities of emotional maturity in both partners, suggests the capacity to learn from experience and a pattern of growth in adaptability.

Another example that comes frequently to attention in the foster home study is the applicant who recalls intense feelings of rebellion against his own parents, acknowledges the feeling of criticism of the parents, but, in adulthood has come to view his own part in those struggles with some objectivity and acceptance of both his own earlier problems in growing up and the realistic difficulties he presented to the parents. Usually this maturation is accompanied by healthy emancipation from the dependent relationship either in the direction of the development of warmth and affection in an adult relationship with the parents or some degree of acceptance or tolerance for their own and their parents' differences.

The adult who continues to carry with him, unmodified, the pervasive, intense, bitter feelings of childhood hurt or anger toward his parents has not been able to use his subsequent relationship experiences for growth. Such feelings would be likely to interfere with his own parenting capacities in the foster care relationships.

The pattern of response to the foster home study is a parallel area of observation which is especially pertinent to the degree of adaptability necessary in foster parents and serves as a check against the findings of the history. Can the applicants make a reasonable adaptation to working with each other and with the agency staff in areas that need to be explored in the study process? This relates to some of the most obvious aspects of the study, such as the management of appointments, the concrete information needed, the use of references, and the like. It relates also to the quality of communication. On the practical level, making and keeping appointments, working out suitable arrangements for privacy and submitting a written application—all become important in assessing the applicants' adaptiveness in relation to agency supervised foster-parenting. In respect to communication one sometimes finds that the applicants have company each time the caseworker visits (by appointment); or bring a parent or friend to the interviews; or the husband refuses to arrange an interview, wanting to leave the entire matter in the hands of his wife; or the applicants talk compulsively, thus effectively shutting out the opportunity for genuine communication.

Any study activity that is handled in a way that seriously interferes with the study process and its requirements suggests that the adaptivity of the applicants does not include the capacity for a realistic assessment of foster parenthood, of their own needs and wishes, and the expectations of the agency. The behavior represents defenses that are nonadaptive in this situation. When the actions are not too gross and pervasive, they may simply be clues to the necessity to look further to try to determine whether there is enough flexibility in adaptive behavior to meet the tasks of foster parenting.

The freedom to learn from experience and from others plays an important part in the development of foster parents just as in development in other life roles. Applicants who have had no experience as foster parents cannot fully comprehend what is involved. In order to make an informed decision about the undertaking, they must be able to learn from the caseworker, in the successive stages of the study, enough to enable them to consider the new information and reconcile it with their prior conceptions and fantasies of foster parenthood. Some of what is communicated may be denied, blocked out, or simply not integrated, but heavily weighted denial suggests lack of sufficient freedom to learn. As applicants become aware of the discrepancy between their preconceptions and the new information introduced by the caseworker, they may go through a period of indecision while they work out and integrate the new information with their personal wishes and needs. This process may well be an indicator of adaptation and realistic assessment rather than resistance.

EGO INTEGRITY AND EGO IDENTITY

The parent who has achieved a level of emotional maturity that enables him to subordinate receiving to giving for its own sake, in the parental role, and responds adaptively to his own needs and to his environment is likely to possess a relatively healthy sexual and social identity and a consistent value system within which the foster child can find security. However, specific attention to this aspect of maturity augments the observations and helps establish a more reliable picture of the personality organization. Under the pressure of rapid changes in social values and expectations, any parent may find himself floundering in uncertainty about his life style and values and expectations in certain areas of conduct. The distinction between serious problems in ego integrity and uncertain parental attitudes and values that result from either a mild internal conflict or the lack of firm cultural support in the community mores is an important one.

Erikson's concepts of ego identity and ego integrity (17) help illuminate the meaning of emotional maturity in its application to the important qualities of foster parenthood. The essential qualities of mature ego identity include continuity and stability in patterns of reaction and a consistent, confident self-concept. These qualities are of great importance to the foster child whose own self-concept is likely to be poorly developed as a result of insufficiently good care or to have been damaged by the drastic environmental changes in his life. For an opportunity to correct the damage and promote the beginnings of a consistent, confident self-concept, the child needs to be able to rely on a predictable approach to life experiences and interpersonal relationships by the foster parents.

Well-developed ego identity in adulthood is reflected in a relatively consistent value system. An adaptive ego calls for flexible adjustment to one's own needs and the environment, but ego integrity maintains the adaptivity within limits that do not violate the core value system. Serious problems in identity and integrity show themselves most readily in a general pattern (as distinct from isolated incidents) of inconsistency or of contradictions between expressed beliefs and overt actions, regardless of how the specific situations are rationalized. The inconsistencies and contradictions are primarily below conscious awareness. Sometimes these contradictions are made apparent by the vociferous protest against disapproved behavior while it is simultaneously or subsequently permitted or encouraged in subtle or indirect ways. For example, the school child knows with unerring intuition when his teacher is self-assured, confident, and unequivocal in her values and in her expectations in regard to his performance and behavior. If he is able to react realistically, he responds to her attitude with the security he experiences in a reliable environment. When the teacher's own lack of integrity is reflected in an atmosphere of uncertainty and vacillation, the child reacts equally directly, feeling the danger from both his own impulses and the unpredictable responses of the teacher. This anxiety, in turn, interferes with learning. His need for ego integrity in adults is the counterpart of the threat of his own unformed or precarious inner controls and self-concept.

The teacher is used here as an illustration because the dynamic interplay is clearly visible in the structured setting of the school. The child reacts to the foster parents just as he does to the teacher in this respect, but the foster parents play the primary role in his development, which takes place within the more intimate, more intense dynamics of the family system.

The prospective foster parent who is persistently unsure of his own value system and subject to vacillation about his major expectations from children in relation to these values leaves the child in a morass of uncertainty, unable to rely on the integrity of adult expectations and consequently unable to develop an internalized sense of values in relation to himself and others.

One of the most frequent examples of parental uncertainty arises in connection with setting essential limits. In the parents' reports, and in their responses to help in the form of reinforcement, one finds the clues to the differential diagnosis. Does the problem about setting limits arise from a serious problem in ego integrity? Or is it the expression of a mild internal conflict? Is it the result of the buffeting of rapidly changing or conflicting standards and modes of behavior within the wider community? Or is it the influence of some misguided or misunderstood psychological guidance derived from child-rearing specialists?

As noted earlier, when the problem arises from serious problems in ego integrity, one is likely to see grave discrepancies between what the parent verbalizes and what he does, and vacillation in regard to whether he believes and means what he says. A case in point is that of a mother who reported that the twelve-year-old foster son refused to abide by the family's curfew. He stayed out late in the evening, wandered around, refused to tell the parents where he was going, and often came home late. He was admonished and then disciplined, to no avail. The foster parents felt helpless. They reported that he did as he pleased; that he defied them; and since he was too old and too big to be restrained physically there was nothing they could do. Their remonstrance and disciplinary measures seemed only to increase his hostility and rebellion and drove him further from them. Consequently, they vacillated about holding to the limits but were extremely angry and agitated about his behavior. The caseworker's efforts to help them hold to reasonable limits were met with resistance. The foster father presented a series of responses to prove that nothing they could do would be effective and they would then be in the position of losing their authority altogether because the boy was able to defy them with impunity and would know that he had the upper hand. Actually, although the parents verbalized disapproval, they tacitly allowed the behavior. This negative response to help is an important diagnostic clue to an underlying lack of personal security and a problem in ego integrity that interferes seriously in the parenting role.

The same situation, in almost exact duplicate, is reported by parents who respond healthily. They say that they don't know what they should do about controls because the other boys in the neighborhood have more flexible hours. How can they explain to the child why he is not allowed to do what others do? It becomes clear that their concern does not arise from internal inconsistency about their own position, but rather from the conflict in neighborhood standards. For example, a teacher reported the situation of a father who said, "I don't always know how to explain my position so that it makes sense to the boys when they tell me that other children are allowed to do these things." The teacher advised him that he didn't always have to be able to explain all of his reasons, since he was thoughtful and was doing what he thought was right and was best for them. Even though they rebelled at times, they relied on him to be consistent. Later, he reported that when the parents learned to accept the verbal protests without undue concern, they observed over a period of time that their children, despite the rebelliousness, knew what was expected and at times even seemed proud of "our family and the way we do things." The ready accessibility to support reflects a relatively healthy state of ego integrity. When mild conflicts are present, the parents require more help, but may be responsive to approaches that are well within the caseworker's helping function.

There is, of course, that group of parents who have full confidence in their own value system, reject values that conflict with their own, and struggle along finding ways to cope with the inevitable child-rearing problems. They have a strong sense of who they are and what they believe. Some find flexible ways of meeting and resolving child-rearing problems; others are relatively inflexible. In either case they do not vacillate uncertainly and they cannot be pushed, pressured, blackmailed, or wheedled into departing from important expectations that reflect their standards and values. Those who are inflexible may strike other adults as rigid and dogmatic—qualities sometimes distasteful to, and deplored by, other adults, and, especially by members of the helping professions. But observation of the reactions of children suggests that forceful belief in one's values gives children sureness and security within which they can incorporate values and learn social skills and standards and it gives them something manifest to rebel against when rebellion is developmentally healthy.

The testing of the value system of surrogate parents by children in foster families and group facilities is a widely recognized phenomenon. Early in placement, or at times of change within the child or in the family, the surrogate parents almost daily may be presented with rebellion, negativism, defiance, and various ingenious efforts to "get away with" forbidden, unacceptable, or even some mild kinds of self-punitive behavior. It is as though the child is saying: How far will you let me go? What can I rely on? How much do you care about me? Foster parents may be less confident in their responses than they would be with their own children, because the foster child is not their own. Consequently, even the least vulnerable foster parent may need help in understanding this behavior and may need guidance and support in responding to it (18).

This phenomenon presents a focus for discussion in the study process which enables the applicants to examine the problem and provides an added opportunity for the caseworker's exploration and observation of patterns of ego integrity.

THE APPLICATION OF THE CONCEPT
OF EMOTIONAL MATURITY

The concept of emotional maturity in the parental role as a developmental state of organization implies continued growth beyond the adolescent organization and throughout life (19). In examining the evidences for a continuing maturational process in the mothering and fathering roles, one is not looking for evidences of perfection or uniform maturity. One is looking for maturity as a dominant theme in personality organization. There are many inherent struggles in family life, in individual development, and in social and work adaptations. In reaction to these struggles there are times of family conflict, regressions, breakdowns in communication and interpersonal stress. But in assessing these problems, the caseworker tries to determine what predominates in the parenting roles and family dynamics. Couples with sufficient emotional maturity for foster parenting reflect a predominant sense of confidence about themselves in their major life roles, a stable sense of values, free energy to give affection and care for the welfare of others, some degree of acceptance of their own needs and capacities, and a realistic perception of the demands of their external environment.

Two foster home studies will be presented to demonstrate and make more graphic the practical applications of the components of maturity that have been discussed. These highly summarized studies illustrate contrasting evidences of maturity and immaturity.

THE WILSON FAMILY: IDENTIFYING
INFORMATION AND FAMILY SITUATION

Mr. and Mrs. Wilson, a young couple in their early thirties, applied for a foster child because, they said, they were aware of the community need. They have been married for eight years and have one child, Mary Lou, aged four. They hope to have more children of their own when they can afford it. They are both college graduates with successful teaching experience. Mrs. Wilson stopped working before the birth of their child. They are intelligent and sophisticated in their intellectual understanding of deprived children and of child development and they are interested in community problems. They present a picture of mutuality of interests, devotion to their daughter, and social attitudes free from bigotry or prejudice. They are respected in their community and in their work relationships.

After telephoning the agency to make the application, Mrs. Wilson could not arrange to come to the agency office for an interview; she said she was unable to get a sitter and asked that the caseworker come to her home. In the initial interview it was learned that the family had purchased a new home and was preparing to move to a new community, but wanted to begin the study. Mrs. Wilson thought they would be settled in about two months and would then be ready to take a foster child. Although they hoped to have a son some day, they wanted a girl at this time because Mr. Wilson was presently carrying two jobs and would not have the necessary time to devote to a boy. They gave these additional reasons for interest in a foster child: 1) Mrs. Wilson now has time to take on more responsibility, but does not want to go back to work. 2) She thought it would be a stimulating experience to work with an agency; her husband agreed that the experience would be good for her.

The Wilsons expressed interest in emotionally disturbed children and evidenced unusual understanding of psychological problems. However, they said they knew it would be difficult for a foster child to accept the amount of attention they felt they needed to give their little girl. The Wilsons thought they could accept a child with family ties and were understanding about the problems of parents who were unable to provide family life for their children. They tended to feel empathy with the withdrawn child in contrast to aggressive children. Mrs. Wilson emphasized that they loved their pets and a child in their home would have to be kind to animals.

Mary Lou

Mary Lou, aged four, is a precocious, attractive little girl. She seems well developed and is in good health. She demands a good

deal of her parents' attention and they are indulgent with her.
They report that her development has been normal. They think
perhaps they spoil her, letting her do pretty much as she wishes.
Although she seems willful, she is responsive to her parents'
wishes. She is with her mother most of the time, as Mrs. Wilson
does not go out very much; she prefers to have friends come to
their home. Mrs. Wilson thinks that a child this age needs to be
with her mother rather than in nursery school. She anticipates that
Mary Lou may have some trouble at first when she goes to school,
because she doesn't like to be separated from her mother but the
mother thinks this will work out in time.

Mrs. Wilson's Background

Mrs. Wilson is attractive and well-groomed. The home is mod-
estly furnished with a "lived-in" look. Mrs. Wilson said she liked
homemaking, and wanted the house to be orderly but that she was
not bothered by the messiness of children or the family pets.

Mrs. Wilson was the eldest of three siblings. She said that she
had a stable, happy childhood. Both her parents were employed in
factory work all through her childhood, at low wages. Her sister
and brother did not have the educational advantages that she had.
They both went to work in factories when they completed high
school. She thinks she was always her parents' favorite, which was
hard on her sister. Her parents thought she was bright and attractive and seemed proud of her, downgrading the sister, who
couldn't seem to please them. The family members now have a
friendly relationship, but are not close. She has noticed that her
parents pay more attention to her child than to the other grandchildren when they are all together.

Mrs. Wilson, although stating that she had a happy childhood,
told of a great many moves and of pressure on her mother to keep
up the home and work outside to supplement the meager income.
Her mother was an excellent housekeeper and cook, gave parties
for the children, and was active in the church. Mrs. Wilson said
she would never be able to do all that her mother did. In high
school she enjoyed the social life and academic work. Her teachers
found her interesting because she had a high I.Q. They encouraged

her to go to college and helped her get a scholarship, although her parents questioned her wish to go to college. They did not see how she could manage it financially. In fact, she didn't enjoy college, as she had high school, because she had to work part-time to supplement her scholarship. As a result she was tired all the time.

After six weeks, the caseworker made the following observations:

The study has not yet been completed because the family moved earlier than originally planned. Although the parents seem to be united, intelligent, and sensitive about children's feelings, there are some problems. The Wilsons are concerned about their new neighborhood. They did not look into this before they bought their home, assuming that it would be all right because the houses and grounds were neat and attractive. They are now worried because there is a delinquent teen-age gang in the area.

Mrs. Wilson often appears tired, but this may be related to the move.

Although the study is incomplete, it is puzzling to know how to select a child for placement in this family. Mrs. Wilson has focused increasingly on a teen-age girl, as if this would solve the problem about reactions their daughter might have and Mrs. Wilson would enjoy the companionship of a teen-ager in the evenings when her husband works.

Subsequently, this study was completed and a teen-age girl was placed in the home. The decision to use this family was based on the many strengths seen in the fully study, especially in regard to the foster mother's talent in working with teen-age girls as a high school advisor, the foster father's support of her activities and willingness to participate when he was needed, and strong recommendations from references regarding their individual and family stability and motivation for work with social problems. The agency's evaluation, however, took into consideration certain recognized problems that had to do with the disequilibrium that might occur with the placement of a teen-ager. Therefore, supportive services such as regular casework service for foster mother and adolescent, as well as recreational and educational services, were planned and carried out from the onset of placement. Nevertheless, the placement was fraught with serious problems and ultimately failed.

Retrospectively, the authors looked at the early interviews to try to determine whether there was substantive evidence of insufficient maturity for foster-parenting.

EVALUATION

The initiation of the application for a foster child at the time the couple was preparing to move probably was the first potential clue to a problem. The unsettling nature of a move, for all family members, is so well known that mature applicants ordinarily postpone their application until they are settled and stabilized in their home and community. The agency, under the pressure of need for foster homes, began the study, hoping that there were compensating strengths.

Mrs. Wilson's inability to go to the agency's office for an interview was another clue. Parents usually are either able to find someone to attend a child in their absence or take the child with them. Mrs. Wilson's inability to handle this suggests some maladaptive problem, possibly in relation to the ego demands of the study process, transportation phobia, or inability to separate from the child.

Next, there are discrepancies between the expressed interest in and understanding of emotional problems and the stated requirements that the foster child must be able to accept the amount of attention they felt they should give their child, must be kind to animals, and, must provide companionship for Mrs. Wilson in her husband's absence. The discrepancies not only suggest some degree of unrealistic expectations but further lead into questions of capacity for object relatedness and for giving. Mrs. Wilson's chief emphasis, despite unusual intellectual understanding of children's needs, was not on the child's needs but rather on the family's needs.

There are other supporting evidences of insufficient capacity for reality testing and adaptiveness. Mrs. Wilson's fatigue, although perhaps realistic under the circumstances, tends to corroborate the unrealistic timing of the application. It is reminiscent of her problem in college in connection with inability to assess her own strength and consequent over-exertion that caused excessive chronic fatigue. Also, the parents' assumption that the foster father's activity would be less important for a girl than a boy is not consistent with their intellectual knowledge of child development and the needs of girls or teen-agers for paternal investment. The foster mother's need for active support from the foster father was not given realistic appraisal by them. The couple's failure to investigate the community before buying a new home was not consistent with their presumed intellectual and professional level of sophistication and their experience in relation to such problems. This leads to the inference that some emotional problems interfered with adequate reality testing.

Further corroboration of insufficient maturity in capacity for giving and receiving is Mrs. Wilson's major emphasis on herself. In her discussions of her child, her family members, her teachers, and a prospective foster child, her chief focus was on their interest in or reaction to her. Even in discussing Mary Lou, she talked about her need to be free to do everything she wished for the child rather than what Mary Lou needed from her. This may seem to be an overly subtle distinction, but in this study it was a clue to a larger pattern of narcissistically oriented adaptation. No identity problems crystallized in these early interviews.

Well-educated, socially liberal, psychologically sophisticated applicants, who seem to have a stable marriage and home life, often appear superficially to be ideal potential foster parents. The presence of a predominant narcissistic adjustment is easily lost in this array of socially desirable qualities. Such applicants are usually well qualified for other types of work, but may not possess sufficient maturity in the specific areas required for foster parenting.

A brief contrasting study follows. The assessment of maturity in these applicants is self-evident, in part because the study was recorded with the issues of adaptivity, capacity for giving and receiving, and ego integrity as the implicit focal points for the study process.

THE AVERY FAMILY

Mr. and Mrs. Avery are a black couple in their early fifties. They have four grown children, who range in age from seventeen to twenty-five. Only the youngest, their seventeen-year-old daughter, is now at home. Of the three boys, one is in the armed forces and two are married and have children. The Averys feel fortunate that their sons married "well." They have good wives and the Averys think they are good parents. Both sons have steady employment handling freight.

The parents became interested in foster care recently when they learned through their church about the acute need for foster homes for black children. They felt that they had been fortunate in having a healthy family and economic security; they loved children, and wanted to share their eight-room home and their love with children who need them.

Mr. and Mrs. Avery had grown up in the South and both their parents were sharecroppers. They came from large families in the same community. All the children helped with farming when they were old enough. It was a hard life, but their parents were honest, stable people who wanted to do their best for their children. Mr. Avery was in the sixth grade when his father died. The extra work on the farm held him up in school and he finished the eighth grade a year late. Mrs. Avery stopped school after the seventh grade to work and help with the younger children in her family.

Mr. and Mrs. Avery moved to a midwestern city when the children were young. This was a difficult adjustment at first, even though their economic situation was greatly improved. Mr. Avery had secured employment as a freight handler and found housing for the family before they moved. In the first year Mr. and Mrs. Avery found it hard to get accustomed to the ways of the city. Mrs. Avery felt that people didn't realize that they had dignity and self-respect in their life on the farm, even though it was a different kind of life. She said proudly that she and her husband had their ways, which were good and unchanging. They lived simply, and had very little economically, but they had respect for each other and solidarity in their family, a cohesive religion in which they were very active, and pleasure in family and community. Mrs. Avery learned about the city gradually. She found work to supplement the family income. She said she appreciated what she learned from her employers and they appreciated her ability to take care of their children. She resented some of the implicitly depreciating attitudes that she encountered but reported them with a kind of ironic tolerance. She saw that people depended on her to take care of their children, even, in some instances, when they were unable to manage the children themselves. She communicated a deep sense of self-assurance in her child-rearing skill, and security in her sense of self-worth.

Mr. Avery and the older children helped look after the younger ones when Mrs. Avery worked. The children adjusted without difficulty to the city once they were well established in school. They were moderately good students. They participated in church activities and found small jobs during summer vacations.

Both parents said, together and in individual interviews, that they didn't have any serious problems rearing their children because "they were kept busy" and "they knew just how far they could go" in their quarrels, disobedience, or misbehavior. When talk didn't do any good, Mrs. Avery made them stay in from play after school, and if they were very bad Mr. Avery used his strap, but it was necessary only a few times with the boys. Their daughter was "sassy" sometimes, but not disobedient about staying out late or fighting, as the boys had sometimes been.

They are gratified with their children and with their ability to provide for them to complete high school. Their daughter is a superior student and they have managed to save enough to help her go to college in the fall. They want to do this because she is intelligent and wants to be a teacher. They think of teaching in terms of making a contribution to people, as well as her own greater economic security in the future.

Mr. and Mrs. Avery had known each other all their lives. They acknowledged philosophically that there had been difficulties in

their relationship, but that they had always patched them up because Mr. Avery would "sit and talk to Mama when she got mad,
and said she was going home to her family."

In talking about foster children, Mrs. Avery observed that rais-
ing children now is different; it is often hard to keep up with the
changes. However, they thought that with the help of the agency
they would be able to learn how to raise foster children because
what they have learned from experience worked out well with the
children Mrs. Avery cared for in families where she had been employed. They thought they could build on this. In their home, both
parents and their daughter were proud of the interior work they
had done themselves. The home was comfortable and bright with
a feeling of warmth. They altered their tentative plans for the use
of space in the course of discussing the various needs of foster children in relation to their age, location of bedrooms, and study
space.

One of the Averys' concerns about foster children focused on the
changing ways of the neighborhood. They are concerned about
violence but they have a quiet involvement and pride in furthering
the development of black culture and participation in changing the
social conditions of their race. They were aware of the problems of
the drug culture in the urban schools, but since their children had
not been pulled into this they hoped they could help other youngsters avoid the problem. They considered the age at which new
children in the school can "stand up for themselves." Their daughter entered actively into considering ways to supervise and protect
foster children during the first few months in school. She expressed
preference for girls, saying she could teach them some of her hob-
bies. Her brothers, older than she, had never been interested and
she had a hard time with so many boys around. Both parents
agreed that in some ways a girl has a hard time with so many
brothers, especially when they tease, but they tried not to allow
much of this. The parents were interested in taking either a
brother and sister or a boy and a girl from two different families.

Throughout the study, Mr. and Mrs. Avery were cooperative in
the procedures and seemed to undertand the agency's policies and
the explanations about the special needs of foster children. The

breadth of their experience with children and the hard life they
had economically, as they grew up, seemed to have given them
strength and tolerance. Although both are limited in formal education, they are articulate and in touch with their feelings, which
they seem to accept with little conflict. They also are perceptive in
regard to rapid social change and what it may mean in rearing
children. Their involvement in their church is strong, but not fa-
natic. They feel that foster children should participate with them
in the church because it is so much a part of the family's social life,
but they are not insistent, as they accept the fact that there may be
factors that will require individual consideration.

When asked what their hopes would be in rearing foster children, Mrs. Avery responded, "We just want to raise them up until
they are grown so they can be someone; I mean, look after themselves and look after their families."

EVALUATION

Adaptation and growth are prominent in the current life of the
family and in the longitudinal histories of the parents. Capacity to
meet the needs of children and to gain gratifications from providing for the family and from maintaining a sense of family solidarity
are important. The strong ego integrity and adaptiveness are seen
in the maintenance of the family's standards and values in the face
of the severe dislocation caused by moving to a different geographical area, an urban culture as contrasted to a rural culture, change
of occupation, and all of the accompanying stresses. The adaptive
functioning is further evidenced in the freedom to accept and acknowledge difficulties and problems in the marriage, child-rearing,
and moving to the city. The fact that none of the problems assumed serious or overwhelming proportions is the reflection of
adaptiveness and capacity for learning and growth.

The capacity for giving in the parental role and for relating to
the children's needs is apparent in their discussions of their children and of prospective foster children. Their total life orientation
is focused on the welfare of the family, and is relatively free from
self-centered ambitions.

WORKING RELATIONSHIP IN THE
STUDY PROCESS

The foster parents' working relationship with the agency begins with the foster home study. The study process sets the beginning course for the subsequent relationship. At its most productive, this is a friendly professional relationship as distinguished from a friendly social relationship. Only the caseworker can set and maintain its professional character. Usually this is conveyed implicitly by the caseworker's conduct. Occasionally, foster parents wish to make the relationship a personal, social one, and occasionally the caseworker allows the relationship to be established on this basis without being fully aware that the social relationship is inconsistent with the professional functions inherent in the role. Sometimes it is necessary to define the reasons for maintaining the relationship on a professional basis. This does not preclude the friendly quality that is essential to the relaxed atmosphere in which foster parents can relate to the mutual tasks. The caseworker's attitude of genuine interest in and respect and appreciation for the foster-parent applicants as individuals and for the family as a whole sets the tone of the relationship. This attitude, combined with the purposeful exploration, direction of interviews, and responsiveness, tends to maintain the essential balance in the relationship. The caseworker's attitude is augmented by other essentials. These include:

1) The establishment of a mutual understanding of the purposes and procedures of the study and what it entails.

2) Clarity regarding areas of information that should be shared in relation to achieving the purposes.

3) Appropriate timing of exploration of sensitive areas of information in relation to the movement in the relationship.

Both the applicant and the caseworker go through an initial period of relative discomfort. Relaxation in the relationship usually is a reciprocal process. The caseworker, as interviewer, however, has the primary responsibility and is in a more auspicious position to help create a relaxed atmosphere in which communication can take place. Ordinarily there is a natural progression which cannot be hurried. It is often in the third session that the applicant and the caseworker experience a noticeable change in their ease of communication. Applicants who have well-functioning egos would not be likely to discuss important stressful aspects of their family life until they understand the relevance and purpose of such communication and have confidence in the understanding of the caseworker.

When a study is completed, the family and the caseworker have shared an important experience which has promoted a positive relationship. The effectiveness of transfer to the foster care caseworker depends in part on the kind of preparation the prospective foster parents have had, in anticipation of the role of the foster care caseworker. In fact, the definition of the supervising caseworker's role is a dynamic part of the study process. The applicants must be informed about the future role of the supervising caseworker in order to respond to the information and to decide whether these role relationships are consistent with their wishes or will be consonant with their ways of adaptation. Reciprocally, their responses, directly and indirectly, contribute to an understanding of the applicants' personalities and their potentialities for functioning effectively in the foster care system.

The Supervisory-Helping Process

The supervisory function of the caseworker in the relationship with the foster parent, as discussed earlier, is an inherent one which derives from the agency's legal, ethical, and professional responsibility for the child's welfare.

The helping function arises from the nature of the foster-parenting task, because it involves the environment of the foster child, the child's impact on that environment, and the welfare of the total foster family. The agency's obligation is to try to develop and maintain an optimal environment for the child within the foster parents' potentialities and to insure, in so far as possible, the welfare of the family engaged in this role. The stresses introduced into the family by the presence of a foster child are the direct concern of the foster care caseworker, in the interest of both the foster child and the foster family. Similarly, other stresses that adversely affect the family are within the domain of the caseworker's professional activity, should the family need and want help of some kind. As will be discussed later, in most instances such help may be appropriately provided directly by the foster care caseworker or, in unusual situations, by referral to a suitable resource.

Theoretical differences among practitioners in regard to the nature of the caseworker's role and the helping process influence practice to some degree, but perhaps not as greatly as the terms of debate might suggest. The experienced, skilled caseworker, regardless of philosophical orientation, draws upon the full range of his knowledge, technical skills, and creativity to promote growth, prevent crises, and resolve problems in his work with foster parents.

In practical experience it has been found that: (a) Most foster parents need and want help. (b) The components and content of this help may vary greatly, since they are determined by the personalities of the foster parents and their life situation, the problems presented by the foster child and his natural family, the skills of the caseworker, and the duration and intensity of the casework relationship.

Components of the supervisory-helping process can be viewed as administrative, educative, and therapeutic. Emotional support is the undergirding of administrative and educative supervision, just as it is in casework treatment.

THE ADMINISTRATIVE COMPONENT

The administrative component of the supervisory-helping relationship embraces the concept of agency responsibility and authority, accountability, and certain areas of decision-making. In order to discharge his responsibilities, the foster care practitioner, trained or untrained, experienced, or inexperienced, must possess, minimally, some special knowledge not otherwise available to the foster parents. Any social worker representing a foster care agency should learn the basic facts about the services of the agency; the child and the child's family; a generic appreciation of the special needs of placed children and the unique tasks and problems of foster parenthood; and how to use the resources of the agency and the community on behalf of the foster child and in support of the foster family. The caseworker's administrative functions include these:

1) The decisions regarding the agency's initial and continuing use of the foster home. (These decisions usually involve casework and administrative participation.)

2) Evaluation of the suitability of a particular child for placement in the home.

3) Sharing of information regarding the agency's services, procedures, mutual roles and responsibilities, and implementation of these services, as needed, throughout the time the foster home is active.

4) Provision of information about the child, his family, and the conditions of his placement, and interpretation of his special needs.

5) Arrangement for the provision of the agency's tangible services, such as financial payments, medical and dental care, diagnostic services, educational aids or guidance and other auxiliary and special services, as needed.

6) Arrangements for family visits and other liaison activities with the child's family.

7) Coordination of activities with schools, courts, and other community organizations.

Some of these functions are educative in effect, and in many aspects of the process the administrative and educative components are inseparable. The administrative aspects of the agency's service are the cornerstone of both the necessary collaboration and the enabling process. They are crucial to an effective foster parent-agency working relationship. The practitioner's ability to discharge the administrative tasks in the context of a positive, supportive relationship, determines to a large extent the degree to which the foster parents will be able to utilize the educative functions of the caseworker's role and the therapeutic function, if it is needed.

Since the total personality of the foster parent is invested and involved in this task, the caseworker, in carrying out the administrative function, must be highly sensitized to the foster parents' emotional investments in the foster child. One of the first requirements of sound administrative supervision is the provision of adequate information and opportunity for genuine participation in the decision-making process with the purpose of arriving at mutually desired goals. Sensitivity to the feelings and wishes of the participants and avoidance of arbitrary decisions, to the greatest possible extent, are essential elements in the participation process.

THE EDUCATIVE COMPONENT

The educative component presupposes that the caseworker possesses technical knowledge and skill in special areas which have an important bearing on the needs of the foster child beyond or different from that possessed by the foster parents; that he recognizes the feelings and needs of the foster parents in the adaptive process; and recognizes the needs of the clients who are served by collaboration between foster parents and agency.

The caseworker, if well trained, has acquired a body of knowledge in child development, psychopathology, parent-child relationships, and family dynamics. With experience he will develop skills in using this knowledge in the educative and therapeutic components of the helping process. Awareness and understanding of the foster parents' feelings about the child and his behavior and about the caseworker are major factors in the effective use of the educative component. Negative feelings tend to block learning. Feelings of frustration, a sense of failure, anger reactive to provocative behavior, over-determined reactions to specific problems—all, stand in the way of learning and of the use of knowledge. Negative reactions to the educative initiatives of the caseworker may reflect a problem in the foster parents' current feelings about themselves, the foster child or his parents, or the caseworker. The opportunity to ventilate and examine feelings in a relationship with an understanding, noncritical person tends to resolve the feelings sufficiently to enable the foster parent to move on to the next step: to understand the child and to find ways to relate and respond to him which are consonant with the foster parents' self-esteem and conducive to the child's growth.[1]

An excerpt from the record of a sixteen-year-old boy will illustrate the application of the educative component combined with therapeutically oriented, enabling techniques in the work with foster parents.

THE KELLY FOSTER FAMILY

Mrs. Kelly began our regular visit saying she just didn't know what to do or even how to think about Eddy's latest problem. On Tuesday, the school counselor called her requesting an immediate school visit. On her arrival, he handed her Eddy's wallet. He said it was found in a class room and turned over to him. In going through the wallet to find identification he found negatives of obscene pictures. He wanted to be sure these were not circulated in the school but he felt it was the parents' or agency's responsibility to deal with this.

Mrs. Kelly was upset about the pictures. Where did Eddy get them? What did this mean? How serious was it? She had not had this experience with her own sons and didn't understand it. She led quickly into another area that seemed to concern her equally: Eddy's carelessness in leaving his wallet around school. Lately he has been absent-minded, preoccupied, and moody. I agreed that we had a problem that needed attention and asked for more details about Eddy's behavior. She elaborated on incidents of forgetfulness, preoccupation, and daydreaming. She feels as though all their work has gone down the drain. Several months back, he had reached a new plateau: he had settled down to studying; he was pleased with his new track record; he had been successful in dating his first girl friend; and he began to think about a part-time job for the first time. I suggested that we consider his present behavior

[1] Relatively mature individuals can be expected to respond realistically to the attitudes and behavior of the caseworker, and consequently this type of help is effective. Foster parents who are less healthy present more complex problems in their use of the relationship and require more extensive help through the use of therapeutically oriented techniques.

in the perspective of his condition three years ago and what had happened since. I recalled some of the problems, and the ways the foster parents had helped Eddy struggle to his recent level of development. Together we reviewed their holding him to limits in doing his school work, encouragement in attending track meets, listening to his complaints, giving him guidance about dating, and the ingenious ways they found to bring him out of his daydreaming with activities and companionship at home and elsewhere. I said this setback may have some current explanation in addition to his adolescent preoccupation with sex. After this review Mrs. Kelly seemed to regain her perspective.

I asked about the job experience. She said she knew it had been rough: going for interviews, being turned down, and trying to fit working hours in with school and fun; the job discipline was new and Eddy worried about the boss, who left a lot of responsibility to others in the shop; but he likes the work as he had always been interested in film developing. Then, she said, "Gosh, he's had a lot on his mind." She asked if his increased preoccupation could be a result of the job. I said it seemed likely; it would be for anyone starting a new job, especially for Eddy, who always became preoccupied when he started anything new.

She recalled that we had discussed this even before Eddy came to their home. I discussed further the current impact of adolescence and growing-up as a part of his preoccupation. She and I had gone over this last fall when he first talked about dating. The first job, too, was part of growing-up, getting ready to be independent. She responded, "Then this isn't going backwards, just the beginning of a new attempt forward—we'll go through another struggle together." We laughed about this, and she said, "Well then, let's get onto these pictures." Simultaneously, we said, "Where did he get them?" The "Why" seemed to fit into his present development, and again we both thought that they may have come from the photography shop. This was a guess, but it fit logically with his concerns about the boss and other employees. Mrs. Kelly moved on to ask how to handle it and who should handle it with Eddy. She didn't think she could or should, considering his age and her discomfort. I agreed, and asked if she had talked with Mr. Kelly about the problem. She hadn't yet, but she planned to do so after talking with me. She had waited because she had some concern about his reaction—she amended this saying, "Well, not really, but I don't want to put any pressure on him to do something he might feel he isn't up to. He has such a good relationship with Eddy, and this is so important." She reminded me he had difficulty about discipline years ago with their second son, although he did all right with the others. I agreed that there should be no pressure but wondered about the three of us discussing this together, leaving the choice about it to Mr. Kelly. If he preferred not to discuss this with Eddy, I would handle it. She knew I'd helped him with similar problems when he was younger and he was accustomed to this, but if Mr. Kelly would talk with him so much the better.

Mr. Kelly, by plan, arrived in time to join us. Mrs. Kelly told him about the wallet incident. He followed closely and sympathetically, then he laughed broadly. He recalled his first experience with "obscene nude pictures" when he was a boy and his embarrassment about it. He thought a man-to-man talk was needed, about what goes on in the working world and "how to cope and keep out of the school teacher's hair." He followed this with a serious discussion and questions about Eddy's present adjustment and what help he needs.

Several days later Mrs. Kelly called to say, "All is well. Dad's talk with Eddy did the trick. He's going around whistling again. He put some money in the bank and has extra green for Saturday's dance."

The caseworker's approaches are governed by the precipitants of the current stress, understanding of the foster parents, the child, and the family dynamics. In this interview the foster mother's anxiety and frustration appear to come from four identifiable sources: (a) anxiety about the sexual incident which represented a new and unexpected problem; (b) the new problem emerging in connection with the recurrence of previous problems that she hoped had been resolved, despite previous intellectual preparation for possible recurrences; (c) a consequent sense of failure; (d) a minor but persistent problem in some aspects of her relationship with the foster father that interfered with communication and joint problem-solving.

Educative and therapeutically oriented approaches illustrated in this case include these:

1) Acknowledgement and clarification of the problem; placing it in appropriate perspective and in the context of related stress precipitants.

2) The translating of psychological concepts from technical terms into the language of the foster parents. (This is a cardinal requirement for effective educative approaches.)

3) Review of the foster parents' past experience with the child and their successful problem-solving techniques. The review tends to cut through the feelings of failure and helplessness, to restore confidence in problem-solving capacities, and release the creative use of the foster parents' own resources. Only after this discussion was Mrs. Kelly able to use her previous knowledge to understand Eddy's current situation and the effects of the new job, which may have caused the regression.

4) Reinforcement and augmentation of knowledge about the child's developmental stage. (Eddy's adolescent heterosexual strivings and the struggle for independence, which further explained the regressive phase.) The objective knowledge tends to correct the sense of personal failure and disappointment, and strengthen cognitive grasp of causes as well as to expand understanding of the child.

5) Reinforcement of the connections between the knowledge and the subsequent response to the child's needs. (In some instances the preferred response is to relax and do nothing, but this is an understood and purposeful response in contrast to frustration or drift.)

6) Encouragement and support of communication between the foster parents in relation to their appropriate roles. This is a therapeutically oriented activity which helps promote and maintain the parental aspect of the marriage relationship, the parent-child relationships, and the family equilibrium.

The school's request that the current episode be discussed with Eddy points up the agency's administrative responsibility as the child's guardian (to see that this is accomplished either directly with the child or by foster parents).

The extent of the use of the educative component, beyond its inherent, minimal use, varies greatly, depending on the child, the extent to which his behavior and development exceed the foster parents' span of understanding and parenting skills at any given time, the patterning of their use of learning, and the caseworker's mastery and skill in using the knowledge that is available.

THE THERAPEUTIC COMPONENT

The therapeutic or treatment component in the supervisory-helping process may be introduced at the initiation of either the foster parents or the caseworker. Since the foster parents' primary role is not that of a client, the therapeutic component in the helping process is not a primary one but rather is invoked temporarily when needed in periods of stress to prevent an undesirable outcome or to restore equilibrium when a crisis occurs that interferes with the primary parenting role. In such situations, the administrative and educative components in the supervisory-helping process may drop into a secondary place temporarily.

No therapeutic approach is more relevant or essential to the maintenance of foster homes than that developed by the crisis theorists and practitioners (20). Crisis theory, first developed and applied to psychiatric problems and later expanded and applied in a variety of preventive mental health programs, has its value for foster family care precisely because: (a) it emphasizes preventive intervention; (b) it identifies certain common stressful events; (c) it defines the dynamics of emotional crises in individuals, families, and groups, which are responsive to short term treatment intervention; (d) it takes advantage of the fact that, "a little help rationally directed and purposefully focused at a strategic time is more effective than extensive help given at a period of less emotional accessibility" (21). The weight of this principle is many times multiplied in the foster care situation, where the loss of the foster home is at stake.

According to Rapoport's analysis, "there are three sets of interacting factors that can produce a crisis: (a) a hazardous event
which poses some threat; (b) a threat to instinctual need which is
symbolically linked to earlier threats that resulted in vulnerability
or conflict; (c) an inability to respond with adequate coping mechanisms" (22).

As in any preventive orientation, foreknowledge of emotionally
hazardous events enables the practitioner to make himself available when a known stress occurs, to evaluate the meaning of the
event to the individual or the family, to assess the family's resources for coping with the event, and to determine whether his
help is needed. In foster family life the most frequently encountered emotionally hazardous events encompass those that are common to families in general and those that are peculiar to the foster
family system in particular. These include:

1) Death or other loss of a family member or other important
person, which can apply also to the child's natural family (23).

2) Loss or change of job involving major role, status, or income
changes of the foster father.

3) Prolonged or serious illness in the foster family.

4) Movement of the foster family to a different home in a
strange community. (The foster child in particular may be acutely
vulnerable to change.)

5) Departure of a family member for residence outside the family (for school, work, service in the armed forces, marriage, etc.).

6) Addition of a person to the foster family (a baby, foster child,
relative).

7) Disruptive behavior or unexpected reappearance of the foster
child's natural parent, or the unexpected action of a court or
agency that threatens the stability of the placement.

8) Problematic behavior of a foster child (or own child) which
threatens shame or disgrace in the community, sets up strong interpersonal tensions in the family, or assails some other acute emotional vulnerability in the foster parents.

The foster care agency's pre-existing and on-going working relationship with the foster family provides an auspicious continuum
within which the caseworker can make preventive contact in emo-

tionally hazardous situations, as well as for therapeutic intervention in crises. Intervention techniques vary in relation to the details of the situation. In general the technical approaches are governed by these dynamics:

1) The individual under stress often is not fully cognizant of the stress precipitants, the coalescence of contributing factors, or their connections between the actual precipitants and the responses.

2) Feelings about the event may be excessively repressed or denied leading to distortion or other pathological results. ·

3) The individual goes through a series of response stages in which his altered behavior may introduce a disequilibrium into the family relationships, setting in motion a set of interactions and transactions that may lead to increasing disequilibrium in other individuals and in the family system.

4) In the foster care system the transactional responses may extend from or be extended into the child's natural family.

The operation of these dynamics and their implications for practice can be seen in a situation, which, when it arises, poses a series of problems: the anticipated death of either parent who is in a terminal illness is a potentially traumatic event in a foster family, as in any family. The caseworker's participation may be the crucial determining factor in the social and psychological outcome. The details of intervention may vary in each situation, but essentially, the approach is designed to afford the foster parent the opportunity to discuss the situation, strengthen his cognitive perception of the events, maintain some awareness of his feelings, drain off tension, and find new ways to use the help of his family members and the resources in the community. The purpose of the caseworker's participation is to facilitate a normal mourning process and recovery.

The knowledge that children as well as adults are better able to cope with loss when they are prepared for it is important in itself, and becomes one of the foci in the reorganization of psychological tasks and activities of the responsible surviving parent.

The natural questions that arise in connection with the foster child are concerned with his special vulnerability to loss and to uncertainty about his future status in the foster home. Measures that insure a climate of stability and continuity for all of the children in the family during the stressful period help to prevent the trauma that commonly results from an atmosphere of impending catastrophic change and interferes with a normal mourning process. In some instances, the future of the family may appear uncertain, but this uncertainty is not ordinarily something that can be acted on advantageously during the period of high emotional stress. Often, the uncertainty may be resolved by clarifying discussions, and the foster parent may be helped to support the natural tendency for family members to draw closer together and provide mutual support in a time of crisis. Removal or contemplation of removal of the foster child at this time should be avoided if at all possible, since removal not only interferes with normal grief reactions, but also reinforces established pathological defenses against a normal process of mourning, and increasingly forecloses the child's opportunities for psychological, and, possibly, physical health. The child's natural parent, too, may be threatened by the event and can best maintain a stable state when given timely help.

An actual crisis in the foster home, as distinct from an emotionally hazardous event, is often revealed to the caseworker by a request for removal of the foster child. The question of removal of a child, when handled through a reciprocal decision-making process, between the caseworker and the foster parents, may result in a rational decision for removal. This should not be confused with a crisis-oriented request which reflects the irrational aspect in the foster parents' reactions to a stressful event. The meaning of the request is usually complex, and cannot be taken at face value as a solution to the crisis.

In many instances the sudden request for removal is essentially a "cry for help"—an unconscious effort to bring the emotional crisis to the attention of someone who is able to intervene therapeutically. As in other types of crisis situations, the foster parents may be unaware of the real precipitant and its ramifications. As in crisis prevention, the key to effective crisis intervention is the immediate availability of the caseworker.

Two contrasting foster home situations will be presented to demonstrate and analyze the use of crisis intervention techniques in response to the foster parents' request for removal of a child.

Mrs. Hunt telephoned, sounding harassed and anxious, and asked the caseworker to come to her home that day. When the caseworker arrived Mrs. Hunt told her, in despair, that she had to ask the agency to find another home for Jane. Since there was a well-established relationship, Mrs. Hunt talked freely. She said she was not able to handle all of the demands of her own children, her sick mother, the pressures arising from Jane's trouble in school, the notes from the teacher, and the children's complaints about Jane's behavior. She gave a detailed account of the family and community stresses, and she wept over the decision she and her husband had reached regarding Jane. The stresses sounded realistic enough, as did the considered decision about Jane. After hearing the foster mother's account fully, the caseworker commented, "You seem to feel at the end of your rope today. When did you start to feel this way?" The foster mother, after some ruminating, said she thought the pressure got too much for her when her mother became ill. With further exploration the foster mother's feelings continued to focus on the grandmother's illness, the necessary running up and down the stairs to take care of her, and trying to keep the children quiet. All of this became unbearable this week when grandmother expressed resentment of Jane, and accused foster mother of having to neglect her for a child that didn't belong to the family.

It became clear that the critical ego stress came from Mrs. Hunt's emotional conflict in her relationship with her mother, and her inability to place realistic limits on her mother's demands. She said, "You can't blame mother; she is getting old and is really suffering." She did not express anger or frustration with her mother or Jane; she simply stated that she could not handle Jane under these conditions. The caseworker put all of this together for her, and then said, "Jane's problems seem to be about the same as always; the children's sporadic quarrels haven't changed much; all of you get exasperated, but you mean a lot to Jane and all of you have invested a lot and wanted this to work. One problem seems to be your concern about limiting yourself in meeting your mother's demands. Remember, we talked about this before in connection with its effect on the children when you get over-tired; you felt then that you were taking it out on the kids, and blamed yourself. I wonder if the problem will be solved by Jane's leaving? Would it be worth-while for you to spend a few sessions with me, to take a closer look at this?"

By agreement, a plan for a temporary period of weekly visits was worked out. The focus of the subsequent interviews shifted, purposively, to an examination of the interpersonal relationship between the foster mother and her mother. Both foster parents were strongly committed to the responsibility of caring for the grandmother in their home. Mrs. Hunt's inability to place realistic limits on grandmother's demands became the focus of treatment. Mrs. Hunt gradually expressed her frustration and resentment, but continued to blame herself for these reactions, feeling that because her mother was old and ill she (Mrs. Hunt) should be able to meet her wishes without resentment. With help, she sorted out the kinds of demands made by her mother which were unrealistic and childish. The caseworker pointed out the negative effects of meeting some of these demands, not just on Mrs. Hunt, but also on her mother, who regressed when dependent demands were met unrealistically; whereas she responded well to support in doing for herself or for others whatever she was capable of managing within the limits of her illness. Grandmother's recently developed resentment of Jane was examined and seen as a childlike jealousy associated with her illness and dependency. Mrs. Hunt began to see that her own frustrations with Jane received reinforcement from her mother's feelings, and she experienced intense anxiety about "being in the middle." Her usual patience and affection for the child were worn thin in part because she had over-drawn her emotional resources. Mrs. Hunt welcomed the caseworker's suggestion that she could pick up the school contacts if this would relieve Mrs. Hunt of a task that seemed too much at present.

After a few sessions, the previous equilibrium in the family was restored. While the foster mother's internal conflict was not resolved, it was modified to a degree that was within her capacity to manage. Thereafter, Mrs. Hunt's continued intellectual insight, combined with the caseworker's support, enabled her to ventilate and dissipate her feelings of frustration when they began to mount. In this, as in other similar situations, the brief period of treatment sets a pattern for handling the recurring tensions within the ongoing casework relationship, from time to time, as necessary.

The therapeutic effect of these sessions derived from:

1) Clarification of the precipitant and its consequences.

2) Ventilation of feelings which had been partly denied, and modification in responses to the stressor (grandmother's demands).

3) Practical relief from a task that created a realistic burden by the appropriate use of the caseworker.

4) And finally, but not least, the active and symbolic giving of the caseworker at a strategic time when the support, understanding, and help are especially important in restoring a balance in the giving-receiving equilibrium.

A second family illustrates a crisis precipitated by what appeared to be the foster mother's over-determined vulnerability to a specific problem in the child, but which was actually touched off by the foster mother's reactions to separation when her son left home for college. In this situation, the link between the foster mother's reaction to a current separation and earlier unresolved problems emerges clearly as a factor in her temporary inability to cope with the stressful event:

Telephone call from Mrs. Davis (foster mother of Patty, aged nine). She said I would have to move Patty. She poured out feelings of anger, frustration, and discouragement, and finally added, "The last straw is her smoking." I arranged for a visit on the following day.

(Note: the Davis family had been through three years of work with this severely disturbed child and at times had wondered if they could help her but had not, at any time, considered giving up.)

When I arrived, Mrs. Davis was still agitated and intensely angry at Patty. She went over the ground covered on the tele-

phone, but now added that she told Patty she had asked me to move her. She discussed it with Mr. Davis first and he agreed that if she feels too upset to manage Patty, it would be better for the child not to be with them. She said when she feels so strongly about something she can't do what is best for Patty. She just loses her temper and shrieks at her. She again inventoried all of the problems Patty had from the beginning: hyper-activity, destructiveness, wandering away from home, trouble with playmates, sex play, school problems, "and now this smoking! She knows I hate smoking." Mrs. Davis talked in circles, bringing up past problems as though they were current, but without the empathy she had for those problems in the past. I made tentative comments along lines of recognizing what she had been through, and tried to remind her of Patty's progress (which we had discussed the previous week). She disagreed, saying Patty was not improving; she was just jumping from problem to problem; and added that the smoking filled her with disgust and anger. I said smoking does seem to be the last straw. Is it worse than running away, distrust, sex play? She immediately said, "Much worse!," caught herself, and laughed self-consciously. After a short silence, she said that her head tells her it isn't so bad, but her guts tell her it's terrible. After another pause, she said, "No wonder I can't help anyone with this problem." She guessed she had to work on herself first, but where to start? It wasn't exactly all Patty's problem. Could we discuss this kind of thing together? Or would it be better just to move Patty? I told her this often happens with foster parents. The child placed by the agency may stir up something that otherwise might never become a problem. We could set up some sessions to try to understand what bothers her so much. She said, "That would help a lot."

Mrs. Davis spontaneously went on to talk about Mr. Davis's smoking. She tried not to nag, but couldn't stop. She thought this strong feeling came from her strict religious upbringing. Smoking, drinking, sex, were part of the "gut reactions." Her parents threw out her eldest sister when she started "partying." She (Mrs. Davis) was then a little girl and frightened that if she displeased her parents she wouldn't have any place to go. Her first year away from home (in college, preparatory for nurse's training) she smoked a cigarette and had a severe anxiety attack. Somewhere I commented that her feelings about smoking seemed to be tied up partly, at least, with feelings about leaving her home or being sent away.

After she had calmed down, Mrs. Davis asked me to talk to Patty about her anger and threat of removal. She thought she must have scared her. She didn't feel that she could discuss it with Patty yet, either alone or with the three of us together. She needed more time to think and talk about this.

I waited for Patty to arrive from school and interviewed her privately. (Note: this was not an unusual procedure. The caseworker had established a pattern of periodic contacts with Patty, throughout her placement, with help focused on her problems of adjustment in her foster home and in school.) We reviewed the smoking episode and Mrs. Davis's threat of removal. Patty was afraid I was going to move her that day. She was relieved that it wasn't so, but cried with fear and anger that foster mother had threatened to send her away. I asked about the smoking episode; how had it come about? She told me she was lonely that day; one of the neighbor boys had cigarettes; she got matches from the kitchen for him. She wanted to know when she had to move. I explained that Mrs. Davis hoped this would not be necessary. She wanted to help Patty grow up, but there are times when she isn't sure about being able to do this because she gets too upset and she knows this is partly her problem. Patty guessed she'd been pretty bad at times, but she'd try harder. This was the best place she had ever been, only she gets so angry at Mom sometimes. We decided to talk about her anger at Mom in our future meetings to help her not do things that get her in trouble.

For the next six weeks, I visited weekly and talked to Mrs. Davis and Patty separately. During the first week Mrs. Davis could not handle this with Patty directly but told her she was glad I was coming to talk with them both about their upset over the smoking.

In the following interviews, Mrs. Davis ventilated some of her early experiences with smoking and the details of her parents' reactions. She thought Patty knew how she felt about smoking and had done this deliberately to hurt her. I agreed that Patty had hit a sore spot, and wondered what had been going on that week that might account for this. Patty had said she was lonely which didn't quite fit her usual feelings. Mrs. Davis recalled that she had been away several afternoons at meetings. This was unusual, but she had thought Patty was far enough along to accept this now and that she had made adequate arrangements with the neighbor. This led to Mrs. Davis's recounting that she had been thinking about going to work part-time on the local hospital staff because the inflation was eating up their income. There had been some discussion of this, in Patty's presence but it was in the talking stage. Mrs. Davis made the connection between these events and Patty's reaction, asking if it was just too much separation for her, too soon.

(Note: Another piece of information that the caseworker possessed fits into the theme of separation and loss that ran through these episodes. Mrs. Davis's son had just left home to enter college. Before this Mrs. Davis had needed and used help to support his growing independence, especially dating, and taking trips away from home.) I pointed out that all the problems we discussed had involved changes and separations in one way or another, and wondered if the recent change in the family, with Fred off at school, had affected Mrs. Davis more than she was aware. This was confirmed in several ways.

Subsequent interviews focused on Mrs. Davis's feelings about Fred's departure, and the conflict she experienced, wanting him to go, knowing it was a good thing for his education and need to grow up, but at the same time feeling his loss in various ways. She recognized that her wish to go to work was partly an effort to adjust to the change. The interactions between her and Patty were retraced. During this period, Mrs. Davis discussed with Patty the issue of threatened removal and smoking. Both foster parents told Patty the family would stay together and work things out.

In this situation, resistance to the educative component of the helping process is seen in Mrs. Davis's angry, compulsive repetition of her complaints and in her disagreement with the caseworker's reminder of the child's progress. This contrasts with the relaxation of tension seen in Mrs. Kelly (p. 267) in response to a similar approach, demonstrating the inefficacy of educative, and some-times supportive, approaches in the face of hostility or resistance caused by psychological conflict. The therapeutic techniques se-lected by the caseworker may vary. In this instance, the case-worker, knowing the foster mother's value system, chose to con-front her with the irrationality of her response by a touch of humor, inherent in the comparison between this symptom and oth-ers, much more serious, which she had been able to accept. The therapeutic issue here is to open up a blocked communication, to make it possible for the foster mother to reveal herself sufficiently for clarification of the causes of her over-reaction in the present sit-uation. She obviously could not explain this rationally; she did not understand it herself. The mutual search for understanding of the precipitating events becomes the essential process to restore reality testing and problem-solving capacities that have been temporarily blocked. Old problems, symbolically associated with the present crisis, emerged spontaneously as Mrs. Davis recalled her experi-ence with her parents, her sister, and the separations from the fam-ily. The early childhood genesis of separation problems was not touched. It was sufficient that Mrs. Davis saw the problem in terms of Fred's departure for school, which she experienced as a loss and a rejection, and linked to the earlier experiences. In this context, she felt Patty's smoking as a rejection, mirroring her own deliber-ate violation of her parents' wishes when she went away to school.

Generally, therapeutic intervention as a component of the super-visory-helping relationship is needed and is employed most effec-tively when a crisis occurs which is connected with the family dynamics and is focused on the foster child. In the Hunt family, the over-stretched ego of the foster mother, brought about by the grandmother's illness, precipitated a crisis in relation to the foster child. In the Davis family, the crisis seemed to be triggered by the child's behavior, but actually the child's behavior proved to be a response to emotional stress in the foster mother that occurred in reaction to a separation when her son left home to go to college. It is implicit that these kinds of crises require a brief period of case-work treatment from the foster care caseworker rather than from any other source. Referral elsewhere would not be feasible or acceptable. Referral to a strange resource holds the hazard of adding stress on top of crisis, and is likely to fail when the removal of the foster child is seen by the foster parents as an alternative means of reducing stress to a manageable level.

A different type of problem sometimes found in foster families is similar to the problem constellation commonly seen in family service agencies. The foster child is not the focus of the problem nor is it limited to the acute personal discomfort caused by a single individual's conflict. The major outlines show a family caught up in interpersonal conflict and inadequate communication that ramifies through the family structure, and threatens the environment as a growth-producing one for all the children. A period of family treatment may be needed. This may best be undertaken by the foster care caseworker since the foster child's welfare is an implicit mutual investment between caseworker and foster parents.

The need for treatment within the foster family often raises the issue of the foster care agency's function and the appropriateness of referral to a clinic or family service agency. In most instances, when short-term treatment is indicated the intricate involvement of the foster child in the family dynamics contraindicates referral elsewhere. The type of situation which can and should be referred elsewhere for treatment is one in which a foster parent needs and wants treatment for intrapsychic problems.

CONCLUSION

Once the foster family becomes a part of the foster care system as the major nurturing agent for the child, any situation or event that threatens the quality or continuity of parental functioning is the proper concern of the caseworker. From the viewpoint of the needs of placed children, it follows inexorably that a narrow or static definition of the caseworker's role or failure to place top priority on the caseworker's availability for service to foster parents is a disservice to the children in many foster homes.

Lack of clarity regarding the reciprocal roles of caseworker and foster parents leads to loss of effectiveness in varying degrees. Mutual understanding of the basic administrative functions of the caseworker forms the foundation for effective collaboration.

Although certain aspects of authority reside in and must be retained by the agency, supervision of the foster home is not an authoritarian process; it is, rather, a process in which the caseworker discharges the agency's responsibilities for: (a) being informed about the child's human and nonhuman environment and his growth responses to the environmental provisions; and (b) providing the supplemental services needed. Decisions that grow out of this process usually are mutual ones. In a relatively few situations it becomes necessary to make administrative decisions in which the foster parents do not concur. The absence of agreement is rare when the sharing and participating process is designed and carried out in each instance for the express purpose of arriving at mutual decisions.

The supervisory-helping process is facilitated by a relationship in which the foster parents experience the support and backing of the caseworker and the agency. Foster parents who are relatively healthy respond realistically to the caseworker's attitude and behavior and to the policies and practices of the agency.

The administrative, educative, and therapeutic components in the supervisory helping process can be defined as separate entities. The administrative functions can be carried out as the primary basic service required from the agency, or the components can be synthesized in a process in which any one may be invoked for primary emphasis, in response to the total situation and the needs of the foster parents, child, and foster family. The educative component is intrinsically interrelated with the administrative component in that the caseworker shares information about the foster child and his family in an ordered pattern which illuminates the connections between the child's known experiences, his current situation, his condition, his behavior, and his needs, inherently demonstrating a dynamic orientation to human development and behavior.

The therapeutic component takes two forms which should be considered separately. (a) Therapeutically oriented techniques may be utilized at any time to facilitate the foster parents' freedom to use the administrative and educative aspects of the supervisory-helping process. (b) Therapeutic intervention in periods of stress or in crises is a short-term psychosocial treatment approach which is based on recognition of identifiable, emotionally hazardous events and utilized in response to a potential or fully developed crisis which threatens the foster parents' parental functioning.

All practitioners, whether or not professionally trained, can develop the knowledge and skills necessary for competently carrying out the administrative functions of the caseworker's role and in so doing perform the basic functions which are indispensable to the foster child's care and to appropriate role relationships. Beyond the use of basic administrative skills, the maintenance of foster homes in many instances may depend heavily on the agency's provision of casework service for preventive and therapeutic intervention in times of stress, regardless of its source.

REFERENCES

1. *Standards for Foster Family Care Services,* Child Welfare League of America, New York, 1959, p. 42.
2. Charlotte Towle, "Evaluating Motives of Foster Parents," *Helping: Charlotte Towle on Social Work and Social Casework,* ed. Helen Harris Perlman, The University of Chicago Press, Chicago, 1969, p. 152.
3. *Standards for Foster Family Care Services,* pp. 14–17.
4. Draza Kline and Helen-Mary Overstreet, *Casework with Foster Parents,* Child Welfare League of America, New York, 1956.
5. Alfred Kadushin, *Child Welfare Services,* The Macmillan Company, New York, 1967, p. 426.
6. Draza Kline, "A Clinical Review of the Gaudet Youth Services Foster Care Program of the Episcopal Community Services of New Orleans," in *New Payment Patterns and the Foster Parent Role,* Benson Jaffee and Draza Kline, Child Welfare League of America, New York, 1970.
7. *Ibid.* Two of the agencies are described in this publication. The third agency referred to is the Illinois Children's Home and Aid Society in which the authors, with others, developed and observed the foster family care program.

8. James Anthony, M.D., and Therese Benedek, M.D., *Parenthood,* Little, Brown and Company, Inc., Boston, 1970. Helene Deutsch, M.D., *Psychology of Women,* Vol. II, "Motherhood," Greene and Stratton, New York, 1945, Chapter 9.

9. Anthony, and Benedek, *Ibid.* Deutsch, *Ibid.* D. W. Winnicott, M.D., *The Maturational Processes and the Facilitating Environment,* International Universities Press, Inc., New York, 1965.

10. Deutsch, *Ibid.,* p. 294.

11. See Benedek, *Ibid.,* for discussion of parenthood as a maturational stage.

12. For discussion of this subject see Draza Kline, "Understanding and Evaluating a Foster Family's Capacity to Meet the Needs of an Individual Child," *The Social Service Review,* Vol. XXXIX, No. 2, June 1960, and in *Changing Needs and Practices in Child Welfare,* Child Welfare League of America, New York, 1960.

13. Towle, *Ibid.,* p. 153.

14. Franz Alexander, M.D., "Emotional Maturity," Illinois Society for Mental Hygiene, *Mental Health Bulletin,* Nov.–Dec. 1948, pp. 2–3.

15. Direct evidence for this observation was provided by foster parents who were interviewed by Kline and are quoted in *New Payment Patterns and the Foster Parent Role.* See pp. 20–23.

16. For discussion of the process and purposes of the foster home study see Draza Kline, "Understanding and Evaluating a Foster Family's Capacity. . . ."

17. Erik Erikson, M.D., *Childhood and Society,* W. W. Norton & Co., New York, 1950.

18. Detailed discussion of testing behavior is presented in Chapter III, pp. 80–82.

19. Benedek, in *Parenthood.*

20. Theoretical formulations of crisis intervention theory and application are presented in *Crisis Intervention: Selected Readings,* Howard J. Parad, ed., Family Service Association of America, New York, 1965.

21. Lydia Rapoport, "The State of Crisis: Some Theoretical Considerations," *The Social Service Review,* Vol. XXXVI, No. 2, The University of Chicago Press, Chicago, 1962, p. 30.

22. Rapoport, *Ibid.* p. 25.

23. *Crisis Intervention: Selected Readings,* "A Framework for Studying Families in Crisis," Howard J. Parad and Gerald Kaplan, M.D. *See also* "Symptomatology and Management of Acute Grief," Erich Lindemann, M.D. and "Generic Features of Families under Stress," Reubin Hill, Ph.D.

CHAPTER VI

TERMINATION, EVALUATION, AND OUTCOME

Termination

Discussion of termination of service has been reserved for the concluding chapter in order to view the closure as the final stage in the service continuum. What takes place in this stage of service is determined in part by the individual and group dynamics which characterize the participants, in part by the current environmental situation and conditions, and in part by the previously established dynamic patterns within the service system. What transpires grows logically out of what has already been established. The agency's philosophic approach to human relationships, child-rearing, the use of knowledge, and the level of priority of human values come into sharp relief. If service has lacked coherent continuity and integration, termination is likely to be unplanned and relationships abruptly terminated. Regardless of agency philosophy and practice, however, the practitioner's wish to avoid confrontation with painful aspects of the separation experience may find expression in well-rationalized abrupt withdrawal from clients or surrogate parents. Recognition of the positive potentials for growth in this final stage of the foster care relationships tends to safeguard against the temptation to short-cut the process. The period of anticipated termination is a period of stress which holds potentialities for trauma or for further growth, and the activity of the caseworker in this stage, as in earlier stages, may be a heavily determining factor in the outcome.

Closure of service to the child, the parents, or the foster parents, may take place by plan or as a result of events that are outside the agency's effective influence and against the agency's recommendation. Planned closure may come about through return of the child to his family, adoption of the child, transfer of the child to a facility under different administrative auspices, or through completion of the unit of service. The planned termination may result from decisions initiated by the parents, the surrogate parents, the agency, or the young person in the process of emancipation. Unplanned termination may be precipitated by the autonomous decision of a parent, or of a court, or independent action of an older adolescent. In any case, the termination has a specific meaning for and influence on the future adaptation of each of the participants. Nurturing relationships, which have extended over a period of time in which a strong degree of reciprocity has been established, are among the most important life relationships.

Termination is not necessarily coterminous for the child, parents, and foster-parents, but since it involves some form of separation, it affects others to varying degrees and introduces a new set of interactions with changing nuances and implications in all of the relationships. Service to the foster parents may be terminated while a child and his family members continue to use service after the child is transferred out of a foster home; or the foster parents may continue to work with the agency on behalf of other children after service to a foster child and his family has terminated, or, under various circumstances, closure of service to child and parent may not be simultaneous. The conditions of the impending termination and the subsequent reactions differ for the different individuals involved. For each, the loss and change have a psychological meaning related in part to the extent of the loss and in part to the psychological make-up of the individual. The loss and disequilibrium are likely to be greatest when the child and the foster parents lose each other and the agency simultaneously. Under any conditions, heightened stress is implicit in this stage of the foster care process.

Under the most auspicious conditions, the closure of service to the child is planned and carried out with the collaboration of all of the participants, utilizing the pre-existing role relationships in providing the supportive and therapeutic help needed by the child. The child whose placement is terminated or who is anticipating closure of service from the agency is highly susceptible to the attitudes of the significant adults in his environment. Consequently the attitudes and feelings of the natural parents and of the current surrogate parents about the impending change are of major importance in influencing the child's adaptation to it. The positive participation of the parent and surrogate parents in the preparation of the child is almost essential in order to provide the optimal opportunity for growth. Such participation of the parents and surrogate parents presupposes that their own preparation and participation in the decision-making process has been adequate. The adults whom the child is leaving must be considered both in their own right, from the viewpoint of their emotional involvement and as participants whose attitudes and reactions to the change will significantly affect the child.

The preventive and therapeutic approaches of the caseworker include some of the same considerations that prevailed during the placement. These are: (a) adequate preparation of the child and the participating adults; (b) clarity regarding the reasons for the change and the steps to be taken; (c) appropriate plans for future contacts with important adults during a planned transitional period and thereafter, as indicated. Implicit in termination, however, is the central distinguishing factor: this plan is usually a change made in response to growth.

The separation experience involved in termination inescapably confronts the placed child again with the reawakening of earlier separation anxieties superimposed on current stress. In the course of this new experience, the personality equilibrium is temporarily disrupted and memories and affects connected with earlier experiences which have been suppressed or repressed may re-emerge. With adequate support from the environment, some spontaneous reworking of the earlier separation experience may take place, correcting some earlier misconceptions and, to some degree, alleviating repressed anxiety. Even without reworking the earlier experience, the opportunity to go through the current separation under conditions in which the child has adequate help to review what has been accomplished, to perceive the important facets of this experience, and to achieve some degree of active mastery in the process through his participation, tends to modify the earlier feeling of helplessness and establish greater confidence in his capacity to cope with change. Some children may need, in addition to the built-in supportive and therapeutic steps in the process, a limited period of treatment to modify an earlier arrest of development and to utilize the current experience for growth. This is especially applicable to young persons who are anticipating the transition to independence. The mobilization of stress in the anticipation of closure of services provides a final opportunity for the agency to help the placed child modify earlier damage and increase his capacity to cope with separation and change.

The technical approaches to helping the child, based on the current diagnostic evaluation, are related to his age and stage of development,[1] the current conditions that bring about closure, and the nature of existing roles and relationships. If the agency relationship has been of sufficient duration and quality to establish the agency as an important parental force in the child's life, the termination of this relationship with the agency, as distinguished from the interpersonal relationship with the caseworker, in itself represents a significant dimension of change with important meaning to the child. Provision for transfer of the agency's parental responsibility requires the availability of a substitute to whom the child can transfer his confidence. The aim of a carefully paced transitional process for re-establishing a child in his own home, for example, or in any other type of facility, under other auspices, is to afford an opportunity for the child to experience the stability and reliability of the new parental force before losing the old one.

The effects of separation of children from the surrogate parents as a planned event, as noted earlier, are heavily influenced by the attitudes of the surrogate parents. Forcible removal of the child, and conflict between the surrogate parents and the agency are far from unknown in many agencies, but these conditions, in most instances, reflect a service process that somewhere has gone awry be-

---

[1] For detailed discussion of this factor, see Chapter III.

fore the point of decision-making regarding the child's replacement. When the surrogate parents resist the move, it is a signal for
the agency to reconsider its decision or re-evaluate the timing of
implementation. A young child who is moved under these conditions not only feels helpless on his own behalf but also the parenting adults are seen as equally powerless to protect him. The damage to the child is so great that replacement under these conditions
should be avoided if the agency has any available option. The
following example shows some of the common complexities of this
type of situation.

A thirty-month-old child was removed from a foster family,
where she had lived since she was fourteen-months-old, to be
placed in an adoptive home. The foster parents had been told
some months earlier that the child was then legally free for adoption. The foster parents were deeply attached to the child but they
were worried about her early deprivation and the emotional problems in her development. Although they wanted her to continue to
grow up as a family member, they did not initiate consideration of
adoption. The agency did not suggest this for consideration because the foster mother was thought to be over-protective and anxious in her care of the child and excessively dependent on her husband and on the caseworker. The caseworker and the agency
supervisory staff considered the foster mother's problems sufficiently serious to anticipate that they would interfere with adequate parenting as the child grew older. The agency decided to re-
place the child when a suitable adoptive home became available.
Thus, the timing of implementation was determined by the external environment. When the decision was shared, the foster mother
did not agree, nor could her husband help her come to terms with
the decision, as he was ambivalent about losing the child. Both
pointed out that they loved her and were "willing to continue her
care." Both described the little girl's anguish when she was separated from them for short periods of time, saying they were afraid
she would be severely upset by removal. An adequate transition
was precluded by the foster mother's anxiety and resistance. On
the day of the move she and the child clung together and wept.

The caseworker intervened firmly and carried the screaming child from the home. In this situation, all of the conditions for a traumatizing separation were present.[2]

A re-evaluation of this situation in the light of pertinent factors which would alter the decision includes these:

1) The child's age and stage of development: at this stage the child's vulnerability to loss of the mothering person is usually at it's height, and separation is contraindicated if there is a choice.

2) The availability of support and help from the mothering person in helping the child cope with the anxiety is especially important at this stage. The child, already terrified by developmental and innate anxiety, is further terrorized by the communicated anxiety of the surrogate parent, whereas a supportive transition would maximize the opportunity for mastery.

3) The foster mother's observed dependence on the caseworker was threatened by termination coincidental with the loss of the child, intensifying her anxiety and resistance. A substantially longer period of preparation is needed when the anticipated loss of the caseworker creates a real psychological threat to the foster parents.

4) The caseworker usually cannot occupy an optimally supportive role with a young child (preschool age) in placement, and must rely heavily on the continuity of existing pre-established role functions to provide the various aspects of help needed by the child.

When the decision-making process has been a fully participating one, involving both foster parents, the agency is unlikely to arrive at a proposed termination which is grossly out of step with the surrogate parents. However, when it occurs that the potential plans for the child have not been mutually shared and a confrontation of differences is reached, the larger perspective usually calls for a change in timing. The purpose of the change is to provide the opportunity for appropriate work with the surrogate parents and for developments in the child which may alter the total equilibrium in the direction of a constructive resolution. It should be kept in mind

---

[2] The child's subsequent development confirmed the traumatic effects of this experience.

that the appearance of seemingly irrational emotional factors in the foster parents' attitudes and the resultant impasse usually do not represent a static situation. It is an ever-changing one with potential changes in the foster child and in the family dynamics. Shifts in the equilibrium of the family system may arise from change in any family member which may alter the situation. Once the negative consequences of forced removal of a young child are recognized, this consideration outweighs the urgency often felt by the agency to achieve what, superficially, appears to be an improved situation for the child. Of course there are exceptional situations in which the current condition of the surrogate parents interferes so seriously in their discharge of the primary parenting role that prompt removal of the child for protective reasons is necessary. Such situations are relatively rare, although they loom large when they occur.

With the older child, the caseworker may play a more substantive role in the termination process since the child is less acutely dependent on the mothering person and verbal communication is an instrument of ego functioning. However, termination of any important relationship at this developmental stage, too, requires the same careful preparation, support, and transition as was discussed earlier in connection with placement.[3]

The young person who is discharged from care to his own responsibility may have entered foster care at any age from infancy to adolescence. When the termination of agency service is anticipated as the final stage in emancipation and self-reliance, the year or two immediately preceding holds both hazards and promise, as does this period for the child reared in his own home. In addition, the approaching emancipation holds specific stresses inherent in the foster care situation. It requires adaptation to the life situation in which the young person does not have the original family as a source of emotional support and practical backing during the period of transition from partial to complete self-reliance. In many instances the foster family or the child-care institution in which the child spends his teen-age years serves in this role, with the aug-

[3] See Chapter III.

mentation of the agency's services. In some cases, however, it is necessary for the agency alone to provide the transitional supports while the young person lives in an independent arrangement.

The usual psychological tasks of adolescence and of termination of foster care are multiplied by the social and technological changes that are present in each succeeding generation, and need special attention from the agency. At the same time, the escalation of tension in the late teen-age period is both necessary and healthy, preparatory to further maturation and further steps in emancipation. Normal events in the environment—discussions about anticipated high school graduation, jobs, or further education—impinge on the established psychological equilibrium as a necessary prerequisite for further mastery of the tasks ahead. At this stage the absence of discussion as well as tension about the future may be a signal of a hiatus in maturational progress which calls for active intervention by the caseworker. Intervention is of critical importance in extreme situations in which the young person fails to show movement in reaching out for preparatory experiences and the foster parents fit into the regressive drive with over-protective or infantilizing attitudes that encourage regression rather than growth. This problem is at the opposite extreme from the problem of forcing growth beyond the adolescent's readiness and may be equally harmful.

The progression through this stage of transition from childhood to adulthood depends not only on the individual's ego growth that has preceded this stage but also on his socialization and the practical preparation for meeting realistic demands. The young person must achieve some degree of reliable work habits, vocational skills, and psychological self-reliance before he becomes fully stabilized in independent young adulthood. For some, work habits and vocational skills may be fairly well established before they enter the first full-time employment, but, for the most part, a period of uneven functioning can be anticipated, as the work adaptation is hampered by both the unstable maturational state and the unconsolidated state of work habits and skills. The foster care agency should be equipped to provide preparatory services well in advance of the first full-time work experience and supportive help for a substantial period thereafter. As noted earlier, in some instances in addition to the practical preparation and supportive services the young person may need a period of regular casework treatment for as much as a year or two to cope with the stresses at this time in his life and to help resolve earlier problems in his feelings about his natural family and his placement. For many young people this is a critical turning point in life and the provision of adequate service may be crucial.

At any age, the termination of the child's interpersonal relationship with the caseworker, if it has been an important one, requires particular attention. The caseworker not only represents the parental force of the agency that has insured continuity in the provision of opportunities for development, but also has provided the child with what becomes a corrective emotional experience in interpersonal relationships. The combined attitudes and attributes of the caseworker's professional self provide a unique experience in interpersonal relationship which usually has greater meaning to the child than is visible or perceived by the caseworker. The caseworker, throughout, as Littner has observed, is "relatively reliable, relatively object-related, relatively non-punitive," and is interested in understanding the child as a unique individual. The child's preparation for termination is proportionately important. One of the most frequent blind-spots of the practitioner is reflected in the tendency to under-evaluate the importance of the relationship to the child and consequently to omit important steps in preparing for its termination. When termination is discussed, the child may not respond overtly either by verbal or nonverbal communication. The failure to respond overtly does not diminish the importance of preparation, if the child will allow it, through verbal information and clarification and through the provision of some period of time for the child to adapt to the knowledge of anticipated closure. Clinical evidence shows that even silent children, who are overtly unresponsive, may make excellent use of the practitioner's communications.

Of course, some of the most careful efforts to provide an adequate period of preparation for termination are frustrated by the child's inability to tolerate the anxiety inherent in the process. In extreme situations, adolescents (and adults) may deal with this anxiety by running away, either figuratively, by not appearing for interviews, or, literally, by precipitously moving to an unknown address.

The return of children to the foster care agency from time to time after termination may serve various purposes. The occasional visit back may be for the purpose of coping with the conflict over the loss involved in termination. It may be the wish to show a person who has been important to him how well he is doing. The placed child who says, "I have known you longer than anyone else," is, in effect, saying: "You have known me longer (or better) than anyone else has known me." The expectation or the hope is that the adult will reflect back to him some ongoing sameness in his essential identity. Thus the adolescent or young adult may return specifically to visit the agency staff member who has known him the longest. If the caseworker has left the agency, this person may be a supervisor, nurse, pediatrician, or executive, depending on his past contacts with individual staff members. Often the purpose of the visit is to communicate a critical need for referral to a helping source or to handle some specific, immediate concern, such as an inquiry about his hereditary background or some noxious experience in his childhood, at a time when he is planning to marry or is expecting to become a parent. The agency's open door to these return visits from its graduates is the ultimate expression of its parental responsibility and consistent with the spirit of the relationship which is responsive to needs. The appropriate service is nearly always of brief duration since long-term service ordinarily is better discharged by an agency or practitioner whose function is designed to provide help with the current problem and who is not associated with the child-rearing functions of the foster care agency.

Termination of the relationship with the parent, as with any client, parallels, in many ways the termination with the child. Preparation, clarity regarding the reasons for closure, an opportunity to take stock of the experience and to anticipate the future, and an open door to discussion of his feelings about the termination are the major technical approaches to helping the parent with the change.

Evaluation and Outcome

In the foregoing discussion of termination, it has been implied that evaluation of the current status of the child and his parents is the basis for planning the approaches to the termination process, just as diagnostic re-evaluation guides planning of services at intervals, as needed, in the course of service. The issue of evaluation, at the point of closure, however, brings into focus added purposes which are related to the other participants in the service system, since each has a stake in the outcome. The specific experiences in each case play a part in the continuing growth and change, not only of the child and his parents, but also of the surrogate parents, the caseworker, and the agency.

The evaluation of outcome, whether formal or informal, may vary greatly in detail, depth, comprehensiveness, and purposes, depending on many variables within different agencies. The goals of service may be particularized for each child and his parents, and related to an assessment of the observable outcome at the point of closure. But the particularized goals for each child and family may be examined, also, within a broader framework. The generalized aims emphasize maturational processes and growth potentials. Broadly viewed, at the time of closure it is hoped that, through the use of the foster care service, the child and his parents have gained some degree of confidence in themselves and trust in others, have learned better ways of coping with stress, and have developed increased capacity to use the resources in their environment to get help when it is needed. The hurt child and the emotionally disturbed parent may absorb these qualities out of identifications made in the total foster care experience with individuals who have reached them emotionally at times and in ways that were specific to their needs. The immediate outcome of care, as observed in developmental detail, does not necessarily foreshadow the long-term outcome. The child, unique in his constitutional endowment and his responses to experience, is in a markedly growing, changing state. His development, viewed at this arbitrarily selected time (to coincide with closure) does not necessarily reveal how much freedom he will have to respond adaptively to future experience, or how his future experiences will influence the outcome of the foster care experience. The child, however, usually will retain what has been invested in a giving relationship with him and will be better off for that investment, whether or not he has been able to respond with observable maturational progress.

At the point of closure, those who have been responsible for providing the enabling environment for the child's maturation must deal with their own feelings in reaction to separation and in reaction to their assessment of the outcome of their work. Whether or not the assessment is a structured one, the participants spontaneously make some form of evaluation of observable progress or lack of progress in the child and of the child's situation in relation to the future. The surrogate parents, who have been close to the child, usually benefit from the caseworker's participation in the evaluation to enlarge their vision, to place the child's current developmental picture in a longitudinal perspective, and to see the ways in which their care has contributed to the child's welfare. Surrogate parents see and experience the termination in part in terms of the motivations that brought them into the service system. These motivations may have been modified in the course of the experience and other motivations may have been added, as new adaptations to the child's needs promote growth in the surrogate parent role. The gratifications of surrogate parenting, which may be highlighted at the time of termination, must be taken into account in any evaluation process that is aimed at promoting growth. The caseworker's helping role in this process is enhanced by his perspective of child development and of the adaptive demands of the surrogate parent role.

Successful experience as a foster parent, regardless of the seeming outcome of the child's care, requires growth and change along lines somewhat different from the maturational lines of natural parenthood. The commitment to the nurture of a foster child is not inherent in our culture, socially or psychologically. The gratifications which consolidate and stabilize the commitment to the role are dependent to some degree on the motivations and to some degree on growth that transcends the inherent frustrations of the task. Since many children placed in foster homes have the capacity to respond to a corrective experience, and since there are many relatively mature foster parents, their gratifications may be derived in part from the child's satisfactory development and in part from their own growth in this special role. In some instances, when the child appears to benefit little from the care that has been provided, the major gratifications must be found in the personal maturation that results from the experience, and from the knowledge that a vital service was provided regardless of the child's capacity to use it.

The caseworker as a participant in the foster care service system has his own set of reactions to closure and to the manifest outcome of each case. As an integral part of professional development, he must grow in his capacity to relate to an ever-widening range of individuals and problems and accept and learn from apparent failures as well as apparent successes with gradually increasing acceptance of his own abilities and limitations. The complexities of foster care services combined with the caseworker's pattern of learning set their own limits on the tempo of learning and the necessary emotional integration of knowledge with practice. As noted by Kubie, "Meaningful education involves a process of maturation which cannot be speeded up materially. This is because growth depends upon our learning from repeated experiences both of success and of failure" (1). The problem for the practitioner is to learn to recognize the application of this principle to his own professional development, as well as to the processes of change and growth in his clients and in the surrogate parents who share the foster care tasks.

Professional maturation of the foster care practitioner requires this ultimate step of learning: to assume responsibility for, and critically appraise, the service he gives, without destructive self-blame. Professional maturation involves a process of coming to terms with the responsible use of one's best skills at each given point in time.

The mature practitioner is able to look back on earlier experience and, when it is indicated, say, "If that situation occurred now, I would handle it differently."

The agency as the primary source of service has its own demands and opportunities for growth and change through its responsiveness to the needs of its clientele. The case-by-case evaluation of outcome at the point of closure has a central position in the procedures through which improvement of services can be obtained. Each agency must find for itself the means of integrating new knowledge from related fields with knowledge gained from ongoing examination of its own practice. Systematic growth in the effectiveness of service is based, in part, on the preservation and expansion of what is tested and found useful and, in part, on elimination of practices that are found deficient, harmful, or unnecessary. Case-by-case evaluation of outcome breeds and nurtures the administrative conviction which is a necessary incentive to leadership in promoting systematic progress.

The process of termination of each case and the evaluation procedure, viewed in the context of a dynamic service system, serve all of the participants as the feedback from which vital changes can be derived as a source of continuously increasing effectiveness in the nurture and treatment of placed children.

REFERENCES

1. Lawrance S. Kubie, M.D., "Unsolved Problems Concerning the Influence of Timing on the Evaluation of Psychotherapy and Education," 1970. Unpublished paper.

ADDITIONAL SELECTED READINGS

Adessa, Sylvester and Audrey Laatsch, "Therapeutic Use of Visiting in Residential Treatment," *Child Welfare,* Vol. XLIV, No. 5, 1965.

Altshul, Sol, "Denial and Ego Arrest," *Journal of the American Psychoanalytic Association,* Vol. XVI, No. 2, 1968.

Babock, Charlotte, "Some Psychodynamic Factors in Foster Parenthood —Part I," *Child Welfare,* Vol. XLIV, No. 9, 1965.

——*Ibid.,* Part II, *Child Welfare,* Vol. XLIV, No. 10, 1965.

Bowlby, John, *Child Care and the Growth of Love,* Penguin Books, Baltimore, Md., 1965.

——"Mother-Child Separation," in Kenneth Soddy, ed., *Mental Health and Infant Development,* Vol. I, New York, Basic Books, 1956.

——*Maternal Care and Mental Health,* Geneva, World Health Organization, 1952.

Brown, Claude, *Manchild in the Promised Land,* The Macmillan Co., New York, 1965. Also paperback, a Signet Book, New American Library, New York.

Casework Treatment of the Family Unit, ten articles reprinted from Social Casework, Family Service Association of America, New York, 1961.

Charnley, Jean, *The Art of Child Placement,* University of Minnesota Press, Minneapolis, Minn., 1955.

Christmas, June Jackson, "Psychological Implications of Long Term Foster Care," *Child Welfare,* Vol. XL, No. 7, 1961.

Coffino, Frances, *Development of a Foster Home,* Child Welfare League of America, Inc., New York, 1955.

Coles, Robert, *Children of Crisis: A Study of Courage and Fear,* Little, Brown and Co., Boston, 1964.

Colvins, Ralph W., "Toward the Development of a Foster Parent Attitude Test," in *Quantitative Approaches to Parent Selection,* Child Welfare League of America, New York, 1962.

Duhl, Gray, and Rizzo, eds., *General Systems Theory and Psychiatry,* Little, Brown and Co., Boston, 1969.

Eissler, K. R., ed., *Searchlights on Delinquency,* International Universities Press, Inc., New York, 1949.

Erikson, Erik, *Identity: Youth and Crisis,* W. W. Norton & Co., Inc., New York, 1968.

——"The Problem of Ego Identity," *Journal of the American Psychoanalytic Association,* Vol. IV, No. 1, 1956.

Fanshel, David, *Foster Parenthood: A Role Analysis,* University of Minnesota Press, Minneapolis, 1966.

——"Specialization within the Foster Parent Role—Part I: Difference between the Foster Parents of Infants and Foster Parents of Older Children," *Child Welfare,* Vol. XXXX, 1961.

Fine, Regina V., "Moving Emotionally Disturbed Children from Institution to Foster Family," *Children,* Vol. XIII, No. 6, 1966.

Fraiberg, Selma H., *The Magic Years,* Charles Scribner's Sons, New York, 1959.

——"A Therapeutic Approach to Reactive Disturbances in Children in Placement," *American Journal of Orthopsychiatry,* Vol. XXXII, No. 1, 1962.

Freud, Anna, "Discussion of John Bowlby's Paper (on "Grief and Mourning in Infancy"), in *The Psychoanalytic Study of the Child,* Vol. XV, International Universities Press, New York, 1960.

——*The Ego and the Mechanisms of Defense,* International Universities Press, New York, 1946.

——"Observations on Child Development," in *The Psychoanalytic Study of the Child,* Vol. VI, International Universities Press, New York, 1951.

Gedanken, Marcia T., "Foster Parent and Social Worker Roles Based on Dynamics of Foster Parenting," *Child Welfare,* Vol. XLV, No. 9, 1966.

Gerard, Margaret W., *The Emotionally Disturbed Child,* papers on Diagnosis, Treatment and Care, Child Welfare League of America, New York.

Glickman, Esther, "The Planned Return of Child to Own Family," *American Journal of Orthopsychiatry,* Vol. XXIII, No. 4, 1953.

Grier, William H., and Price M. Cobbs, *Black Rage,* Basic Books Inc., New York, 1968.

Grinker, Roy R., Sr., ed., "Conceptual Progress in Psychoanalysis," in *Modern Psychoanalysis,* Judd Marmor (ed.), Basic Books, New York, 1968.

Grinker, Roy R., Sr., ed. *Toward a Unified Theory of Human Behavior,* Basic Books, New York, 1967.

Group Homes in Perspective, Child Welfare League of America, New York, 1964.

Hargrave, Vivian, "A Statewide Policy for Permanent Foster Care," *Children*, Vol. XIII, No. 3, 1966.

Hearn, Gordon, ed., *The General Systems Approach: Contributions Toward An Holistic Conception of Social Work*, Council on Social Work Education, New York, 1969.

Herstein, Norman, "The Role of the Supervisor in a Placement Agency," in *Changing Needs and Practices in Child Welfare*, Child Welfare League of America, Inc., New York, 1960.

Herzog, Elizabeth, *About the Poor: Some Facts and Some Fictions*, U.S. Department of Health, Education and Welfare, Social and Rehabilitation Service, Children's Bureau publication number 451, U.S. Government Printing Office, Washington, 1967.

Husbands, Ann, "Developmental Task of the Black Foster Child," *Social Casework*, Vol. 51, 1970.

Hutchinson, Dorothy, *In Quest of Foster Parents*, Columbia University Press, New York, 1943.

Irvine, Elizabeth E., "Children at Risk," in *Crisis Intervention: Selected Readings*, Howard J. Parad, ed., Family Service Association of America, New York, 1965.

Integration and Conflict in Family Behavior, Vol. VI, Report No. 27A, reissued June, 1968, Group for the Advancement of Psychiatry, New York.

Jenkins, Shirley, "Filial Deprivation of Parents of Children in Foster Care," *Children*, Vol. XIV, No. 1, 1967.

——"Separation Experiences of Parents whose Children are in Foster Care," *Child Welfare*, Vol. XLVIII, No. 6, 1969.

Josselyn, Irene, "Evaluating Motives of Foster Parents," *Child Welfare*, Vol. XXXI. No. 2, 1952.

Kay, Neil, "A Systematic Approach to Selecting Foster Parents," *Case Conference*, Vol. XIII, No. 2, 1966.

Katz, Daniel and Robert L. Kohn, *The Social Psychology of Organizations*, John Wiley and Sons, New York, 1966. pp. 14–70.

Kintner, Richard, and Herbert A. Otto, "The Family-Strength Concept and Foster Family Selection," *Child Welfare*, Vol. XLIII, No. 7, 1964.

Kline, Draza, "Teaching Notes on Child Placement," in *Services to Families and Children in Public Welfare*, II, Annandale, Turnpike, 1963.

Kline, Draza, and Helen-Mary Overstreet, "Maintaining Foster Homes through Casework Skills," *The Social Service Review*, Vol. XXII, No. 3, 1948.

Korner, Harold, "Differential Diagnosis as it Affects the Choice of Placement for the Acting-Out Child," *Child Welfare*, Vol. XLII, No. 1, 1963.

Lawder, Elizabeth A., "Toward a More Scientific Understanding of Foster Family Care," *Child Welfare*, Vol. XLIII, No. 2, 1964.

Lewis, Richard S., Alfred A. Strauss, Laura E. Lehtinen, *The Other Child: The Brain Injured Child*, Grune and Stratton, New York, 1960.

Lorand, Sandor, and Henry I. Schneer, eds., *Adolescents: Psychoanalytic Approach to Problems and Therapy*, Paul B. Hoeber, Inc., Medical Division of Harper and Brothers, New York, 1961.

Low, Seth, *Foster Care of Children, Major National Trends and Prospects*, U.S. Department of Health, Education and Welfare, Children's Bureau, Washington, 1966.

Maas, Henry S., "Children in Long-Term Foster Care," *Child Welfare*, Vol. XLIII, No. 6, 1969.

Maas, Henry S., "The Young Adult Adjustment of Twenty Wartime Residential Nursery Children," *Child Welfare*, Vol. XLII, No. 2, 1963.

——and Richard E. Engler, *Children in Need of Parents*, Columbia University Press, New York, 1959.

Mahler, Margaret S., *Helping Children to Accept Death*, The Child Study Association of America, New York.

Malcolm X, *The Autobiography of Malcolm X*, Grove Press Inc., New York, 1964.

Maluccio, Anthony N., "Selecting Foster Homes for Disturbed Children," *Children*, Vol. XIII, No. 2, 1966.

Meeting the Crisis in Foster Family Care and Adults who were Foster Children, Reprinted from *Children*, Vol. 13, No. 1, U.S. Department of Health, Education and Welfare, Children's Bureau, 1966.

Meier, Elizabeth G., "Adults who were Foster Children," *Children*, XIII, No. 1, 1966.

——*The Foster Care of Children with Psychotic Mothers*, Child Welfare League of America, Inc., New York, 1955.

——"Current Circumstances of Former Foster Children," *Child Welfare*, Vol. XLIV, No. 4, 1965.

——"An Inquiry into the Concepts of Ego Identity and Ego Diffusion," in *The Expanding Theoretical Base of Casework*, Family Service Association of America, New York, 1958, reprinted 1964.

——"Implications of Parental Mental Illness for the Foster Care Caseworker," *Child Welfare*, Vol. XLIV, No. 6, 1965.

Moss, Sidney Z., "Integration of the Family into the Child Placement Process," *Children*, Vol. 15, No. 6, 1968.

Ness, Claire M., "The Agency, The Foster Parent, and the Child; Partners in Communication," *Child Welfare*, Vol. XXXIX, No. 1, 1960.

O'Connell, Marie H., *Foster Home Services to Children: Helping the Child to Use Foster Home Care*, Child Welfare League of America, New York, 1953.

Parad, Howard J., ed., *Ego Psychology and Dynamic Casework*, Family Service Association of America, New York, 1958.

Perlman, Helen H., *Persona: Social Role and Personality*, University of Chicago Press, Chicago, 1968.

Pearson, Gerald H., *Psychoanalysis and the Education of the Child*, W. W. Norton & Co., Inc., New York, 1954.

Piaget, Jean, *The Moral Judgment of the Child*, A Free Press Paperback, The Macmillan Co., New York, 1965.

——*Play, Dreams, and Imitation in Childhood*, The Norton Library, New York, 1962.

Radinsky, Elizabeth K., *et al.*, "Recruiting and Serving Foster Parents," in *Today's Child and Foster Care*, Child Welfare League of America, 1963.

Redl, Fritz, and David Wineman, *Children Who Hate*, The Free Press Paperback Edition, New York, 1965.

——*Controls from Within*, Free Press, Glencoe, Ill., 1952.

Reid, William J., Ann W. Shyne, *Brief and Extended Casework*, Columbia University Press, New York, 1969.

Reiner, Beatrice Simox, and Irving Kaufman, *Character Disorders in Parents of Delinquents*, Family Service Association of America, New York, 1959.

Richman, Leon H., "Differential Planning in Child Welfare," *Child Welfare*, Vol. XXXVII, No. 7, 1958.

Rose, John A., "Re-evaluation of the Concept of Separation for Child Welfare," *Child Welfare*, Vol. XLI, No. 10, 1962.

Rubenstein, Helen, "After Care, Who Cares?," *Child Welfare*, Vol. XLIV, No. 4, 1967.

Schoenberg, Carl, "Criteria for Determining Need for Foster Home Care," *Journal of Jewish Communal Service*, Spring, 1957.

Schur, Max, "Discussion of Dr. Bowlby's Paper" (on "Grief and Mourning in Infancy"), in *The Psychoanalytic Study of the Child*, Vol. XV, International Universities Press, New York, 1960.

Shyne, Ann W., *The Need for Foster Care*, Child Welfare League of America, New York, 1969.

Simon, Bernece K., *Relationship between Theory and Practice in Social Casework*, National Association of Social Workers, New York, 1960.

Spitz, René, and K. M. Wolf, "Anaclitic Depression: An Inquiry into the Genesis of Psychiatric Conditions in Early Childhood," *The Psychoanalytic Study of the Child*, Vol. 1, International Universities Press, New York, 1945.

Stevenson, Olive, "The First Treasured Possession: A Study of the Part Played by Specially Loved Objects and Toys in the Lives of Certain Children," with Preface by D. W. Winnicott, in *The Psychoanalytic Study of the Child*, Vol. IX, International Universities Press, New York, 1954.

Stone, Helen, *Reflections on Foster Care: A Report of a National Survey of Attitudes and Practices*, Child Welfare League of America, Inc., New York, 1969.

Taylor, Delores A., and Philip Starr, "Foster Parenting: An Integrative Review of the Literature," *Child Welfare*, Vol. XLVI, No. 7, 1967.

Today's Child and Foster Care, Child Welfare League of America, New York, 1963.

Towle, Charlotte, "Evaluating Motives of Foster Parents: *Discussion*," *Child Welfare*, Vol. XXXI, No. 2, 1952.

——*The Learner in Education for the Professions*, The University of Chicago Press, Chicago, 1954.

Weinstein, Eugene A., *The Self-Image of the Foster-Child*, Russell Sage Foundation, New York, 1960.

Wildy, Lois, "The Professional Foster Home," in *Foster Family Care for Emotionally Disturbed Children*, Child Welfare League of America, New York, 1962.

Winnicott, D. W., *The Family and Individual Development*, Basic Books, New York, 1953.

Wolins, Martin, and Irving Piliavin, *Institution or Foster Family: A Century of Debate*, Child Welfare League of America, Inc., New York, 1964.

Zober, Edith, and Merlin Taber, "The Child Welfare Agency as Parent," *Child Welfare*, Vol. XLIV, No. 7, 1965.

INDEX